the new classics

A definitive collection of classics for every modern cook from *donna hay magazine*

HarperCollins*Publishers*Ltd

the new classics

I've compiled these recipes from *donna hay magazine* to create this ultimate collection of classics with our signature twist. It's designed to help you build your repertoire, taking old favourites and pairing them with modern flavours and seasonal ingredients, or offering an entirely new take instead. I hope this essential book inspires you to create a whole new list of go-to classics.

Donna

CONTENTS

Ingredients marked with an asterisk have a glossary entry

A Sunday family roast, a golden pie, a simple sweet pudding...
these are just a few of the dishes that have become classics,
whether for their combination of flavours, their ease of preparation
or their comforting nature. So why not freshen up your favourites
with modern flavours to give you a whole new cooking repertoire.

SAVOURY

eggs + cheese
pasta, noodles + rice
soups
beef
chicken + duck
pork
lamb
seafood
pies + tarts
salads + sides

EGGS + CHEESE

If you have eggs in the fridge, you have a meal on the table. Nature's versatile packages make quick quiches, easy frittatas and omelettes, perfect for a speedy dinner. Here we partner eggs with their best friend, cheese.

simple homemade ricotta

ricotta-stuffed zucchini flowers

simple homemade ricotta

3 cups (750ml) milk
1 cup (250ml) double (thick) cream*
½ teaspoon sea salt flakes
2 tablespoons lemon juice

Line a sieve with muslin and place over a large bowl. Heat the milk, cream and salt in a large heavy-based saucepan over high heat and bring to the boil, stirring continuously. Add the lemon juice, reduce the heat to low and cook for 2 minutes. Remove from the heat and allow to stand for 5 minutes. Pour the milk mixture into the prepared sieve and set aside at room temperature for 1 hour to strain. Discard the whey+ and place the ricotta in an airtight container in the fridge for up to 5 days. MAKES 1 CUP (200G)
+ Whey is the liquid that remains after the milk solids have been strained.

parmesan baked ricotta with marinated olives

olive oil, for brushing
1 cup (80g) finely grated parmesan
2 cups (400g) fresh ricotta (see recipe, above)
½ cup (70g) grated ricotta salata*
sourdough bread, to serve
marinated olives
550g mixed olives
1 cup (250ml) olive oil
6 cloves garlic, peeled
8 bay leaves
1 long red chilli*, halved
rind of 1 lemon, removed with a vegetable peeler

Preheat oven to 180°C (350°F). Cut 2 x 30cm-squares of non-stick baking paper. Place 1 square on a baking tray, brush with oil and sprinkle with ½ cup (40g) parmesan. Place the ricotta and ricotta salata in a bowl and mix to combine. Place the ricotta mixture on the baking paper and sprinkle with remaining parmesan. Top with the remaining baking paper square and fold the edges to form a parcel. Bake for 25–30 minutes or until puffed and golden.

While the ricotta is baking, make the marinated olives. Place the olives, oil, garlic, bay leaves, chilli and lemon rind in a baking dish and bake for 15–20 minutes. Serve the baked ricotta warm with the olives and sourdough. SERVES 4

ricotta-stuffed zucchini flowers

1 tablespoon finely grated lemon rind
⅔ cup (130g) fresh ricotta (see recipe, left)
⅓ cup basil leaves, chopped
½ cup (40g) finely grated pecorino*
½ teaspoon dried chilli flakes
20 zucchini (courgette) flowers, baby zucchini attached
1 cup (150g) cornflour (cornstarch)
½ cup (75g) self-raising (self-rising) flour, plus extra, for dusting
1¼ cups (430ml) iced water
vegetable oil, for frying
baby purple and green basil leaves, to serve
lemon salt
1 tablespoon sea salt flakes
1 tablespoon finely grated lemon rind

To make the lemon salt, place the salt and lemon rind in a small bowl and rub together with your fingertips to combine. Set aside.

Place the lemon rind, ricotta, basil, pecorino and chilli flakes in a bowl and mix to combine. Gently spoon 1 teaspoon of the mixture into each zucchini flower and twist the petals to enclose.

Place the cornflour, self-raising flour and water in a bowl and mix with a butter knife until just combined (the mixture will be a bit lumpy). Allow to stand for 10 minutes. Heat 1cm of oil in a large, deep saucepan over high heat until hot. Dust the zucchini flowers in the extra flour and dip into the batter. Cook, in batches, for 2–3 minutes or until puffed and golden. Drain on absorbent paper. Top the zucchini flowers with purple and green basil and the lemon salt to serve. SERVES 4

parmesan baked ricotta with marinated olives

HOW TO COOK soufflé omelette

basic soufflé omelette

3 eggs, separated
3 tablespoons single (pouring) cream*
sea salt and freshly cracked black pepper
unsalted butter, for frying
3 tablespoons finely grated parmesan
3 tablespoons finely grated cheddar
finely grated parmesan, extra, to serve

STEP 1 Whisk to combine the egg yolks, cream, salt and pepper.
Place the eggwhites in a clean bowl and whisk until soft peaks form.
Gently fold the eggwhites through the egg yolk mixture.
STEP 2 Melt a little butter in an 18cm non-stick frying pan over
medium-low heat. Add the egg mixture and cook for 2–3 minutes.
STEP 3 Sprinkle the mixture with the cheeses and cook for a further
2–3 minutes or until the base of the omelette is golden and just set.
Using an egg flip, gently fold the omelette over and serve immediately
sprinkled with the extra parmesan. Serve with toast and a rocket
(arugula) salad, if desired. **MAKES 1**

RECIPE NOTES
*By separating the eggs and folding the whipped whites
through the yolk mixture, you are creating an airy and
fluffy omelette that rises like a soufflé.*

basic soufflé omelette

zucchini slice

three cheese soufflé

three cheese soufflé

melted unsalted butter, for brushing
2 tablespoons finely grated parmesan
30g unsalted butter
¼ cup (35g) plain (all-purpose) flour
⅔ cup (160ml) milk
4 eggs, separated
½ cup (100g) fresh ricotta (see recipe, page 14)
½ cup (60g) grated gruyère*
½ cup (40g) grated parmesan, extra
½ teaspoon English mustard powder
sea salt and cracked black pepper
1 eggwhite, extra
grated parmesan and toasted sourdough bread, to serve

Preheat oven to 200°C (400°F). Brush 2 x 2¼ cup-capacity (560ml) ovenproof dishes with butter and sprinkle with 2 tablespoons parmesan. Refrigerate until required.

Melt the butter in a saucepan over low heat. Add the flour and cook for 1 minute. Gradually add the milk and bring to the boil, stirring, for 2 minutes or until the mixture is thick and smooth. Remove from the heat. Add the egg yolks, ricotta, gruyère, extra parmesan, mustard powder, salt and pepper and mix to combine.

Place the eggwhites and extra eggwhite in a bowl and using a hand-held electric mixer, whisk until stiff peaks form. Add ⅓ of the eggwhites to the cheese mixture and fold through with a metal spoon to combine. Add the remaining eggwhites and fold through gently to combine. Pour into the prepared dishes, place on a baking tray and bake for 15–20 minutes or until puffed and set. Sprinkle with parmesan and serve with the sourdough. SERVES 4
Tip: The soufflé should still have a slight wobble in the centre when removed from the oven

---

TRY THIS WITH...
pecorino
goat's cheese
blue cheese

zucchini slice

1 tablespoon olive oil
1 onion, finely chopped
2 cloves garlic, crushed
4 rashers bacon, rind removed and chopped
450g zucchini (courgette), grated
200g feta, crumbled
200g ricotta
½ cup (40g) finely grated parmesan
¼ cup chopped chives
sea salt and cracked black pepper
6 eggs
1 cup (150g) self-raising (self-rising) flour, sifted

Preheat oven to 180°C (350°F). Heat the oil in a large non-stick frying pan over high heat. Add the onion, garlic and bacon and cook for 5 minutes or until light golden. Place in a bowl with the zucchini, feta, ricotta, parmesan, chives, salt and pepper and mix to combine. Place the eggs and flour in a bowl and mix well to combine. Add to the zucchini and mix to combine. Spoon into a lightly greased 20cm x 30cm tin lined with non-stick baking paper and smooth with a palette knife. Bake for 40–45 minutes or until golden and cooked through. Cut into slices to serve. SERVES 8–10
Tip: Cut the zucchini slice into 8–10 portions and place in air-tight containers separated with non-stick baking paper. Freeze for up to three months.

pumpkin, chorizo and kale frittata

1kg kent pumpkin (squash), peeled and chopped
4 fresh chorizo*, cases removed and torn
1 tablespoon olive oil
sea salt and cracked black pepper
100g kale, stems removed and torn
150g soft goat's cheese, crumbled
⅓ cup (95g) store-bought caramelised onion relish
8 eggs
1 cup (250ml) single (pouring) cream*

Preheat oven to 220°C (425°F). Place the pumpkin and chorizo in a 30cm heavy-based shallow pan or baking dish, drizzle with oil and sprinkle with salt and pepper. Roast for 15 minutes or until the pumpkin is light golden and just tender. Remove from the oven and reduce the oven temperature to 200°C (400°F). Add the kale, goat's cheese and caramelised onion to the dish and mix gently. Place the eggs, cream, salt and pepper in a bowl and whisk to combine. Pour over the vegetables and cheese and bake for 30–40 minutes or until puffed and golden. SERVES 4–6

pumpkin, chorizo and kale frittata

HOW TO COOK quiche

1 2
3 4

basic quiche

2 cups (300g) plain (all-purpose) flour
1 teaspoon sea salt flakes
150g cold unsalted butter, chopped
1 egg, lightly beaten
1 tablespoon cold milk
filling
1 tablespoon olive oil
1 large brown onion, cut into thin wedges
200g bacon, rind removed and thinly sliced
1 tablespoon thyme leaves
3 eggs
⅓ cup (80ml) single (pouring) cream*
¼ cup (60ml) milk
½ cup (25g) finely grated gruyère*
sea salt and cracked black pepper

STEP 1 Place the flour, salt and butter in a food processor and process for 1 minute or until the mixture resembles fine breadcrumbs. Add the egg and milk and process until a smooth dough forms. Flatten the dough into a disc shape, cover in plastic wrap and refrigerate for 30 minutes. Roll the dough out between two sheets of non-stick baking paper to 4mm thick. Line a lightly greased 22cm loose-bottomed, fluted tart tin with the pastry and refrigerate for 30 minutes.

STEP 2 Preheat oven to 200°C (400°F). Trim the edges of the pastry and prick the base with a fork. Line with non-stick baking paper and fill with baking weights. Bake for 15 minutes, remove paper and weights and bake for a further 10–15 minutes or until the pastry is light golden. Set aside.

STEP 3 Reduce the oven temperature to 180°C (350°F). To make the filling, heat the oil in a large, non-stick frying pan over high heat. Add the onion and bacon and cook, stirring occasionally, for 8–10 minutes or until golden. Remove from the heat, stir through the thyme and set aside. Place the eggs, cream, milk, cheese, salt and pepper in a bowl and whisk to combine. Spoon the onion mixture into the tart shell and pour over the egg mixture. Bake for 25–30 minutes or until set and golden. Rest for 10 minutes before serving. **SERVES 4**

RECIPE NOTES
Chilling the dough will help prevent shrinkage while baking. Always keep your dough well covered in plastic wrap while it's resting in the fridge; this will help prevent it from drying out.

basic quiche

chorizo and roasted capsicum quiche

1 x quantity shortcrust pastry (see basic recipe, page 22)
1 teaspoon olive oil
1 dried chorizo*, thinly sliced
3 eggs
⅓ cup (80ml) single (pouring) cream*
¼ cup (60ml) milk
½ cup (40g) finely grated manchego*
sea salt and cracked black pepper
⅓ cup (80g) store-bought char-grilled capsicum (bell pepper),
    sliced and drained
⅓ cup (110g) store-bought caramelised onion relish
baby spinach leaves and shaved manchego*, to serve

Preheat oven to 200°C (400°F). Follow steps 1 and 2 of the basic recipe (page 22) and bake the pastry shell as instructed.
Reduce the oven temperature to 180°C (350°F). Heat the oil in a medium, non-stick frying pan over medium heat. Add the chorizo and cook for 1–2 minutes each side or until light golden. Drain on absorbent paper. Place the eggs, cream, milk, cheese, salt and pepper in a bowl and whisk to combine. Place the chorizo, capsicum and onion into the pastry shell and pour over the egg mixture. Bake for 25–30 minutes or until set and golden. Rest for 10 minutes. Serve with the spinach and manchego. SERVES 4

chilli crab and lemon quiches

1 x quantity shortcrust pastry (see basic recipe, page 22)
3 eggs
⅓ cup (80ml) single (pouring) cream*
¼ cup (60ml) milk
1 tablespoon finely grated lemon rind
sea salt and cracked black pepper
350g cooked crab meat+, drained on absorbent paper
½ teaspoon dried chilli flakes
baby (micro) herbs, to serve (optional)

Preheat oven to 200°C (400°F). Following steps 1 and 2 of the basic recipe (page 22), rolling the pastry out to 3mm thick and lining 6 x 8cm lightly greased loose-bottomed, fluted tart tins. Bake for 15 minutes, remove paper and weights and bake for a further 5–10 minutes or until the pastry is light golden. Set aside.
Reduce the oven temperature to 180°C (350°F). Place the eggs, cream, milk, lemon rind , salt and pepper in a bowl and whisk to combine. Divide the crab and chilli flakes between the tart shells and pour over the egg mixture. Bake for 20–25 minutes or until set and golden. Rest for 5 minutes. Top with herbs to serve. SERVES 4
+ *You can buy picked and cooked crab meat from your local fishmonger.*

spinach and ricotta quiche

1 x quantity shortcrust pastry (see basic recipe, page 22)
3 eggs
⅓ cup (80ml) single (pouring) cream*
¼ cup (60ml) milk
½ cup (40g) finely grated parmesan, plus extra, to serve
sea salt and cracked black pepper
250g frozen spinach, thawed and drained on absorbent paper
½ cup (100g) ricotta

Preheat oven to 200°C (400°F). Follow steps 1 and 2 of the basic recipe (page 22), lining a 11.5cm x 34cm lightly greased loose-bottomed, fluted tart tin with the pastry. Bake as instructed.

Reduce the oven temperature to 180°C (350°F). Place the eggs, cream, milk, cheese, salt and pepper in a bowl and whisk to combine. Spoon the spinach and ricotta into the tart shell and pour over the egg mixture. Bake for 25–30 minutes or until set and golden. Rest for 10 minutes. Sprinkle with the extra cheese to serve. SERVES 4

tomato and goat's cheese quiches

1 x quantity shortcrust pastry (see basic recipe, page 22)
3 eggs
⅓ cup (80ml) single (pouring) cream*
¼ cup (60ml) milk
½ cup (15g) finely grated parmesan
sea salt and cracked black pepper
150g soft goat's cheese
180g truss cherry tomatoes
1 teaspoon olive oil, for brushing
2 tablespoons oregano leaves
watercress sprigs, to serve

Preheat oven to 200°C (400°F). Follow steps 1 and 2 of the basic recipe (page 22), lining 2 x 12.5cm lightly greased loose-bottomed, fluted tart tins with the pastry. Bake as instructed.

Reduce temperature to 180°C (350°F). Place the eggs, cream, milk, cheese, salt and pepper in a bowl and whisk to combine. Divide the egg mixture and goat's cheese between the tart shells. Brush the tomatoes with oil and sprinkle with salt and pepper. Add to the tarts with the oregano leaves and bake for 25 minutes. Loosely cover with aluminium foil and bake for a further 10–15 minutes or until set and golden. Rest for 10 minutes. Top with watercress sprigs to serve. SERVES 4

potato and goat's cheese frittata

mushroom, pumpkin and taleggio quiche

herb and mozzarella mushrooms with garlic toast

potato and goat's cheese frittata

350g waxy potatoes, peeled and chopped
1 fresh chorizo*, sliced
1 tablespoon olive oil
4 eggs
¾ cup (180ml) single (pouring) cream*
100g goat's curd*
⅓ cup (100g) store-bought caramelised onion relish

Preheat oven to 200°C (400°F). Place the potato, chorizo and oil in a 1.5 litre-capacity ovenproof dish and toss to coat. Roast for 30 minutes or until golden. Place the eggs and cream in a bowl and whisk until well combined. Pour over the potato and chorizo and top with the goat's curd and caramelised onion. Cook for 15–20 minutes or until the egg is set and the top is golden. SERVES 2

herb and mozzarella mushrooms with garlic toasts

8 thin slices baguette
olive oil, for brushing
sea salt and cracked black pepper
1 clove garlic, halved, for rubbing
40g unsalted butter
400g pine mushrooms*, halved
2 sprigs rosemary
¼ cup sage leaves
250g fresh buffalo mozzarella*, torn

Heat a char-grill pan or barbecue over high heat. Brush the bread with oil and sprinkle with salt and pepper. Char-grill or barbecue the bread for 2–3 minutes or until golden. Rub with the garlic and set aside.

Melt the butter in a large non-stick frying pan over high heat. Add the mushrooms, rosemary, sage, salt and pepper and cook for 5 minutes or until golden. Top with the mozzarella and place under a preheated hot grill (broiler) for 2–3 minutes or until melted. Serve with the garlic toasts. SERVES 4

Tip: The buffalo mozzarella will melt into delicious golden pools with its characteristic stringy texture. Dip the bread into the cheese. If you don't have a char-grill pan, simply toast the bread and rub with the garlic.

mushroom, pumpkin and taleggio quiche

600g butternut pumpkin (squash), thinly sliced
olive oil, for drizzling
6 portobello mushrooms
150g flat pancetta*, finely chopped
200g taleggio*, rind removed and sliced
6 eggs
sea salt and cracked black pepper
finely grated parmesan, to serve
parmesan pastry
2 cups (300g) plain (all-purpose) flour
1 cup (80g) finely grated parmesan
150g cold unsalted butter, chopped
1 teaspoon sea salt flakes
1 egg
1 tablespoon cold milk
1 eggwhite

Preheat oven to 200°C (400°F). Place the pumpkin on a baking tray and drizzle with oil. Place the mushrooms and pancetta on a separate baking tray and drizzle with oil. Cook for 20 minutes or until tender. Set aside.

Reduce temperature to 180°C (350°F). To make the parmesan pastry, place the flour, parmesan, butter and salt in the bowl of a food processor and process for 1–2 minutes or until the mixture resembles fine breadcrumbs. Add the egg and milk and process for 2 minutes or until a smooth dough forms. Wrap in plastic wrap and refrigerate for 30 minutes. Roll out between 2 sheets of non-stick baking paper to a 30cm round. Line the base and sides of a lightly greased 22cm spring-form cake tin with the pastry. Prick the base with a fork, line with non-stick baking paper and fill with baking weights, uncooked rice or beans. Bake for 15 minutes, remove the paper and weights, brush with the eggwhite and bake for a further 10 minutes or until cooked through and golden. Set aside to cool.

Reduce temperature to 160°C (325°F). Layer the pumpkin, mushrooms, pancetta and taleggio in the pastry shell. Whisk to combine the eggs and salt and pepper and pour the mixture into the pastry shell. Cover tightly with aluminium foil and bake for 1 hour 30 minutes or until cooked through. Sprinkle with the parmesan to serve. SERVES 6–8

roasted garlic and potato soufflés with salsa verde

spinach and ricotta dumplings with tomato salsa

roasted garlic and potato soufflés with salsa verde

2 heads garlic
1 tablespoon olive oil
1 cup (300g) rock salt
1 x 250g starchy potato, brushed clean
melted unsalted butter, for brushing
2 tablespoons finely grated pecorino*
30g unsalted butter, extra
¼ cup (35g) plain (all-purpose) flour
⅔ cup (160ml) milk
4 eggs, separated
1 cup (80g) finely grated pecorino*, plus extra, to serve
1 teaspoon hot English mustard
sea salt and white cracked pepper
1 eggwhite, extra
salsa verde
1 cup mint leaves
1 cup flat-leaf parsley leaves
¼ cup chopped chives
2 cloves garlic, crushed
2 tablespoons white wine vinegar
2 tablespoons olive oil

Preheat oven to 180°C (350°F). Drizzle the garlic with oil and wrap with aluminium foil. Place the rock salt in a baking tray and top with the garlic and potato. Bake for 1 hour or until the garlic and potato are softened. Allow to cool slightly. Cut the potato in half and scoop the flesh into a bowl. Peel the garlic, add to the potato, and mash until smooth. Set aside.

Increase the oven temperature to 200°C (400°F). Brush 4 x 1¾ cup-capacity (430ml) ovenproof dishes with the melted butter and sprinkle with the 2 tablespoons of pecorino to coat. Refrigerate until ready to use.

Melt the extra butter in a small saucepan over medium heat. Add the flour and cook, whisking, for 1 minute. Gradually add the milk and whisk continuously for 2 minutes or until thick and smooth. Add to the potato mixture with the egg yolks, 1 cup (80g) pecorino, mustard, salt and pepper and mix to combine. Place the eggwhites and extra eggwhite in a bowl and, using a hand-held electric mixer, whisk until stiff peaks form. Using a metal spoon, gently fold the eggwhites through the potato mixture. Divide between the prepared dishes, place on a baking tray and bake for 15–18 minutes or until puffed and golden.

While the soufflés are cooking, make the salsa verde. Place the mint, parsley, chives, garlic, vinegar, oil, salt and pepper in a small food processor and process to combine. Drizzle the soufflés with the salsa verde, sprinkle with extra pecorino and serve immediately. MAKES 4

three-cheese semolina gnocchi with gremolata

1.5 litres milk
2 cups (320g) semolina*
6 egg yolks
200g taleggio*, rind removed and chopped
sea salt and cracked black pepper
8 sprigs marjoram
1 cup (100g) grated mozzarella
1 cup (80g) grated parmesan
gremolata
⅓ cup chopped flat-leaf parsley leaves
1 tablespoon chopped marjoram leaves
¼ cup (60ml) olive oil
1 tablespoon lemon juice
1 tablespoon shredded lemon zest
1 clove garlic, crushed

To make the gremolata, place the parsley, marjoram, oil, lemon juice, zest and garlic in a bowl and mix to combine. Set aside.

Pour the milk in a large saucepan over medium heat. Bring to the boil and gradually whisk in the semolina. Using a wooden spoon, stir for 2–3 minutes or until cooked through. Remove from the heat, add the egg yolks, taleggio, salt and pepper and stir until well combined. Spoon the mixture into a lightly greased 20cm x 30cm slice tin and refrigerate for 2–3 hours or until set. Cut the gnocchi into 12 x 4cm x 10cm rectangles and place on a lightly greased oven tray. Top with the marjoram and sprinkle with the mozzarella and parmesan. Grill (broil) under a preheated hot grill (broiler) for 2–3 minutes or until the cheese is golden and melted. Top with the gremolata to serve.
SERVES 10–12

three-cheese semolina gnocchi with gremolata

caramelised fennel, kale and goat's curd quiche

spinach and ricotta dumplings with tomato salsa

200g baby spinach leaves, wilted, dried and chopped
1 cup (200g) fresh ricotta (see recipe, page 14)
⅔ cup (50g) finely grated parmesan, plus extra, to serve
⅓ cup (50g) plain (all-purpose) flour, plus extra, for dusting
2 eggs
⅓ cup chopped chives
1 clove garlic, crushed
40g unsalted butter
tomato salsa
300g mixed cherry tomatoes, halved
12 white anchovy fillets*, chopped
1 cup mint leaves
1 clove garlic, crushed
2 tablespoons olive oil
1 tablespoon white wine vinegar
sea salt and cracked black pepper

To make the tomato salsa, place the tomatoes, anchovy, mint, garlic, oil, vinegar, salt and pepper in a bowl and toss to combine. Set aside.

Place the spinach, ricotta, parmesan, flour, eggs, chives, garlic, salt and pepper in a bowl and mix until a sticky dough forms. Roll tablespoonfuls of the mixture into balls and roll in the extra flour. Cook, in batches, in a large saucepan of boiling water for 3–4 minutes or until firm and floating to the surface. Remove with a slotted spoon and set aside.

Melt the butter in a non-stick frying pan over high heat. Add the dumplings and cook for 2 minutes each side or until golden. Serve with the tomato salsa and extra parmesan. SERVES 4

caramelised fennel, kale and goat's curd quiche

½ cup (125ml) sherry vinegar*
½ cup (90g) brown sugar
sea salt and cracked black pepper
500g baby fennel, trimmed and halved
2 eggs
1 cup (250ml) single (pouring) cream
1 teaspoon Dijon mustard
2 sheets store-bought butter puff pastry, thawed
30g kale leaves, blanched and chopped
⅓ cup goat's curd*, plus extra, to serve

Preheat oven to 220°C (425°F). Place the vinegar, sugar, salt and pepper in a small deep-sided baking tray. Add the fennel, cut-side down, and roast for 35–40 minutes or until sticky and tender. Reduce temperature to 180°C (350°F). Place the eggs, cream, mustard, salt and pepper in a bowl and whisk to combine. Trim the pastry and use to line a lightly greased 34cm x 12cm loose-bottomed tin, overlapping the sheets in the centre. Top with the kale and fennel, cut-side up. Pour over the egg mixture and place spoonfuls of the goat's curd around the fennel. Bake for 40 minutes or until just set and golden. Serve with extra goat's curd. SERVES 4

TRY THIS WITH...
silver beet
mascarpone
dried chilli flakes

PASTA, NOODLES + RICE

More than just a side act, silky pasta, slippery noodles and fluffy rice feature in these heart-warming, simple and versatile recipes that are geared to both quick weeknight cooking and relaxed weekend feasts.

slow-cooked lamb shank pasta with pesto

chilli-crumbed mac 'n' cheese

slow-cooked lamb shank pasta with pesto

2 tablespoons olive oil
1.2kg lamb shanks
1 brown onion, chopped
3 cloves garlic, crushed
1 cup (250ml) dry white wine
2 x 400g cans cherry tomatoes
4 sprigs thyme
1 cup (250ml) water
375g dried lasagne sheets+
125g fresh buffalo mozzarella*, torn
pesto
3 cups basil leaves
½ cup (125ml) olive oil
⅓ cup (25g) finely grated parmesan
sea salt and cracked black pepper

To make the pesto, place the basil, oil, parmesan, salt and pepper in the bowl of a food processor and process until well combined. Set aside.

Heat the oil in a large heavy-based saucepan over high heat. Add the lamb and cook for 1–2 minutes each side or until browned. Remove from the pan and set aside. Add the onion and garlic and cook for 1–2 minutes or until softened. Add the wine, tomato, thyme and water and stir to combine. Return the lamb to the pan and bring to the boil. Reduce the heat to low, cover and simmer for 2 hours or until the lamb is tender and falling off the bone. Remove the lamb from the pan and shred the meat from the bones with a fork, discarding the bones. Return the meat to the sauce.

Break the lasagne sheets into rough pieces and cook in a large saucepan of salted boiling water for 8–10 minutes or until al dente. Drain and return to the pan. Add the shredded lamb and sauce and toss to combine. Top with the mozzarella and spoon over the pesto to serve. SERVES 4–6
+ *Sold fresh or dried, lasagne sheets are traditionally used for the dish of the same name, but are also good to break into large pieces and serve with a very chunky sauce.*

chilli-crumbed mac 'n' cheese

400g macaroni
¾ cup (185ml) single (pouring) cream*
1¼ cups (310ml) milk
1½ cups (180g) grated cheddar
½ cup (40g) finely grated parmesan
2 cups (140g) fresh breadcrumbs
½ teaspoon dried chilli flakes
1 clove garlic, crushed
50g unsalted butter, melted

Preheat oven to 200°C (400°F). Cook pasta in a large saucepan of salted boiling water for 6 minutes or until al dente. Drain and return to the pan.

Add the cream, milk, cheddar and parmesan and cook, stirring, over low heat for 3–4 minutes or until the pasta is thoroughly coated. Spoon into a large baking dish.

Place the breadcrumbs, chilli flakes, garlic and butter in a bowl and toss until well combined. Sprinkle over the pasta mixture and bake for 6–8 minutes or until golden and crispy. SERVES 4–6

chorizo, lentil and goat's curd pasta

400g conchiglie (small shell pasta)
2 tablespoons olive oil, plus extra, for drizzling
2 dried chorizo*, sliced
200g Swiss brown mushrooms, sliced
3 cloves garlic, sliced
¾ cup (185ml) dry sherry
1 x 400g can lentils, rinsed and drained
sea salt and cracked black pepper
125g goat's curd*

Cook the pasta in a large saucepan of salted boiling water for 6–8 minutes or until al dente. Drain and keep warm.

Heat the oil in a large non-stick frying pan over high heat. Add the chorizo, mushroom and garlic, cook for 1–2 minutes or until browned. Add the sherry and lentils and cook for 2 minutes or until reduced slightly. Add the pasta, salt and pepper and cook for 1 minute. Top with the goat's curd and drizzle with oil to serve. SERVES 4–6

chorizo, lentil and goat's curd pasta

paper bag seafood linguine

summer bolognese

paper bag seafood linguine

400g linguine
16 green (raw) prawns (shrimp), peeled with tails intact
600g clams (or pippies)
½ cup (125ml) dry white wine
120g unsalted butter, chopped
4 cloves garlic, sliced
sea salt and cracked black pepper
1 tablespoon lemon juice
olive oil, for drizzling
¼ cup roughly chopped flat-leaf parsley leaves
lemon wedges and crusty bread, to serve

Preheat oven to 180°C (350°F). Cook the pasta in a large saucepan
of salted boiling water for 10–12 minutes or until al dente. Drain and
set aside. Cut 4 x 40cm pieces of baking paper. Use the paper to line
4 x 3 cup-capacity (750ml) bowls. Divide pasta between the bowls
and top with the prawns, clams, wine, butter, garlic, salt and pepper.
Bring the ends of each piece of paper together to enclose and secure
tightly with kitchen string. Bake for 35–40 minutes or until the prawns
are cooked through and clams are open. Drizzle with lemon juice and
oil and sprinkle with parsley. Serve with lemon wedges and bread.
SERVES 4

baked tomato and ricotta shells

400g conchiglioni (large shell pasta)
2½ cups (500g) ricotta
½ cup (40g) finely grated parmesan
1 cup (100g) grated mozzarella
1 egg
2 x 400g cans chopped tomatoes
250g cherry tomatoes, halved
2 cloves garlic, sliced
1 cup (250ml) chicken stock
1 teaspoon caster (superfine) sugar
sea salt and cracked black pepper

Preheat oven to 200°C (400°F). Cook the pasta in a large saucepan
of salted boiling water for 8 minutes. Drain and rinse under cold
running water. Set aside.
   Place the ricotta, parmesan, mozzarella and egg in a bowl and mix
until well combined. Set aside. Place the canned tomatoes, cherry
tomato, garlic, stock, sugar, salt and pepper in a large baking dish and
stir to combine. Spoon the ricotta mixture into the pasta shells and
place in the baking dish. Bake for 20 minutes or until the cheese is
golden. SERVES 4–6

summer bolognese

400g spaghetti
¼ cup (60ml) olive oil
500g beef mince (ground beef)
3 cloves garlic, crushed
2 tablespoons thyme leaves
2 teaspoons dried chilli flakes
sea salt and cracked black pepper
2 teaspoons caster (superfine) sugar
2 tablespoons tomato paste
½ cup (125ml) dry white wine
1 tablespoon finely grated lemon rind
2 tablespoons lemon juice
2 tablespoons red wine vinegar
400g mixed cherry tomatoes, halved
½ cup (90g) Ligurian olives*
baby (micro) basil leaves and finely grated parmesan, to serve

Cook the pasta in a large saucepan of salted boiling water for
10–12 minutes or until al dente. Drain and keep warm. Heat
1 tablespoon of the oil in a large, non-stick frying pan over high
heat. Add the mince, garlic, thyme and chilli and cook, breaking
up any lumps with a wooden spoon, for 6–8 minutes or until
browned. Add the salt, pepper, sugar and tomato paste and cook
for 4–5 minutes. Add the wine and cook, stirring occasionally,
for a further 3–4 minutes or until the liquid is reduced. Toss the
pasta with the remaining oil, lemon rind, lemon juice and vinegar.
Add the mince, tomatoes and olives and toss to combine. Top with
basil leaves and sprinkle with parmesan to serve. SERVES 4–6

HOW TO COOK pasta

1 2
3 4

basic pasta

2⅔ cups (400g) OO flour*, plus extra, for dusting
4 eggs
butter, finely grated pecorino* and cracked black pepper, to serve

STEP 1 Place the flour in a bowl and make a well in the centre. Add the eggs and use a fork to lightly whisk, bringing the flour into the centre until the dough begins to come together and all the flour has been combined. Turn out onto a lightly floured surface and knead for 3–4 minutes or until the dough is smooth. Cover in plastic wrap and set aside for 30 minutes to rest.

STEP 2 Divide the dough into 4 equal-sized portions (approx. 150g each). Set the pasta machine to position 1 and pass one dough portion through the machine. Repeat 5–6 times, folding the dough onto itself each time and adding extra flour if necessary.

STEP 3 Set the pasta machine to position 2 and pass the dough through once. Repeat on each setting until you reach position 5. Lay the sheets of pasta on trays lined with non-stick baking paper. Repeat with remaining pasta portions.

STEP 4 For cut pasta, attach the pasta cutting rollers to the machine and using the spaghetti cutter, pass the pasta sheets through the machine once. Place the pasta on trays lined with non-stick baking paper dusted with flour or hang over a wooden spoon for 30–60 minutes⁺. Cook the pasta in a large saucepan of salted boiling water for 3–5 minutes or until al dente. Drain, return to the pan, stir through the butter and pecorino and sprinkle with pepper to serve.

SERVES 4

+ This helps to prevent the pasta from sticking, however you could also cook it straight away.

RECIPE NOTES

When making larger quantities of pasta, keep in mind that the ratio will always be 100g of flour to 1 egg. So whether you're serving four people or 14, this ratio will ensure perfect pasta every time.

basic pasta

slow-cooked beef ragu pasta

slow-cooked beef ragu pasta

1 x 1kg piece beef brisket, cut into 4 pieces
plain (all-purpose) flour, for dusting
¼ cup (60ml) olive oil
1 brown onion, thickly sliced
3 cloves garlic, peeled
1 cup (250ml) red wine
2 cups (500ml) beef stock
1 cup (250ml) water
1 x 400g can cherry tomatoes
4 bay leaves
2 tablespoons tomato paste
1 tablespoon caster (superfine) sugar
400g caserecci or rigatoni
sea salt and cracked black pepper
½ cup basil leaves
finely grated parmesan, to serve

Preheat oven to 180°C (350°F). Dust the beef in flour, shaking to remove any excess. Heat 2 tablespoons of oil in a heavy-based saucepan over high heat. Cook the beef for 2–3 minutes each side or until browned. Remove from the pan and set aside.

Reduce heat to low, add the remaining oil, onion and garlic and cook for 6–8 minutes or until softened. Increase the heat to high. Add the wine and cook, scraping the bottom of the pan, for 2–3 minutes or until the liquid is reduced by half. Add the stock, water, tomatoes, bay leaves, tomato paste and sugar and stir to combine. Return the beef to the pan, cover with a tight-fitting lid, transfer to the oven and roast for 2 hours. Remove the lid and roast for a further 30 minutes. Remove beef from the pan and shred the meat using 2 forks, discarding any fat. Return the meat to the sauce and mix to combine. Set aside.

Cook the pasta in a large saucepan of salted boiling water for 10–12 minutes or until al dente. Drain, return to the pan with the beef sauce, salt, pepper and toss to combine. Top with basil and sprinkle with parmesan to serve. SERVES 4–6

pumpkin and nutmeg gnocchi with salami and oregano butter

60g unsalted butter
⅓ cup (60g) finely chopped spicy salami
12 sprigs oregano
1 tablespoon shredded lemon zest
1 tablespoon lemon juice
pumpkin and nutmeg gnocchi
500g starchy potatoes
500g butternut pumpkin (squash)
rock salt, for baking
½ cup (40g) finely grated pecorino*
⅔ cup (100g) plain (all-purpose) flour, sifted
sea salt and cracked black pepper
½ teaspoon finely grated nutmeg
2 egg yolks

To make the pumpkin and nutmeg gnocchi, preheat oven to 180°C (350°F). Place the potatoes and pumpkin on a baking tray filled with rock salt and bake for 1 hour or until soft and skins are crispy. Allow to cool slightly. Cut potatoes and pumpkin in half, scoop the flesh into a bowl and mash until smooth. Add the pecorino, flour, salt, pepper and nutmeg and mix to combine. Add the egg yolks and stir until mixture comes together. Knead on a lightly floured surface for 1 minute or until a soft dough forms. Roll the dough into a 6cm-round log. Cut into 1.5cm-thick discs and place on a lightly floured tray. Cook the gnocchi, in batches, in a large saucepan of salted boiling water for 3–4 minutes or until firm and floating to the surface. Remove with a slotted spoon.

Melt the butter in a large non-stick frying pan over medium heat. Add the salami and oregano and cook for 2–3 minutes or until crisp. Add the gnocchi, and cook for a further 4–5 minutes or until golden. Add the lemon zest, lemon juice, salt and pepper and toss gently to combine before serving. SERVES 4
Tip: The pumpkin will make this dough softer than regular gnocchi dough; you may need to add extra flour as you knead.

pumpkin and nutmeg gnocchi with salami and oregano butter

porcini gnocchi with creamy mushroom sauce

porcini gnocchi with creamy mushroom sauce

3 tablespoons olive oil
⅓ cup sage leaves
3 cloves garlic, thinly sliced
200g Swiss brown mushrooms, sliced
100g chestnut mushrooms, halved
1 cup (250ml) single (pouring) cream
porcini gnocchi
1kg starchy potatoes
rock salt, for baking
1 cup (25g) dried porcini mushrooms*
½ cup (40g) finely grated parmesan
⅔ cup (100g) plain (all-purpose) flour, sifted
sea salt and cracked black pepper
2 egg yolks

To make the porcini gnocchi, preheat oven to 180°C (350°F). Place the potatoes on a baking tray filled with rock salt and bake for 1 hour or until soft and skins are crispy. Allow to cool slightly. Cut in half, scoop the flesh into a bowl and mash until smooth. Place the porcini mushrooms in a bowl with 2 cups (500ml) boiling water. Set aside for 5 minutes. Drain well, reserving ¼ cup (60ml) of the soaking liquid. Finely chop the porcini and add to the potato with the parmesan, flour, salt and pepper and mix to combine. Add the egg yolks and stir until the mixture just comes together. Turn out onto a lightly floured surface and knead for 1 minute or until a soft dough forms. Divide into 2 equal portions and roll each piece into a 64cm-long rope. Cut into 2cm-long pieces and place on a lightly floured tray. Set aside.

Heat 2 tablespoons oil in a large frying pan over medium heat. Add the sage and cook for 1–2 minutes or until crispy. Remove the sage, drain on absorbent paper and set aside. Add the remaining oil to the pan with the garlic and Swiss brown mushrooms and cook, stirring occasionally, for 5–6 minutes. Add the chestnut mushrooms, salt and pepper and cook for a further 3–4 minutes. Add the cream and reserved porcini liquid. Bring to the boil and cook for 3–4 minutes or until reduced slightly.

Cook the gnocchi, in batches, in a large saucepan of salted boiling water for 3–4 minutes or until firm and floating to the surface. Remove with a slotted spoon. Add the gnocchi to the sauce, mix gently to combine and top with the sage leaves to serve. SERVES 4

white bean, olive and basil cannelloni

450g ricotta
1 cup (80g) finely grated parmesan, plus extra, to serve
⅓ cup (40g) pitted black olives, chopped
½ cup chopped basil leaves, plus extra leaves, to serve
1 x 400g can white (cannellini) beans, drained and rinsed
sea salt and cracked black pepper
1½ cups (375ml) tomato purée (passata)
½ cup (125ml) chicken stock
12 fresh lasagne sheets
2 cups (200g) grated mozzarella

Preheat oven to 180°C (350°F). Place the ricotta, parmesan, olives, basil, beans, salt and pepper in a bowl and mix well to combine. Pour the tomato purée, stock, salt and pepper in a separate bowl and mix to combine. Divide half the tomato mixture between 4 x 12cm, 2 cup-capacity (500ml) baking dishes. Set aside.

Place ¼ cup of the ricotta mixture at the short end of each lasagne sheet and roll to enclose. Trim and divide the cannelloni between the baking dishes. Top with the remaining tomato mixture and sprinkle with the mozzarella. Cover with aluminium foil and bake for 20 minutes. Remove the foil and bake for a further 10 minutes or until the pasta is cooked. Top with the extra parmesan and basil leaves to serve. SERVES 4

TRY THIS WITH...
spinach and ricotta
pumpkin and ricotta
beef mince and tomato

white bean, olive and basil cannelloni

HOW TO COOK polenta

1 2
3 4

basic soft polenta

2 cups (500ml) chicken stock
1½ cups (375ml) milk
1 cup (170g) instant polenta
30g unsalted butter, chopped
¼ cup (20g) finely grated parmesan
sea salt and cracked black pepper

STEP 1 Pour the stock and milk into a large saucepan over medium heat and bring to the boil.
STEP 2 Gradually whisk the polenta into the milk and stock mixture. (See recipe notes, below.)
STEP 3 Cook, stirring, for 2–3 minutes, or until thickened.
STEP 4 Remove from heat, add the butter, parmesan, salt and pepper, and stir to combine. SERVES 4

RECIPE NOTES
It's very important to gradually add the polenta to the hot stock while whisking continually. This will prevent any lumps from forming and give the polenta a perfectly smooth texture. Serve the polenta with braised meat dishes such as osso buco and lamb shanks.

basic soft polenta

grilled polenta with mushrooms and ricotta

1 x quantity basic soft polenta (see recipe, page 54)
4 field mushrooms
olive oil, for brushing
100g ricotta and store-bought pesto, to serve

Make the basic polenta recipe, substituting the milk with 1½ cups (375ml) extra chicken stock[+]. Spoon into a lightly greased 20cm x 30cm tin lined with non-stick baking paper and smooth the top. Refrigerate for 30 minutes or until set.

Cut the polenta into 6 pieces. Heat a char-grill pan or barbecue over high heat. Brush the polenta and mushrooms with oil and char-grill or barbecue the mushrooms for 10 minutes. Remove from the heat. Char-grill or barbecue the polenta for 5–6 minutes each side or until golden. Top the polenta with the mushrooms and ricotta and drizzle with the pesto to serve. SERVES 4
+ For this dish, you will need a total of 3½ cups (875ml) chicken stock.

one-pan chorizo, olive and feta polenta

1 x quantity basic soft polenta (see recipe, page 54)
2 tablespoons chopped basil leaves
1 dried chorizo*, sliced
¼ cup (20g) pitted green olives, sliced
50g feta, crumbled
2 bocconcini*, roughly torn
150g truss cherry tomatoes

Make the basic polenta recipe. Add the basil and spoon into a 20cm frying pan with an ovenproof handle, top with the chorizo, olives, feta, bocconcini and tomatoes. Grill (broil) under a preheated hot grill (broiler) for 8 minutes or until the top is golden and cheese is melted. SERVES 4

herbed polenta chips

1 x quantity basic soft polenta (see recipe, page 54)
1 tablespoon chopped rosemary leaves
1 tablespoon oregano leaves
1 tablespoon thyme leaves
olive oil, for brushing
store-bought aioli or mayonnaise, to serve

Make the basic polenta recipe, substituting the milk with 1½ cups (375ml) extra chicken stock[+]. Add the herbs and stir to combine. Spoon the mixture into a lightly greased baking tray and spread to 1cm thick[++]. Refrigerate for 30 minutes or until set.

Preheat oven to 220°C (425°F). Cut the polenta into 2cm x 10cm fingers and brush with oil. Place on a lightly greased baking tray and bake for 20–25 or until golden and crisp. Serve with mayonnaise or aioli. SERVES 4
+ For this dish, you will need a total of 3½ cups (875ml) chicken stock.
++ After removing from the heat, the polenta will set and become firm on standing. If you're serving soft, creamy polenta it will need to be eaten straight away. If setting polenta, it's important to spread it out while it's still warm before allowing it to set.

creamed corn polenta with crispy skin chicken

4 x 300g chicken supremes, skin on[+]
olive oil, for drizzling
5 sprigs sage
1 x quantity basic soft polenta (see recipe, page 54)
¼ cup (30g) cheddar
½ cup (130g) store-bought creamed corn
1 tablespoon chopped sage leaves, extra
steamed green beans, to serve

Preheat oven to 220°C (425°F). Place the chicken on a baking tray, drizzle with olive oil and top with the sage. Roast for 20–25 minutes or until golden and cooked through.

While the chicken is cooking, make the basic polenta recipe, substituting the parmesan with the cheddar. Add the corn and extra sage and stir to combine. Spoon onto plates, top with the chicken and sage and serve with green beans. SERVES 4
+ A chicken supreme is a boneless cut of breast fillet with the wingtip still attached.

pork, veal and fennel meatballs with spaghetti

risotto with maple-glazed bacon

pork, veal and fennel meatballs with spaghetti

2 tablespoons olive oil
4 cups basic homemade tomato sauce (see recipe, page 167)
    or store-bought tomato purée (passata)
600g spaghetti
finely grated parmesan, to serve
pork, veal and fennel meatballs
1 cup (70g) fresh breadcrumbs
¼ cup (60ml) milk
2 teaspoons sea salt flakes
2 teaspoons fennel seeds
1 teaspoon dried chilli flakes
500g pork mince (ground pork)
500g veal mince (ground veal)
1 tablespoon finely grated lemon rind
1 egg yolk
½ cup (40g) finely grated parmesan
2 tablespoons chopped thyme
2 cloves garlic, crushed
cracked black pepper

To make the pork, veal and fennel meatballs, place the breadcrumbs and milk in a large bowl and allow to stand for 5 minutes. Place the salt, fennel and chilli flakes in a mortar and pestle and grind to combine. Add the salt mixture to the breadcrumbs with the pork, veal, lemon rind, egg yolk, parmesan, thyme, garlic and pepper and mix for 2–3 minutes or until the mixture comes together. Roll tablespoonfuls of the mixture into balls. Heat the oil in a large, non-stick frying pan over high heat. Cook the meatballs, in batches, for 5–6 minutes until browned. Remove from the pan and keep warm. Add the tomato sauce to the pan and bring to the boil. Reduce heat to medium and cook for 5 minutes.

While the sauce is cooking, cook the pasta in a large saucepan of salted boiling water for 10–12 minutes or until al dente. Drain and transfer to a large dish. Add the meatballs to the sauce and stir gently to combine. Top the pasta with the meatballs and sauce and sprinkle with parmesan to serve. SERVES 4–6

risotto with maple-glazed bacon

6 rashers bacon, rind removed
½ cup (125ml) maple syrup
1.5 litres chicken stock
60g unsalted butter
1 brown onion, finely chopped
2 cups (400g) arborio rice*
½ cup (125ml) dry sherry
½ cup (40g) finely grated parmesan
sea salt and cracked black pepper
½ cup (40g) shaved pecorino*

Preheat oven to 160°C (325°F). Place the bacon and maple syrup in a bowl and toss to coat. Place the bacon on a baking tray lined with non-stick baking paper and cook for 8–10 minutes or until golden, crisp and caramelised. Set aside and keep warm.

Heat the stock in a saucepan over medium heat. Melt the butter in a large saucepan over medium heat. Add the onion and cook for 5 minutes or until softened. Add the rice and sherry and cook, stirring, for 1–2 minutes or until the sherry is absorbed. Gradually add the hot stock, 1 cup (250ml) at a time, stirring for 25–30 minutes or until the stock is absorbed and the rice is tender. Remove from the heat and stir through the parmesan, salt and pepper. Divide between bowls and top with the bacon and pecorino to serve. SERVES 4

spring pea and mint risotto

2 cups mint leaves, roughly chopped
1 teaspoon sea salt flakes
1 tablespoon olive oil
75g unsalted butter, chopped
1 brown onion, finely chopped
2 cloves garlic, crushed
⅓ cup (80ml) dry white wine
2 cups (400g) arborio rice*
1.5 litres hot chicken stock
½ cup (40g) finely grated parmesan
2 cups (240g) fresh or frozen peas, thawed
200g sugar snap peas, trimmed, blanched and halved
sea salt and cracked black pepper
crème fraîche* and snow pea (mange tout) tendrils, to serve

Place the mint and salt in a mortar and pestle and pound until a rough paste forms. Add the oil, stir to combine and set aside. Melt 25g butter in a saucepan over medium heat. Add the onion and garlic and cook, stirring occasionally, for 4–5 minutes or until softened. Add the wine and cook for 2 minutes. Add the rice and cook, stirring, for 1–2 minutes. Add the stock, 1 cup (250ml) at a time, adding more once absorbed, and cook, stirring, for 20–25 minutes or until the rice is al dente. Remove from the heat and stir through the remaining ingredients. Top with the crème fraîche and tendrils to serve. SERVES 4

spring pea and mint risotto

HOW TO COOK paella

1 2
3 4

basic paella

½ tablespoon olive oil
1 dried chorizo*, sliced
3 x 125g chicken thigh fillets, roughly chopped
1½ cups (300g) arborio rice*
¼ cup (60ml) sherry vinegar*
2½ cups (625ml) chicken stock
300g mussels, cleaned
350g green (raw) prawns (shrimp), unpeeled
⅓ cup (40g) frozen peas, thawed
flat-leaf parsley leaves, to serve
tomato sauce
6 cloves garlic, peeled
1 onion, roughly chopped
200g store-bought roasted capsicum (bell pepper)
10 threads saffron
1 tablespoon thyme leaves
2 teaspoons sweet paprika*
2 teaspoons smoked paprika*
1 x 400g can crushed tomatoes
sea salt and cracked black pepper

STEP 1 To make the tomato sauce, place the garlic, onion, capsicum, saffron, thyme, sweet and smoked paprika, tomatoes, salt and pepper in a food processor and process until smooth. Set aside.

STEP 2 Heat the oil in a 4-litre capacity non-stick frying pan or paella pan over high heat. Add the chorizo and cook for 1–2 minutes or until golden. Add the chicken and cook for a further 2–3 minutes or until browned.

STEP 3 Add the rice and cook, stirring, for 1 minute. Add the vinegar and cook for 1 minute or until absorbed. Stir through the stock and tomato sauce and bring to the boil.

STEP 4 Push the mussels and prawns into the rice and reduce heat to low. Cook for 15 minutes without stirring. Increase heat to medium and cook for a further 4 minutes. Remove paella from the heat, top with the peas, cover with aluminium foil and set aside to rest for 15–18 minutes or until the liquid is absorbed. Top with parsley leaves to serve. SERVES 4

RECIPE NOTES
It's important to cover the paella with aluminium foil and allow it to rest for some time to ensure the rice absorbs any of the remaining liquid. This will help the paella to form a delicious crust on both the top and base.

basic paella

seafood paella

½ tablespoon olive oil
500g salmon fillet, skin off, cut into pieces
2 dried chorizo*, sliced
1½ cups (300g) arborio rice*
¼ cup (60ml) sherry vinegar*, plus 2 tablespoons, extra
2½ cups (625ml) chicken stock
1 x quantity tomato sauce (see recipe, page 62)
500g clams (vongole)
8 mussels, cleaned
¼ cup chopped coriander (cilantro) leaves
¼ cup (60ml) olive oil

Heat the oil in a 4 litre-capacity non-stick frying pan over high heat.
Add the salmon and cook for 3–4 minutes or until browned. Remove
from pan and set aside. Add the chorizo to the pan and cook for 2–3
minutes or until browned. Add the rice and cook, stirring, for 1 minute.
Add the vinegar and cook for 1 minute or until absorbed. Stir through
the stock and tomato sauce and bring to the boil. Return the salmon
to the pan, push the clams and mussels into the rice and reduce heat
to low. Cook for 15 minutes without stirring. Increase heat to medium
and cook for a further 4 minutes. Remove paella from the heat, cover
with aluminium foil and set aside to rest for 15–18 minutes or until the
liquid is absorbed. Mix to combine the coriander, oil and extra vinegar
and serve with the paella. SERVES 4

pork belly, calamari and tomato paella

900g pork belly, skin removed and roughly chopped
100g squid tubes, sliced
1½ cups (300g) arborio rice*
¼ cup (60ml) sherry vinegar*
2½ cups (625ml) chicken stock
1 x quantity tomato sauce (see recipe, page 62)
200g mixed tomatoes, halved
½ cup baby spinach leaves

Heat a 4 litre-capacity non-stick frying pan over high heat. Add the
pork belly and cook for 5 minutes or until browned. Add the squid
and cook for a further 2–3 minutes or until browned. Add the rice
and cook, stirring, for 1 minute. Add the vinegar and cook for 1 minute
or until absorbed. Stir through the stock and tomato sauce and bring
to the boil. Reduce heat to low and cook for 15 minutes without
stirring. Increase heat to medium and cook for a further 4 minutes.
Remove paella from the heat, add the tomatoes, cover with
aluminium foil and set aside to rest for 15–18 minutes or until the
liquid is absorbed. Top with the spinach leaves to serve. SERVES 4

chickpea and artichoke paella

1 tablespoon olive oil
1½ cups (300g) arborio rice*
1 teaspoon dried chilli flakes
1 x 400g can chickpeas (garbanzos), drained and rinsed
¼ cup (60ml) sherry vinegar*
2½ cups (625ml) chicken stock
1 x quantity tomato sauce (see recipe, page 62)
300g store-bought marinated artichoke hearts, halved
1 tablespoon shredded lemon zest
½ cup mint leaves

Heat the oil in a 4 litre-capacity non-stick frying pan over high heat.
Add the rice, chilli and chickpeas and cook, stirring, for 1 minute.
Add the vinegar and cook for 1 minute or until absorbed. Stir through
the stock and tomato sauce and bring to the boil. Reduce heat to low
and cook for 15 minutes without stirring. Remove paella from the
heat, top with the artichoke, cover with aluminium foil and set aside
to rest for 15–18 minutes or until the liquid is absorbed. Top with the
lemon zest and mint leaves to serve. SERVES 4

prawn, asparagus and chorizo paella

½ tablespoon olive oil
2 dried chorizo*, sliced
1½ cups (300g) arborio rice*
¼ cup (60ml) sherry vinegar*
2½ cups (625ml) chicken stock
1 x quantity tomato sauce (see recipe, page 62)
500g green (raw) prawns (shrimp), unpeeled
340g asparagus, trimmed and thinly sliced+
½ cup dill leaves

Heat the oil in a 4 litre-capacity non-stick frying pan over high heat.
Add the chorizo and cook for 2–3 minutes or until browned. Add the
rice and cook, stirring, for 1 minute. Add the vinegar and cook for
1 minute or until absorbed. Stir through the stock and tomato sauce
and bring to the boil. Push the prawns into the rice and reduce heat
to low. Cook for 15 minutes without stirring. Increase heat to medium
and cook for a further 4 minutes. Remove paella from the heat,
add the asparagus, cover with aluminium foil and set aside to rest for
15–18 minutes or until the liquid is absorbed. Top with the dill to serve.
SERVES 4
+ Thinly slice the asparagus lengthways using a vegetable peeler.

chicken and pork larb

sesame-crusted salmon with pickled daikon

chilli-salt salmon noodles

chicken and pork larb

3 carrots, thinly sliced[+]
2 tablespoons sea salt flakes
1 cup (250ml) white vinegar
¼ cup (55g) caster (superfine) sugar
250g vermicelli rice noodles
500g chicken mince (ground chicken)
500g pork mince (ground pork)
2 tablespoons chilli jam*
1 tablespoon sambal oelek*
¼ cup (60ml) oyster sauce
¼ cup (60ml) Chinese rice wine*
2 long red chillies*, chopped
3 cloves garlic, crushed
5cm piece (25g) fresh ginger, peeled and grated
1 teaspoon sesame oil
½ cup (125ml) chicken stock
coriander (cilantro) leaves, sliced green onions (scallions), sliced red
    onion and thinly sliced Lebanese cucumbers, to serve

Place the carrot and salt in a bowl and toss to combine. Set aside
for 10 minutes. Rinse to remove salt, drain and rinse again with cold
water. Place the vinegar and sugar in a saucepan over low heat and
cook, stirring, until sugar is dissolved. Bring to the boil and simmer
for 5 minutes. Allow to cool slightly before pouring over the carrot.
Refrigerate for 10 minutes.

Place the noodles in a bowl and cover with cold water. Set aside
for 15 minutes or until the noodles are softened. Drain and set aside.

Place the chicken, pork, chilli jam, sambal oelek, oyster sauce,
rice wine, chilli, garlic, ginger and sesame oil in a bowl and mix to
combine. Heat a large, non-stick frying pan over high heat. Add the
mince and cook, breaking up any lumps with a wooden spoon, for
6–8 minutes or until browned. Add the noodles and stock and cook,
stirring, for a further 1–2 minutes. Top the larb with coriander leaves,
green onion, red onion, cucumber and carrot to serve. SERVES 6
+ *Thinly slice the carrots using a vegetable peeler with a julienne attachment.*

sesame-crusted salmon with pickled daikon

500g daikon*, peeled and thinly sliced
1 tablespoon sea salt flakes
¼ cup (60ml) rice vinegar*
¼ cup (55g) white sugar
1 tablespoon white sesame seeds
1 tablespoon black sesame seeds
4 x 150g salmon fillets, skin on
320g soba noodles*
¼ cup (60ml) kecap manis*
3 green onions (scallions), thinly sliced
¼ cup pickled ginger*

Place the daikon in a non-metallic bowl and sprinkle with the salt.
Set aside for 30 minutes. Rinse well. Place the vinegar and sugar
in a small saucepan over high heat and bring to the boil. Allow to
cool slightly and pour over the daikon. Set aside.

Place the sesame seeds on a tray and mix to combine. Press the
salmon, skin-side down, into the sesame seeds to coat.

Heat a large non-stick frying pan over medium heat and cook the
salmon, skin-side down, for 3 minutes. Turn and cook for a further
2 minutes or until cooked to your liking.

Cook the noodles in a large saucepan of boiling water for 4–5
minutes or until softened. Drain, return to the saucepan with the
kecap manis and toss to coat. Top the noodles with the salmon,
green onion and ginger and serve with the daikon. SERVES 4

chilli-salt salmon noodles

¼ cup (60ml) kecap manis*
2 cloves garlic, crushed
3cm piece (15g) fresh ginger, peeled and finely grated
½ cup (125ml) water
1 tablespoon dried chilli flakes
1 tablespoon sea salt flakes
4 x 180g salmon fillets, skin removed
1 tablespoon vegetable oil
200g Swiss brown mushrooms, halved
200g dried flat rice noodles, cooked
1 cup coriander (cilantro) leaves

Place the kecap manis, garlic, ginger and water in a bowl and mix
to combine. Set aside.

Place the chilli flakes and salt on a tray and mix to combine.
Press both sides of the salmon into the chilli salt to coat. Slice each
fillet into 1cm-thick pieces. Heat the oil in a large wok or non-stick
frying pan over high heat. Add the salmon and cook, in batches,
for 1 minute each side. Remove from the pan and set aside. Add the
mushroom and cook for 2 minutes. Add the sauce and cook for
4 minutes or until the mushroom is tender. Top the noodles with
the salmon, mushroom and coriander to serve. SERVES 4

SOUPS

There are few things more comforting than a generous helping of soup. From delicate and invigorating broths to creamy, silken soups and robust vegetable-based bowls, there's plenty here to help warm the heart and soul.

french onion soup

spicy chicken dumpling soup

french onion soup

1 tablespoon olive oil
6 brown onions, sliced
3 cloves garlic, sliced
¼ cup (60ml) dry white wine
1.5 litres beef stock
slices of sourdough bread and grated gruyère*, to serve

Heat the oil in a saucepan over low heat. Add the onion and garlic and cook for 5–6 minutes or until softened. Add the wine and stock, increase the heat to high and cook for 10 minutes. Top the bread slices with the cheese and grill (broil) under a preheated hot grill (broiler) until melted. Place the toasts on the soups to serve. SERVES 4

spicy chicken dumpling soup

200g chicken mince (ground chicken)
1 green onion (scallion), chopped
1 tablespoon hoisin sauce*
1 small red chilli*, chopped
24 wonton wrappers*
water, for brushing
chicken soup
1 litre chicken stock
3 slices fresh ginger
1 long red chilli*, sliced
2 tablespoons soy sauce
¼ teaspoon sesame oil
1 bunch bok choy*, chopped
coriander (cilantro) to serve.

Combine the chicken mince, green onion, hoisin sauce and chilli. Place 1½ teaspoons of the mixture on a wonton wrapper and brush edges with water. Fold over to enclose and press edges to seal. Repeat with remaining mixture and wrappers. Place the stock, ginger, chilli, soy sauce and sesame oil in a saucepan and bring to the boil. Add the wontons and cook for 4–5 minutes. Add the bok choy and cook for 1 minute. Top with chilli and coriander to serve. SERVES 4

clam chowder

1 tablespoon olive oil
1 brown onion, chopped
3 cloves garlic, crushed
2 sprigs thyme
650g starchy potatoes, peeled and chopped
¼ cup (60ml) dry white wine
1 litre fish stock
1kg clams (vongole)
2 cups (500ml) milk
chopped flat-leaf parsley leaves, to serve

Heat the oil in a saucepan over high heat. Add the onion, garlic and thyme and cook for 3–4 minutes. Add the potatoes, wine and stock and cook for 20 minutes. Add the clams and milk and cook for 3–4 minutes. Sprinkle with the parsley to serve. SERVES 4

potato and leek soup with porcini oil

50g unsalted butter
4 leeks, white part only, sliced
1kg starchy potatoes, peeled and chopped
2 cups (500ml) chicken stock
2 cups (500ml) water
2 cups (500ml) milk
sea salt and cracked black pepper
porcini oil
10g dried porcini mushrooms*
⅓ cup (80ml) olive oil
crispy leeks
2 tablespoons olive oil
1 leek, white part only, thinly sliced

Melt the butter in a saucepan over low heat. Add the leek and cook for 5 minutes or until softened. Increase the heat to high, add the potato, stock and water and bring to the boil. Reduce the heat to low and cook for 20 minutes or until the potato is tender.

While the soup is cooking, make the porcini oil and crispy leeks. To make the porcini oil, place the porcini and oil in a small saucepan over low heat. Cook for 10 minutes. Strain and set aside.

To make the crispy leeks, heat the oil in a frying pan over high heat. Add the leek and cook for 1–2 minutes or until golden and crisp. Drain on absorbent paper. Set aside.

Remove the soup from the heat and using a hand-held blender, blend until smooth. Stir through the milk, salt and pepper. Return to the heat and cook for 2–3 minutes or until warmed through. Divide the soup between bowls, spoon over the porcini oil and top with crispy leeks to serve. SERVES 4-6

clam chowder

potato and leek soup with porcini oil

roasted garlic and pumpkin soup
+ cheesy leek and polenta madeleines

tofu and pumpkin laksa

roasted garlic and pumpkin soup

1 x 2kg butternut pumpkin (squash), seeds removed and halved
1 brown onion, halved
1 head garlic, cloves separated
olive oil, for drizzling
3 cups (750ml) water
½ cup (125ml) single (pouring) cream*
1 teaspoon freshly grated or ground nutmeg
sea salt and cracked black pepper

Preheat oven to 200°C (400°F). Place the pumpkin, cut-side up, on a baking tray with the onion and garlic and drizzle with oil. Roast for 50–55 minutes or until the pumpkin is golden and cooked through. Scoop the pumpkin and onion from their skins and place in a food processor. Squeeze the garlic cloves from their skins and add to the processor. Add 1 cup (250ml) water and process until smooth. Transfer the mixture to a saucepan over medium heat. Add the remaining water, cream, nutmeg, salt and pepper and cook until the soup is heated through. Serve with cheesy leek and polenta madeleines (see recipe, below). SERVES 4

cheesy leek and polenta madeleines

20g unsalted butter
1 leek, trimmed and sliced
⅓ cup (80ml) buttermilk
⅓ cup (55g) instant polenta
2 tablespoons plain (all-purpose) flour, sifted
¼ teaspoon bicarbonate of (baking) soda, sifted
½ cup (40g) grated cheddar
¼ cup chopped chives
sea salt and cracked black pepper
20g unsalted butter, extra, melted
1 egg

Preheat oven to 180°C (350°F). Melt the butter in a non-stick frying pan over medium heat. Add the leek and cook for 5 minutes or until softened. Place the leek and buttermilk in a food processor and process until smooth. Place the polenta, flour, bicarbonate of soda, cheese, chives, salt and pepper in a bowl and mix well to combine. Add the extra melted butter, egg and leek mixture and stir until smooth. Spoon into 16 lightly greased madeleine moulds+ and bake for 10–12 minutes or until cooked when tested with a skewer. Turn out onto a rack to cool. MAKES 16
+ Madeleine moulds are available from kitchenware stores.

tofu and pumpkin laksa

1 tablespoon vegetable oil
⅔ cup (185g) store-bought laksa paste*
2 cups (500ml) chicken stock
800ml coconut milk
2 tablespoons fish sauce*
800g pumpkin, peeled and sliced
400g broccolini, trimmed and chopped
250g dried vermicelli rice noodles, cooked
300g silken tofu*, sliced
4 green onions (scallions), thinly sliced
1 cup coriander (cilantro) leaves
2 long red chillies, sliced

Heat the oil in a large saucepan over high heat. Add the laksa paste and cook for 1 minute or until fragrant. Add the stock, coconut milk and fish sauce and bring to the boil. Add the pumpkin and cook for 12 minutes or until tender. Add the broccolini and cook for a further 2 minutes or until tender. Divide the noodles between bowls and spoon over the soup. Top with the tofu, green onion, coriander and chilli to serve. SERVES 4

———————

TRY THIS WITH...
snow peas
snake beans
gai larn

HOW TO COOK chicken soup

1

2

basic chicken soup

2 stalks celery, chopped
1 carrot, peeled and chopped
1 cup (220g) risoni or small pasta
sea salt and cracked black pepper
chopped flat-leaf parsley leaves, to serve
chicken stock
1 x 1.5kg whole chicken
1 brown onion, chopped
2 cloves garlic, chopped
2 stalks celery, chopped
1 carrot, peeled and chopped
4 bay leaves
1 teaspoon black peppercorns
2.5 litres water or enough to cover

STEP 1 To make the chicken stock, place the chicken, onion, garlic, celery, carrot, bay leaves, peppercorns and water in a large saucepan over high heat. Bring to the boil, cover and reduce the heat to low. Cook for 1 hour or until the chicken is cooked through.
STEP 2 Use a large metal spoon to occasionally skim the foam from the surface. Remove the chicken from the stock and allow to cool slightly.
STEP 3 Remove the skin and discard. Shred the chicken meat from the bones, discarding the bones, and set aside.
STEP 4 Strain the stock, discarding the vegetables. Return the stock to the pan with the celery, carrot, risoni, shredded chicken, salt and pepper. Cook over high heat for 10–15 minutes or until the vegetables are tender. Top with parsley to serve. SERVES 6

RECIPE NOTES
Skimming the foam from the surface of the stock removes the impurities so it will have a cleaner, sweeter flavour and look clear instead of cloudy.

basic chicken soup

ham, lentil and kale soup

celeriac and potato soup

creamy cauliflower soup

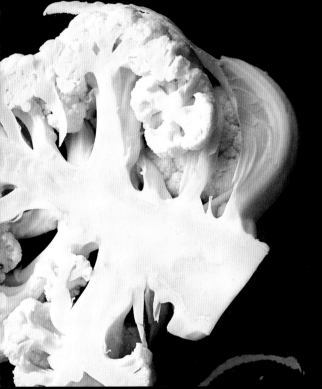

½ cup (125ml) single (pouring) cream
sea salt and cracked white pepper
parmesan cauliflower crumbs
100g chopped cauliflower
2 tablespoons olive oil
¼ cup (20g) finely grated parmesan

Melt the butter in a saucepan over low heat. Add the onion, garlic,
thyme and bay leaf and cook for 5–8 minutes or until onion has
softened. Add the cauliflower, potato, stock and milk, increase heat
to medium and cook for 25–30 minutes or until cauliflower and
potato are tender. Remove from the heat and using a hand-held
blender, blend until smooth. Stir through the cream, salt and pepper.
    While the soup is cooking, make the crumbs. Mix to combine the
cauliflower, oil and parmesan. Heat a non-stick frying pan over high
heat. Cook the cauliflower, stirring, for 2 minutes or until golden and
crisp. Top soup with cauliflower crumbs to serve. SERVES 4

SAVOURY | soups

BEEF

Whether it's the perfect steak, a Sunday beef roast with all the trimmings, or slowly braised cuts such as brisket or ribs, this compilation of flavoursome recipes is sure to make your list of go-to classics.

horseradish beef with roasted beetroot

sticky asian beef ribs

corned beef with cabbage, leek and cauliflower mash

horseradish beef with roasted beetroot

2 tablespoons grated fresh horseradish*
2 cloves garlic, crushed
1 x 2.6kg (4-bone) beef rib roast
sea salt and cracked black pepper
2 bunches sage
1kg mixed beetroot, rinsed and halved
10 eschalots* (French shallots), peeled
½ cup (125ml) balsamic vinegar
1 tablespoon olive oil
¼ cup (45g) brown sugar

Preheat oven to 220°C (425°F). Place the horseradish and garlic
in a bowl and mix to combine. Rub the beef with the horseradish
mixture and sprinkle with salt and pepper. Tie the sage to the
underside of the beef using kitchen string and place in a roasting dish.
Place the beetroot, eschalots, vinegar, olive oil and sugar in a bowl
and toss to coat. Add to the roasting dish with the beef and roast
for 20 minutes. Reduce temperature to 200°C (400°F) and roast
for a further 40–50 minutes. Cover and set aside for 10 minutes
to rest before carving. Serve the beef with the beetroot and
eschalots. SERVES 6-8

sticky asian beef ribs

2kg beef short ribs
6 sticks cinnamon
6 whole star anise
5cm piece (25g) ginger, peeled and sliced
2 cloves garlic, unpeeled
¼ cup (45g) brown sugar
¾ cup (180ml) oyster sauce
¾ cup (180ml) Chinese black vinegar*
1 cup (250ml) water

Preheat oven to 180°C (350°F). Place the beef, cinnamon, star anise,
ginger, garlic, sugar, oyster sauce, vinegar and water in a baking dish
and cover tightly with aluminium foil. Roast for 2 hours. Remove foil
and roast for a further 30 minutes or until tender and sticky.
SERVES 4-6

corned beef with cabbage, leek and cauliflower mash

1 x 2kg piece beef brisket, trimmed and cut into 2 pieces
sea salt and cracked black pepper
1 tablespoon sea salt flakes, extra
1 teaspoon black peppercorns
4 bay leaves
1 stalk celery, trimmed and chopped
1 carrot, peeled and chopped
1 brown onion, sliced
6 cloves garlic, peeled
2 cups (500ml) sherry vinegar*
2 cups (350g) brown sugar
leek and cabbage mash
1kg starchy potatoes, peeled and chopped
1kg cauliflower, chopped
½ cup (120g) sour cream
50g butter
sea salt and cracked black pepper
2 tablespoons olive oil
200g speck*, chopped
3 leeks, trimmed and sliced
300g white cabbage, sliced

Sprinkle the beef with salt and pepper. Place in a large heavy-based
saucepan over high heat with the extra salt, peppercorns, bay leaves,
celery, carrot, onion, garlic, vinegar, sugar and enough water to cover,
and bring to the boil. Reduce heat to low, cover, and cook, using a
spoon to skim any foam from the surface, for 3–3½ hours or until
tender. Remove beef from the cooking liquid and use 2 forks to shred
into large pieces. Strain the cooking liquid, reserving 3 cups. Set aside
and keep warm.

To make the leek and cabbage mash, place the potato in a large
saucepan of salted cold water and bring to the boil. Cook for
15 minutes, add the cauliflower and cook for a further 5 minutes or
until tender. Drain and return the potato and cauliflower to the pan
with the sour cream, butter, salt and pepper, and mash until smooth.
Set aside and keep warm.

Heat 1 tablespoon oil in a large non-stick frying pan over high heat.
Add the speck and cook for 5 minutes or until crispy. Set aside.
Add the remaining oil to the pan with the leek and cabbage and cook
for 5 minutes or until softened. Add the speck, leek and cabbage to
the potato and cauliflower mash and mix to combine. Set aside and
keep warm. Place the reserved cooking liquid in a large non-stick
frying pan over high heat and bring to the boil. Cook for 5 minutes
or until reduced slightly. Serve the brisket with the cabbage and leek
mash and pan sauce. SERVES 6

HOW TO COOK roasted beef

1 2
3 4

classic pepper-roasted beef

1kg beef scotch fillet, trimmed
olive oil, for brushing
¼ cup (40g) cracked black pepper
sea salt flakes

STEP 1 Preheat oven to 180°C (350°F). Using a small, sharp knife, trim any excess fat and sinew from the beef.

STEP 2 Cut a metre-long piece of kitchen string. Starting at the end of the beef furthest from you, secure the string in the centre at the top of the beef with a knot, leaving a little 'tail' of string about 10cm long.

STEP 3 Pull the long end of the string down from the knot. At about 2cm, use your finger to create a hook in the string. Holding the string in place with your finger, wrap the tail of the string around the beef, bringing it back to your finger, before threading it through the hook. Pull the string down from the hook to create another 2cm section. Repeat along the length of the beef at 2cm intervals. Once at the end, take the string under the beef, weave through the strings on the underside and secure to the tail of string at the end where you started.

STEP 4 Brush beef with oil and roll in pepper. Sprinkle with salt. Heat a large frying pan over high heat. Cook the beef for 1–2 minutes each side or until browned.

STEP 5 Place on a baking tray and roast for 50–55 minutes for medium rare or until cooked to your liking. Cover and allow to rest for 10 minutes before slicing. Slice to serve. SERVES 4-6

SERVE WITH...
Crispy roasted potatoes, blanched green beans and your favourite condiments, such as horseradish, gravy or mustard.

classic pepper-roasted beef

prosciutto and caramelised onion roasted beef

1kg beef scotch fillet, trimmed
olive oil, for brushing
sea salt and cracked black pepper
12 slices prosciutto
¼ cup (75g) store-bought caramelised onion relish, plus extra,
  to serve

Preheat oven to 180°C (350°F). Brush the beef with oil and sprinkle
with salt and pepper. Heat a large frying pan over high heat. Cook the
beef for 1–2 minutes each side or until browned. Set aside. Arrange
the prosciutto slices on a cutting board or clean benchtop, making
sure they overlap. Top the prosciutto with the caramelised onion.
Place the beef in the middle of the prosciutto and fold over to enclose.
Secure with kitchen string (see technique, page 92). Place on a
baking tray, brush with oil and roast for 50–55 minutes for medium
rare or until cooked to your liking. Slice and serve with extra
caramelised onion. SERVES 4-6

mustard roasted beef

3 tablespoons wholegrain mustard
1 teaspoon cracked black pepper, plus extra, for sprinkling
1 clove garlic, crushed
1 x 1.5kg scotch fillet, trimmed and tied (see page 92)
sea salt
1 tablespoon olive oil
steamed green beans, to serve

Preheat oven to 180°C (350°F). Place the mustard, pepper and
garlic in a bowl and mix to combine. Sprinkle the beef with salt and
extra pepper. Heat the oil in a large non-stick frying pan over high
heat. Cook the beef for 2 minutes each side or until browned.
Remove from the pan and spread evenly with the mustard mixture.
Place on a baking tray lined with non-stick baking paper and roast
for 50–60 minutes for medium rare or until cooked to your liking.
Allow to rest for 10 minutes before slicing. Serve with steamed
green beans. SERVES 4-6

roasted beef with porcini salt

20g dried porcini mushrooms*
1 tablespoon sea salt flakes
1 tablespoon olive oil
1 x 1.5kg scotch fillet, trimmed and tied (see page 92)
roasted garlic and field mushrooms, to serve

Preheat oven to 180°C (350°F). Place the porcini in a small food
processor and process until finely crumbled. Add the salt and pulse to
combine. Spread the porcini salt evenly over the beef fillet. Heat
the oil in a large non-stick frying pan over high heat. Cook the beef
for 2 minutes each side or until well browned. Remove from the pan
and place on a baking tray lined with non-stick baking paper. Roast
for 50–60 minutes for medium rare or until cooked to your liking.
Allow to rest for 10 minutes before slicing. Serve with roasted garlic
and field mushrooms. SERVES 4–6

tarragon horseradish beef

1 cup tarragon leaves
1 tablespoon store-bought horseradish cream*
½ teaspoon sea salt flakes, plus extra, for sprinkling
1 teaspoon cracked black pepper, plus extra, for sprinkling
1 x 1.5kg scotch fillet, trimmed and tied (see page 92)
1 tablespoon olive oil
roasted potatoes, to serve

Preheat oven to 180°C (350°F). Place the tarragon, horseradish,
salt and pepper in a small food processor and process to form a
paste. Sprinkle the beef with the extra salt and pepper. Heat the
oil in a large non-stick frying pan over high heat. Cook the beef for
2 minutes each side or until well browned. Remove from the pan
and spread evenly with the tarragon mixture. Place on a baking tray
lined with non-stick baking paper and roast for 50–60 minutes
for medium rare or until cooked to your liking. Allow to rest for
10 minutes before slicing. Serve with roasted potatoes. SERVES 4–6

texan-style barbecue brisket

1 x 2kg piece beef brisket, trimmed
1 head garlic, halved
2 cups (350g) brown sugar
3 cups (750ml) beef stock
1 cup (250ml) white vinegar
2 ancho chillies*
barbecue sauce
2 cloves garlic, crushed
¼ cup (60ml) maple syrup
¼ cup (45g) brown sugar
2 teaspoons smoked paprika*
2 tablespoons Worcestershire sauce
2 cups (560g) tomato purée (passata)
1 teaspoon cayenne pepper
¼ cup (60ml) malt vinegar
2 teaspoons mustard powder

Place the beef, garlic, sugar, stock, vinegar and chillies in a large, heavy-based saucepan over high heat and bring to the boil. Reduce heat to low, cover with a tight-fitting lid, and cook for 4 hours or until tender. Remove the beef from the pan, place in a baking dish and set aside. Discard the cooking liquid.

To make the barbecue sauce, place the garlic, maple syrup, brown sugar, paprika, Worcestershire sauce, tomato purée, cayenne pepper, vinegar and mustard powder in a saucepan over low heat and cook, stirring, for 2–3 minutes or until the sugar is dissolved. Increase heat to high and bring to the boil for 5 minutes or until thickened. Pour half the barbecue sauce over the beef and turn to coat, reserving the remaining barbecue sauce. Place in the fridge for 1 hour to marinate.

Preheat oven to 200°C (400°F). Place the beef on a baking tray and cook, brushing every 5 minutes with the barbecue sauce, for 15–20 minutes or until dark and sticky. Slice and serve with the reserved barbecue sauce. SERVES 6
Tip: For this recipe, ask your butcher for a piece of brisket with an even thickness, as it will be sliced rather than shredded.

pancetta beef burger with tarragon mayonnaise

1 cup (70g) fresh breadcrumbs
2 tablespoons milk
500g beef mince (ground beef)
1 clove garlic, crushed
1 tablespoon tomato paste
1 tablespoon Worcestershire sauce
2 tablespoons chopped flat-leaf parsley leaves
sea salt and cracked black pepper
12 slices round pancetta*
6 ciabatta or crusty bread rolls, halved and toasted
spinach leaves, store-bought caramelised onion relish,
    sliced aged cheddar and gherkins (dill pickles), to serve
tarragon mayonnaise
½ cup (150g) whole-egg mayonnaise
1 teaspoon Dijon mustard
1 tablespoon chopped tarragon leaves

To make the tarragon mayonnaise, place the mayonnaise, mustard and tarragon in a bowl and mix to combine. Set aside.

Place the breadcrumbs and milk in a bowl and set aside for 5 minutes or until the milk is absorbed. Add the mince, garlic, tomato paste, Worcestershire sauce, parsley, salt and pepper and mix until well combined. Shape into 6 large, flat patties. Place a slice of pancetta on each side of the patties. Heat a large, non-stick frying pan or barbecue over high heat. Add the patties and cook, in batches, for 4 minutes each side or until cooked to your liking. Spread the rolls with the tarragon mayonnaise and top with the spinach leaves, patties, caramelised onion and cheddar. Serve with the gherkins.
MAKES 6

texan style barbecue brisket

pancetta beef burger with tarragon mayonnaise

the new steak sandwich

salted rump steak
+ roasted potatoes with chimichurri

the new steak sandwich

20g unsalted butter
12 large Swiss brown mushrooms
8 slices sourdough bread
olive oil, for brushing
4 x 100g scotch fillet steaks
160g taleggio*, sliced
50g watercress sprigs
rosemary and porcini salt
1 tablespoon dried porcini mushrooms*
1 tablespoon chopped rosemary leaves
2 tablespoons sea salt flakes
horseradish mayonnaise
⅓ cup (100g) whole-egg mayonnaise
2 tablespoons horseradish cream*

To make the rosemary and porcini salt, place the porcini and rosemary in a small food processor and process until finely chopped. Add the salt and process until just combined. Set aside.

To make the horseradish mayonnaise, place the mayonnaise and horseradish cream in a bowl and mix to combine. Set aside.

Melt the butter in a char-grill pan over medium heat. Add the mushrooms and cook for 6–8 minutes or until tender. Remove from the pan and set aside. Brush the bread with oil and cook for 2 minutes each side or until golden. Set aside. Brush the steaks with oil, sprinkle with half the rosemary and porcini salt and cook for 1 minute. Turn steaks over, top with the taleggio and cook for a further 3–4 minutes or until cheese is melted. Spread half the bread slices with the horseradish mayonnaise and top with the steaks, mushrooms and watercress. Top with the remaining bread slices and serve with the remaining rosemary and porcini salt. MAKES 4

salted rump steak

1kg rump steak, cut into large pieces
1 tablespoon olive oil
1 cup (300g) rock salt
cracked black pepper

Thread the steak onto metal skewers and rub with oil. Place on a baking tray and cover completely with the rock salt. Place in the fridge for 1 hour. Wipe with absorbent paper to remove the rock salt and sprinkle with pepper. Heat a char-grill pan or barbecue over high heat. Add the skewers and cook for 7 minutes each side for medium- rare or until cooked to your liking. Serve with chimichurri sauce (see right). SERVES 4

TRY THIS WITH...
other cuts of beef
whole fish

roasted potatoes with chimichurri

1.5kg large starchy potatoes, peeled and chopped
2 tablespoons olive oil
100g wild rocket (arugula) leaves, to serve
chimichurri
⅓ cup chopped flat-leaf parsley leaves
1 tablespoon chopped oregano
2 teaspoons chopped rosemary
1 teaspoon smoked paprika*
½ teaspoon dried chilli flakes
1 clove garlic, crushed
1 bay leaf
3 tablespoons red wine vinegar
3 tablespoons olive oil
sea salt and cracked black pepper

To make the chimichurri, place the parsley, oregano, rosemary, paprika, chilli flakes, garlic, bay leaf, vinegar, oil, salt and pepper in a bowl and mix to combine. Set aside.

Preheat oven to 220°C (425°F). Place the potato in a large saucepan of salted cold water over high heat and bring to the boil. Cook for 10 minutes or until the potato is just tender. Drain, return the potato to the pan and cook for 1 minute to remove any excess moisture. Shake the pan to fluff the potato. Place on a baking tray, drizzle with the oil, sprinkle with salt and pepper and roast for 40–45 minutes or until crisp and golden. Serve the potatoes with the chimichurri and rocket leaves. SERVES 4–6

grilled beef tacos

1 brown onion, sliced
2 long red chillies*
2 cloves garlic
2 tablespoons vegetable oil
2 sprigs coriander (cilantro), chopped
1 teaspoon ground coriander (cilantro)
1 x 500g rump steak, trimmed
1 x quantity cornmeal or flour tortillas (see recipes, page 280)
lettuce leaves, sour cream and lime wedges, to serve

Heat a char-grill pan or barbecue over high heat. Char-grill or barbecue the onion, chillies and garlic, turning frequently, for 4–5 minutes or until softened. Place the onion mixture in a food processor with the oil, coriander stalks and powder and process until a paste forms. Place the beef in a bowl and pour over the paste. Cover with plastic wrap and refrigerate for 2 hours or overnight to marinate.

Preheat a char-grill pan or barbecue over high heat. Char-grill or barbecue the beef for 4–5 minutes each side for medium-rare or until cooked to your liking. Set aside. Slice the beef and serve in the tortillas with lettuce, sour cream, guacamole, char-grilled chillies, salsa roja (see recipes, page 176), and lime wedges. SERVES 8

grilled beef taco

chilli mince taco

chilli mince tacos

2 tablespoons vegetable oil
2 brown onions, sliced
3 cloves garlic, crushed
300g veal mince (ground veal)
300g sausage mince
1 teaspoon ground cumin
½ teaspoon dried chilli flakes
½ teaspoon hot paprika*
¼ cup oregano leaves
2 tablespoons lime juice
1 quantity cornmeal or flour tortillas (see recipes, page 280)
sour cream, chopped red chilli, coriander (cilantro) and lime wedges,
    to serve

Heat the oil in a large non-stick frying pan over high heat. Add the
onion and garlic and cook for 2–3 minutes or until softened. Add the
mince and cook, breaking up any lumps with a wooden spoon, for
4–5 minutes or until browned. Add the cumin, chilli flakes, paprika,
oregano and lime juice and mix well to combine. Serve the mince in
the tortillas with sour cream, chilli, salsa cruda (see recipes, page 216),
pickled chillies (see recipe, below), coriander (cilantro) and lime
wedges. SERVES 8

SAUCES + CONDIMENTS
pickled chillies: Place 10 long red chillies, 10 long green chillies and
2 sprigs coriander (cilantro) in a 2-litre capacity sterilised glass jar.
Place 3 cups (750ml) white wine vinegar, 3 cups (750ml) water,
4 halved cloves of garlic, ¾ cup (165g) caster (superfine) sugar and
1 tablespoon mustard seeds in a saucepan over high heat and cook for
2–3 minutes or until sugar is dissolved. Pour over the chillies and seal
jar. Allow to sit overnight. Refrigerate after opening. MAKES 2 LITRES

coconut chilli sambal

1½ cups (150g) grated fresh coconut+
2 tablespoons fish sauce*
1 tablespoon lime juice
1 tablespoon finely chopped palm sugar*
1 cup coriander (cilantro) leaves
1 long green chilli*, roughly chopped

Place the coconut, fish sauce, lime juice, sugar, coriander and chilli
in a small food processor and process until coarsely chopped. SERVES 4
+ *To use a fresh coconut, drain the juice by inserting a metal skewer
in the indented eye. Crack the shell with a sharpening steel or hammer.
Gently prise the flesh from the shell using a butter knife. Grate with a
box grater or Microplane. If you can't find fresh coconut, you could also
use moistened coconut flakes.*

beef rendang

1 tablespoon peanut oil
1 x 1.5kg piece beef brisket, halved
sea salt flakes
1½ cups rendang curry paste (see recipe, below)
800ml coconut milk
1½ cups (375ml) water
2 tablespoons fish sauce*
6 kaffir lime leaves*
1 stalk lemongrass, bruised
¼ cup (60ml) lime juice
coconut and chilli sambal (see recipe, left), to serve

Preheat oven to 180°C (350°F). Heat the oil in a large, heavy-based
saucepan over high heat. Sprinkle the beef with salt and cook for
4–5 minutes each side or until well browned. Set aside.
    Add the curry paste and cook, stirring, for 1–2 minutes or until
fragrant. Add the coconut milk, water, fish sauce, lime leaves and
lemongrass and bring to the boil. Return the beef to the pan and cover
with a tight-fitting lid. Roast for 2 hours, turn and roast, uncovered
and turning the meat occasionally, for a further 1 hour or until the
beef is tender and the sauce reduced. Add the lime juice and stir to
combine. Top with the coconut and chilli sambal to serve. SERVES 4

rendang curry paste

2 tablespoons coriander (cilantro) seeds
¼ teaspoon white peppercorns
½ cup (40g) desiccated coconut
3 long red chillies*, roughly chopped
2 eschalots* (French shallots), roughly chopped
4 cloves garlic, roughly chopped
6cm piece (30g) fresh galangal*, peeled and roughly chopped
6cm piece (30g) fresh ginger, peeled and roughly chopped
2cm piece (10g) fresh turmeric*, peeled and roughly chopped
1 stalk lemongrass, white part only, sliced
4 kaffir lime leaves*, shredded
1 tablespoon dark palm sugar*
2 tablespoons peanut oil

Heat a small frying pan over medium heat. Add the coriander
seeds and peppercorns and toast, shaking the pan frequently,
for 2–3 minutes or until fragrant and light golden. Place in a small
food processor and process until ground. Return the pan to the
heat, add the coconut and cook, shaking the pan frequently, for
2–3 minutes or until toasted. Add the coconut to the spices with
the chilli, eschalot, garlic, galangal, ginger, turmeric, lemongrass,
lime leaves, sugar and oil and process, scraping down the sides of
the bowl, until smooth. MAKES 1½ CUPS (375ML)

beef rendang

HOW TO COOK stir-fry

2
4

beef stir-fry

400g rump steak, cut into strips
1 teaspoon sea salt flakes
2 teaspoons freshly cracked black pepper
2 tablespoons peanut oil
2 long red chillies*, thinly sliced
5cm piece (25g) fresh ginger, peeled and thinly sliced
4 cloves garlic, thinly sliced
300g snow peas (mange tout)
½ cup (75g) roasted unsalted cashew nuts
¼ cup (60ml) soy sauce
1 teaspoon caster (superfine) sugar
1 cup coriander (cilantro) leaves
1 cup Thai basil leaves
steamed rice and lime wedges, to serve

STEP 1 Sprinkle the beef with the salt and pepper to coat.
STEP 2 Heat half the oil in a large wok or non-stick frying pan over high heat. Add the chilli, ginger and garlic and cook, stirring, for 1–2 minutes or until golden. Remove with a slotted spoon and set aside.
STEP 3 Heat the remaining oil and cook the beef, in batches, for 30 seconds each side or until well browned.
STEP 4 Add the snow peas and cashews with the reserved chilli mixture, soy sauce and sugar and cook, stirring, for 2–3 minutes or until the snow peas are tender and the sauce has reduced.
STEP 5 Top with the coriander and basil and serve with steamed rice and lime wedges. SERVES 4

RECIPE NOTES
It's important to cook the beef in batches so it sears and browns evenly. If you overload the wok, it will begin to stew rather than fry and caramelise.

beef stir-fry

spiced rump steak with tomato chutney

prosciutto wrapped eye fillet steak with ale jus
+ horseradish yorkshire puddings

prosciutto-wrapped eye fillet steaks with ale jus

2 slices prosciutto, halved lengthways
2 tablespoons store-bought caramelised onion relish
2 x 200g centre-cut eye fillet steaks, trimmed and at
    room temperature
olive oil, for brushing
ale jus
2 cloves garlic, crushed
1 tablespoon tomato paste
¼ cup (85g) store-bought caramelised onion relish
1 sprig rosemary
330ml dark ale
1 cup (250ml) beef consommé
sea salt and cracked black pepper

To make the ale jus, heat a saucepan over medium heat. Add the garlic, tomato paste and caramelised onion and cook, stirring, for 1 minute. Add the rosemary, ale, consommé, salt and pepper and cook for 25–30 minutes or until reduced by half. Strain, set aside and keep warm.

Preheat oven to 200°C (400°F). Place 2 prosciutto slices, overlapping, on top of each other and spread with caramelised onion. Repeat with remaining prosciutto and onion. Wrap each steak with the prosciutto pieces and tie with kitchen string. Sprinkle with salt and pepper and brush with oil. Heat a large ovenproof frying pan over medium heat. Add the steaks and cook for 2 minutes each side. Transfer to the oven and cook for a further 5 minutes for medium-rare or until cooked to your liking. Loosely cover the steaks with aluminium foil and allow to rest for 3–4 minutes. Spoon over the ale jus to serve. SERVES 2

horseradish yorkshire puddings

2 eggs
⅔ cup (160ml) milk
1 tablespoon store-bought horseradish cream*
½ cup (75g) plain (all-purpose) flour
40g ghee*, melted

Preheat oven to 220°C (425°F). Place the eggs, milk and horseradish in a bowl and whisk to combine. Gradually add the flour and whisk until smooth. Set aside for 30 minutes. Divide the ghee between 6 x ½ cup-capacity (125ml) muffin tins. Place the tins on a tray and cook for 5–7 minutes or until the ghee is just smoking. Remove from the oven and divide the batter between the tins. Bake for 20–25 minutes or until puffed and golden. SERVES 2

char-grilled sirloin steak with pink peppercorn and whisky sauce

2 x 200g sirloin steaks, trimmed and at room temperature
olive oil, for brushing
sea salt and cracked black pepper
pink peppercorn and whisky sauce
1 tablespoon olive oil
1 tablespoon unsalted butter
2 eschalots* (French shallots), chopped
2 cloves garlic, crushed
2 cups (500ml) beef stock
1 tablespoon pink peppercorns
¼ cup (60ml) single (pouring) cream*
2 tablespoons whisky

To make the pink peppercorn and whisky sauce, heat the oil and butter in a large frying pan over medium heat. Add the eschalot and garlic and cook, stirring, for 4 minutes or until softened. Add the stock and cook for 12–15 minutes or until reduced by half. Strain the sauce and return to the pan, discarding the eschalot and garlic. Add the peppercorns, salt, cream and whisky and cook for 3 minutes. Set aside.

Preheat a char-grill pan or barbecue over high heat. Brush the steaks with oil and sprinkle with salt and pepper. Cook the steaks for 3 minutes each side for medium-rare or until cooked to your liking. Serve the steaks with the peppercorn sauce. SERVES 2

crispy potato and gruyère dominoes

1kg large starchy potatoes, peeled and thinly sliced
50g unsalted butter, melted
½ cup (30g) finely grated gruyère*
sea salt flakes

Preheat oven to 200°C (400°F). Cut the potato slices into 8cm x 5cm rectangles. Place in a large bowl with the butter, cheese and salt and toss to combine. Place 8–10 potato slices, overlapping by 1cm, on a baking tray lined with non-stick baking paper. Repeat with the remaining potato. Bake for 25–30 minutes or until golden and crisp. SERVES 2

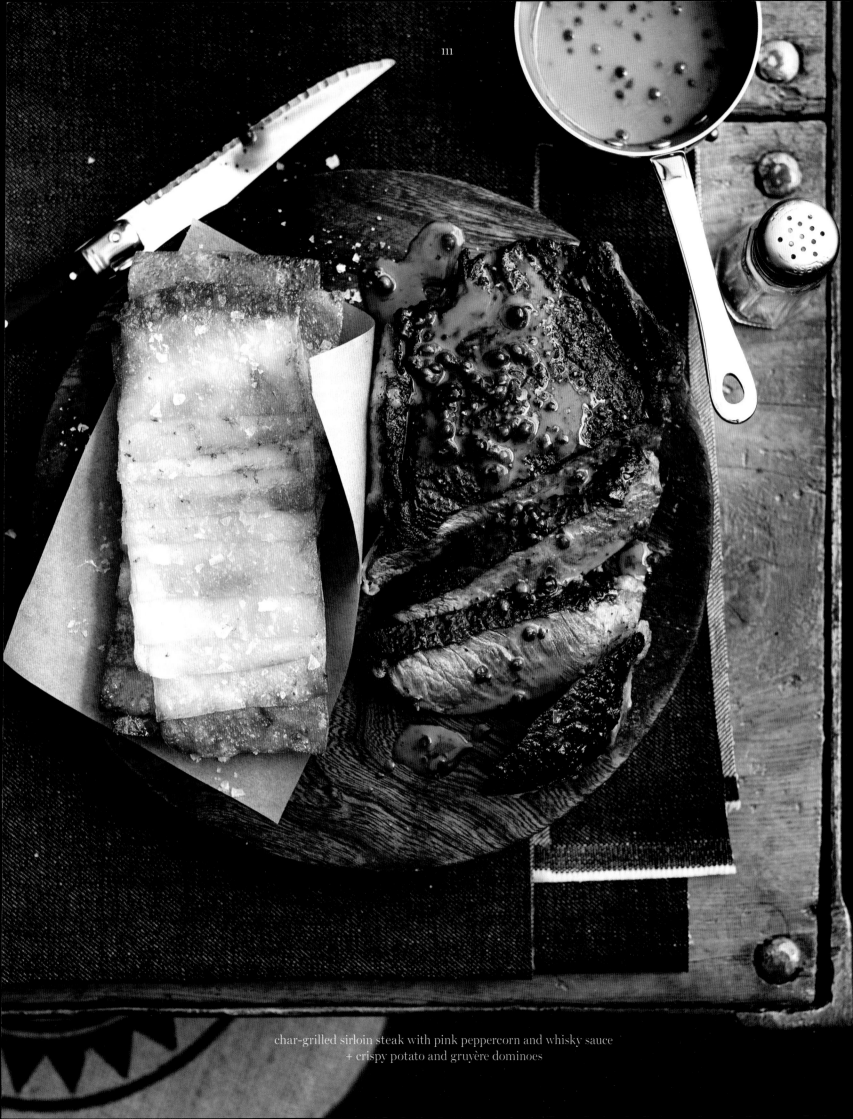

char-grilled sirloin steak with pink peppercorn and whisky sauce
+ crispy potato and gruyère dominoes

t–bone steak with thyme and garlic butter
+ jerusalem artichoke and potato chips with mustard salt

t-bone steak with thyme and garlic butter

60g unsalted butter
2 tablespoons olive oil
1 x 850g t-bone steak (2.5cm-thick), trimmed and at
    room temperature
sea salt and cracked black pepper
6 sprigs thyme
6 cloves garlic, unpeeled

Heat the butter and oil in a large frying pan over high heat for
1–2 minutes or until the butter starts to foam. Sprinkle the steak
with salt and pepper. Add the thyme, garlic and steak to the pan and
cook for 4–5 minutes each side, spooning the butter over the steak,
for medium-rare or until cooked to your liking. Drizzle the steak with
the butter to serve. SERVES 2

jerusalem artichoke and potato chips with mustard salt

vegetable oil, for deep-frying
300g waxy potatoes, thinly sliced
300g Jerusalem artichokes*, thinly sliced
mustard salt
1 tablespoon yellow mustard seeds
1 tablespoon sea salt flakes

To make the mustard salt, place the mustard seeds in a small frying
pan over medium heat and cook, stirring, for 1–2 minutes or until
fragrant. Place the mustard seeds and salt in a mortar and pestle
and pound until combined. Set aside.
    Heat the oil in a large saucepan over medium heat until the
temperature reaches 180°C (350°F) on a deep-frying thermometer.
Cook the potato, in batches, for 2–3 minutes or until golden and
crisp. Drain on absorbent paper. Cook the artichoke, in batches, for
3–4 minutes or until golden and crisp. Drain on absorbent paper.
Sprinkle the chips with the mustard salt and serve immediately.
SERVES 2
*Tip: The potatoes and Jerusalem artichokes can be sliced in advance and
kept in separate bowls covered with water to ensure they don't brown.
Just be sure to drain them well before cooking. Use a mandolin slicer
or vegetable peeler to thinly slice the chips.*

spiced rump steak with tomato chutney

2 teaspoons yellow mustard seeds
1 teaspoon fennel seeds
½ teaspoon coriander (cilantro) seeds
1 tablespoon sea salt flakes
½ teaspoon cracked black pepper
1 x 600g rump steak, trimmed and at room temperature
olive oil, for brushing
tomato chutney
500g Roma tomatoes, chopped
1 brown onion, chopped
3 sprigs thyme
1 teaspoon yellow mustard seeds
½ cup (125ml) malt vinegar
⅓ cup (75g) caster (superfine) sugar
sea salt and cracked black pepper

To make the tomato chutney, place the tomato, onion, thyme,
mustard seeds, vinegar, sugar, salt and pepper in a large frying pan
over medium heat and cook, stirring occasionally, until the sugar is
dissolved. Reduce heat to low and cook, stirring occasionally, for a
further 20–30 minutes or until thickened[+].
    Place the mustard, fennel and coriander seeds in a small frying pan
over medium heat and cook, stirring, for 1–2 minutes or until fragrant.
Place in a food processor with the salt and pepper and process until
coarsely ground. Rub the steak with the spice mixture. Preheat a
char-grill pan or barbecue over high heat. Brush the steak with oil and
cook for 2 minutes each side for medium-rare or until cooked to your
liking. Set aside to rest for 2–3 minutes before slicing. Serve with the
tomato chutney. SERVES 2
*+ The tomato chutney makes 2 cups (500ml) and will keep in the
refrigerator for up to 2 weeks.*

crispy pan-fried kale, eschalots and potatoes

400g starchy potatoes, peeled and chopped
40g unsalted butter
1 tablespoon olive oil
sea salt and cracked black pepper
6 eschalots* (French shallots), peeled
100g kale, stems removed and roughly chopped

Place the potato in a saucepan of cold salted water over high heat. Bring to the boil and cook for 5 minutes or until partially cooked. Drain and set aside. Heat the butter and oil in a non-stick frying pan over medium heat. Add the potato, salt and pepper and cook, stirring occasionally, for 10 minutes. Add the eschalots and cook for 5 minutes or until the potato is golden and the eschalots are tender. Increase the heat to high, add the kale and cook for a further 3 minutes or until the kale is just crisp around the edges. SERVES 2

oven-roasted rib-eye steak with porcini and port butter

1 x 600g rib-eye steak, trimmed and at room temperature
olive oil, for brushing
sea salt and cracked black pepper
porcini and port butter
½ cup (10g) dried porcini mushrooms*
⅓ cup (80ml) boiling water
2 eschalots* (French shallots), finely chopped
½ cup (125ml) port
125g unsalted butter, softened
1 tablespoon finely chopped flat-leaf parsley leaves
1 tablespoon finely chopped thyme
sea salt and cracked black pepper

To make the porcini and port butter, place the porcini and boiling water in a bowl and set aside for 10 minutes to soak. Drain, reserving the liquid, and finely chop. Place the porcini, reserved liquid, eschalot and port in a small saucepan over medium heat and bring to the boil. Cook for 6–7 minutes or until most of the liquid has evaporated. Place in a large bowl and allow to cool slightly. Add the butter, parsley, thyme, salt and pepper and mix to combine. Place the butter in the centre of a sheet of non-stick baking paper and shape into a 20cm-long log. Roll to enclose, wrap in aluminium foil, twisting the ends to seal, and refrigerate for 30 minutes or until firm+.

Preheat oven to 200°C (400°F). Brush the steak with oil and sprinkle with salt and pepper. Heat a large ovenproof frying pan over high heat. Cook the steak for 3–4 minutes each side. Transfer to the oven and cook, turning halfway, for a further 15 minutes for medium-rare or until cooked to your liking. Loosely cover the steak with aluminium foil and set aside to rest for 6–8 minutes. Slice the butter and serve with the steak. SERVES 2
+ *The porcini and port butter will keep in the freezer for up to 2 months.*

SERVE THE BUTTER WITH...
roasted beef
chicken
boiled potatoes

oven-roasted rib-eye steak with porcini and port butter
+ crispy pan-fried kale, eschalots and potatoes

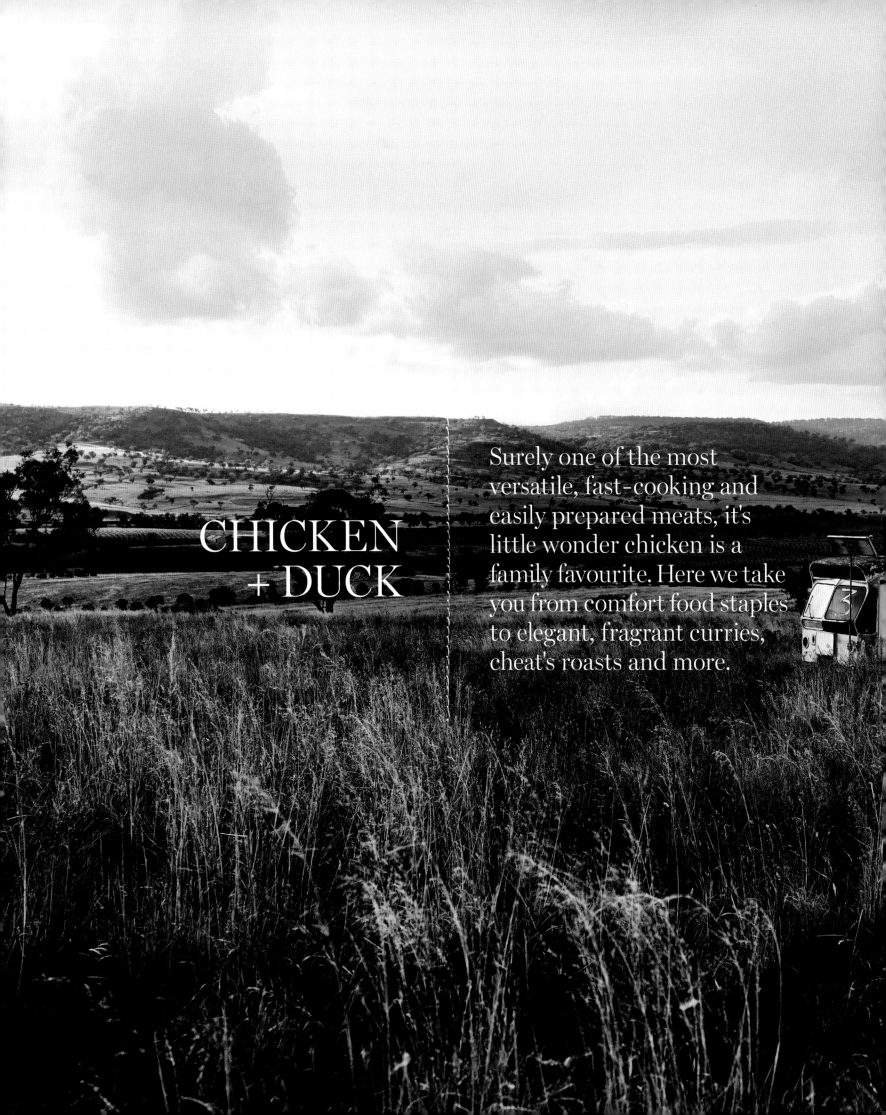

CHICKEN + DUCK

Surely one of the most versatile, fast-cooking and easily prepared meats, it's little wonder chicken is a family favourite. Here we take you from comfort food staples to elegant, fragrant curries, cheat's roasts and more.

twiced-cooked chicken with ginger and coriander salt

sticky chinese-style chicken

chicken master stock

twice-cooked chicken with ginger and coriander salt

1 x quantity chicken master stock (see recipe, below)
rice flour, for dusting
vegetable oil, for deep-frying
lime wedges, to serve
ginger and coriander salt
15g crystallised ginger*
1½ tablespoons sesame seeds
2 tablespoons chopped coriander (cilantro) leaves
½ teaspoon dried chilli flakes
⅓ cup (40g) sea salt flakes

Make the chicken master stock by following the recipe below. Remove the cooked chicken from the broth and place on a baking tray. Allow to cool to room temperature before placing in the refrigerator for 1 hour.

To make the ginger and coriander salt, pound the ginger and sesame seeds in a mortar and pestle until a paste forms. Add the coriander and chilli flakes and pound to combine. Stir through the salt. Set aside.

Chop the chicken into 12–14 pieces and dust in the rice flour. Heat the oil in a deep saucepan over medium heat until temperature reaches 180°C (350°F) on a deep-frying thermometer. Deep-fry the chicken, in batches, for 3–4 minutes or until golden. Drain on absorbent paper and toss in half the ginger and coriander salt. Serve with the remaining salt and lime wedges. SERVES 8

chicken master stock

5 green onions (scallions), cut into lengths
1 brown onion, peeled and quartered
2 long red chillies*
100g fresh ginger, peeled and sliced
6 cloves garlic, bruised
¼ cup (60ml) light soy sauce
1 cup (250ml) Chinese cooking wine*
¼ cup (60ml) caster (superfine) sugar
4 litres water
1 x 1.8kg whole chicken

Place the green onion, onion, chillies, ginger, garlic, soy, cooking wine, sugar and water in a large saucepan over high heat and bring to the boil. Add the chicken, breast-side down, and return to the boil. Reduce heat to medium and cook for 20 minutes. Remove from the heat, cover with a tight-fitting lid and allow to stand for 1 hour. SERVES 4–6
Tip: You can strain the broth and use to make soups and shred the chicken for salads and sandwiches. Freeze for up to three months.

sticky chinese-style chicken

1 x quantity chicken master stock (see recipe, left)
6 whole star anise
4 sticks cinnamon
peel of 1 orange
1 teaspoon Chinese five-spice powder*
char sui marinade
¼ cup (60ml) oyster sauce
¼ cup (60ml) Chinese cooking wine*
⅓ cup (115g) char siu (Chinese barbecue) sauce*
¼ cup (60ml) corn syrup

Make the master stock by following the recipe, adding 3 star anise and 2 sticks cinnamon to the broth. Remove the cooked chicken from the broth and allow to cool to room temperature before placing in the refrigerator for 30 minutes.

Preheat oven to 200°C (400°F). To make the char sui marinade, pour the oyster sauce, cooking wine, char sui and corn syrup in a saucepan over high heat and bring to the boil. Reduce heat to low and cook for 5 minutes, stirring occasionally, or until thickened. Allow to cool slightly.

Place the remaining star anise and cinnamon in the cavity of the chicken with the orange peel and five-spice. Secure the legs with kitchen string. Place the chicken on a lightly greased wire rack on a baking tray lined with aluminium foil and brush with the char siu marinade. Roast for 35–40 minutes, brushing with the marinade every 10 minutes, or until sticky and glazed. SERVES 4-6

chinese-poached chicken

sticky lime and ginger chicken

chinese-poached chicken

3 cloves garlic, peeled
5cm piece (25g) fresh ginger, peeled and sliced
3 whole star anise
2 sticks cinnamon
½ teaspoon Sichuan peppercorns*
1 teaspoon Chinese five-spice powder*
1 long red chilli*, halved
1 cup (250ml) Chinese rice wine*
½ cup (125ml) dark soy sauce
peel of 1 orange
2 litres water
½ cup (125ml) oyster sauce
¼ cup (35g) brown sugar
6 x 220g chicken supremes+, skin on
ginger and green onion dressing
5cm piece (25g) fresh ginger, peeled and grated
3 green onions (scallions), finely sliced
1 tablespoon white vinegar
½ tablespoon sesame oil

Place the garlic, ginger, star anise, cinnamon, peppercorns, five-spice, chilli, rice wine, soy sauce, orange peel, water, oyster sauce and sugar in a large saucepan over high heat. Bring to the boil and reduce heat to a gentle simmer. Add the chicken and cook for 7 minutes. Cover with a tight-fitting lid and remove from the heat. Allow to stand for 20 minutes.

To make the ginger and green onion dressing, place the ginger, green onion, vinegar and sesame oil in a bowl and stir to combine. Slice the chicken and pour over a little of the poaching liquid. Serve with the dressing. SERVES 6
+ *Chicken supremes are breast fillets with the wing tip still attached.*

roasted turkey with pear and sage stuffing and roasted garlic butter

10 cloves garlic, unpeeled
1½ tablespoons olive oil, plus extra, for brushing
60g unsalted butter, softened
sea salt and cracked black pepper
1 brown onion, sliced
2 pears, peeled and finely chopped
2 cups (140g) fresh breadcrumbs
¼ cup sage leaves, chopped
50g unsalted butter, melted, extra
1 x 4kg whole turkey
2 cups (500ml) chicken stock

Preheat oven to 160°C (325°F). Place the garlic on a baking tray, drizzle with ½ tablespoon oil and roast for 20 minutes or until softened. Squeeze the garlic cloves from their skins, place in a bowl and mash. Add the butter, salt and pepper and mix to combine.

Heat the remaining oil in a large non-stick frying pan over high heat. Add the onion and cook for 5 minutes or until light golden. Add the pear and cook for a further 5–7 minutes, stirring occasionally, or until the pear is golden. Place the breadcrumbs, sage, extra butter, salt and pepper, and onion and pear mixture in a large bowl and mix to combine.

Increase the oven temperature to 180°C (350°F). Rinse the turkey and pat dry with absorbent paper. Gently loosen the skin and push the roasted garlic butter underneath. Spoon the pear and sage stuffing into the cavity, secure with a skewer and tie the legs with kitchen string. Place the turkey on a lightly greased wire rack in a baking dish. Brush with oil, sprinkle with salt and pepper, and pour the stock into the dish. Cover with lightly greased aluminium foil and roast for 1 hour 15 minutes. Remove the foil and roast for a further 45–60 minutes, basting every 15 minutes with the stock, or until the skin is golden and juices run clear when tested with a skewer+. Cover the turkey with aluminium foil and allow to rest for 20 minutes before carving. SERVES 6–8
+ *When cooking stuffed turkey, allow 18–20 minutes cooking time per 500g (including the weight of the stuffing).*

roasted turkey with pear and sage stuffing and roasted garlic butter

roasted duck with sage and garlic potatoes

sticky lime and ginger chicken

⅓ cup (80ml) honey
2 tablespoons oyster sauce
1 tablespoon lime juice
5cm piece (25g) fresh ginger, peeled and finely grated
2 cloves garlic, crushed
¼ cup (60ml) water
2 tablespoons peanut oil
8 x 125g chicken thigh fillets, trimmed and cut into strips
1 lime, thinly sliced
600g gai larn* (Chinese broccoli), chopped and blanched
shredded green onion (scallion) and steamed rice, to serve

Place the honey, oyster sauce, lime juice, ginger, garlic and water
in a bowl and mix to combine. Set aside.
    Heat the oil in a large wok or non-stick frying pan over high heat.
Add the chicken and cook, in batches, for 6 minutes or until cooked
through. Add the honey mixture and lime and bring to the boil.
Cook for a further 2–4 minutes or until thickened slightly. Arrange
the gai larn on a plate and top with the chicken and green onion.
Spoon over the pan sauce and serve with the rice. SERVES 4

roasted duck with sage and garlic potatoes

2 tablespoons red wine vinegar
2 tablespoons caster (superfine) sugar
1 x 2kg whole duck
sea salt flakes
1kg waxy potatoes, peeled
1 tablespoon olive oil
6 cloves garlic
20 eschalots* (French shallots)
1 bunch sage

Preheat oven to 200°C (400°F). Combine the vinegar and sugar.
Set aside. Prick the duck skin with a skewer and place in a deep-sided
dish. Cover with boiling water and set aside for 1 minute. Remove the
duck from the water and pat dry with absorbent paper. Overlap the
folds of the skin over the cavity and secure with a skewer. Place in a
baking dish and sprinkle with salt. Toss the potatoes with oil and add
to the dish. Roast for 30 minutes, brushing the duck every 10 minutes
with the vinegar. Add the garlic, eschalots and sage and cook for
a further 30 minutes, brushing every 10 minutes with the vinegar,
or until golden and cooked through. SERVES 4

spicy char-grilled chicken tacos

4 x 125g chicken thigh fillets, trimmed
1 teaspoon onion powder
¼ teaspoon chilli powder
1 teaspoon oregano
1 teaspoon paprika*
vegetable oil, for brushing
1 x quantity cornmeal or flour tortillas (see recipes, page 280)
mint, coriander (cilantro), chopped chilli and lemon wedges, to serve

Place the chicken, onion and chilli powder, oregano and paprika in a
bowl and toss to coat. Preheat a char-grill pan or barbecue over high
heat. Brush chicken with oil and char-grill or barbecue for 4–5 minutes
each side or until cooked through. Slice chicken and serve in tortillas
with pickled onion (see recipe, page 216), salsa verde (see recipe,
page 272), mint, coriander, chilli and lemon wedges. SERVES 8

chicken skewers with spicy peanut sauce

2 tablespoons peanut oil, plus extra, for brushing
4 long red chillies*, chopped
4 cloves garlic, crushed
1 teaspoon sea salt flakes
2 cups (300g) roasted unsalted peanuts
⅔ cup (180g) grated dark palm sugar*
1 cup (250ml) boiling water
6 x 160g chicken breast fillets, each sliced into 8 strips
24 bamboo skewers, soaked in water
Thai basil leaves and lime wedges, to serve

Place the peanut oil, chilli, garlic, salt, peanuts, palm sugar and
boiling water in a food processor and process until a thick sauce
forms. Transfer half the sauce, reserving the remaining sauce, to a
bowl with the chicken and toss to coat. Place in the fridge for 1 hour.
    Preheat a char-grill pan or barbecue over high heat. Thread the
chicken onto skewers, brush with oil and cook for 3–4 minutes each
side or until cooked through and golden. Serve the skewers with the
reserved peanut sauce, basil leaves and lime. SERVES 4-6

spicy char-grilled chicken taco

chicken skewers with spicy peanut sauce

HOW TO COOK butterflied chicken

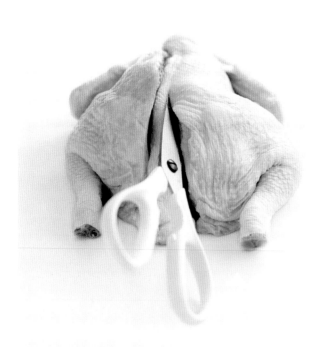

1

2

spice-roasted chicken

1 teaspoon dried chilli flakes
3 cloves garlic, crushed
½ teaspoon smoked paprika*
1 teaspoon dried oregano leaves
1 tablespoon shredded lemon zest
¼ cup (60ml) red wine vinegar
¼ cup (60ml) olive oil
sea salt and cracked black pepper
1 x 1.6kg whole chicken, butterflied

STEP 1 Preheat oven to 200°C (400°F). Position the chicken,
breast-side down, so the back is facing up and the drumsticks are
pointing towards you. Using sharp kitchen scissors or chicken
shears, cut closely along either side of the backbone and remove.
STEP 2 Turn the chicken, breast-side up, and press down firmly
on the breastbone to flatten the chicken. Tuck the wing tips under
before roasting.
STEP 3 Place the chilli flakes, garlic, paprika, oregano, lemon zest,
vinegar, oil, salt and pepper in a bowl and mix well to combine.
STEP 4 Place the chicken on a baking tray, pour over the chilli mixture
and spread over the chicken to coat. Roast for 45 minutes, brushing
with the pan juices halfway through, or until cooked through and
golden. SERVES 4

TIPS + TRICKS
*Butterflying a chicken allows it to cook faster and more
evenly. You can cook butterflied chicken on a barbecue.
Simply pop the barbecue lid on after 5 minutes to act
like an oven.*

RECIPE NOTES
*As a general rule, chicken will take 20-25 minutes per
500g at 200°C (400°F) to cook.*

spice-roasted chicken

garlic and thyme roasted chicken

60g unsalted butter, softened
3 cloves garlic, crushed
1 tablespoon thyme leaves
sea salt and cracked black pepper
1 x 1.8kg whole chicken, butterflied (see technique, page 130)
4 sprigs thyme, extra
1 lemon, halved
olive oil, for drizzling

Preheat oven to 200°C (400°F). Place the butter, garlic, thyme, salt and pepper in a bowl and mix well to combine. Gently loosen the skin off the breast meat and push the butter mixture under the skin. Place the chicken on a baking tray with the extra thyme and lemon and drizzle with oil. Roast for 45 minutes, brushing with the pan juices halfway through, or until cooked through and golden. SERVES 4

spiced soy chicken

5 sticks cinnamon
3 whole star anise
1 x 1.8kg whole chicken, butterflied (see technique, page 130)
1 tablespoon soy sauce
1 tablespoon brown sugar
¼ cup (60ml) water
½ teaspoon Chinese five-spice powder*

Preheat oven to 200°C (400°F). Place the cinnamon and star anise on a baking tray lined with non-stick baking paper and top with the chicken. Place the soy, sugar, water and five-spice in a small saucepan over medium heat and cook, stirring, for 1 minute. Brush the soy mixture over the chicken and transfer to the oven. Roast for 35–45 minutes or until golden and the juices run clear. SERVES 4

ginger, chilli and lime chicken

3 long red chillies*, deseeded and roughly chopped
5cm piece (25g) fresh ginger, peeled and roughly chopped
3 cloves garlic
2 tablespoons peanut oil
1 teaspoon sea salt flakes
1 x 1.8kg chicken, butterflied (see technique, page 130)
1 lime, halved

Preheat oven to 200°C (400°F). Place the chilli, ginger, garlic, oil and salt in a small food processor and process to form a rough paste. Place the chicken on a roasting tray lined with non-stick baking paper. Rub the paste evenly over the chicken, add the lime to the roasting tray and roast for 35–45 minutes or until golden and the chicken is cooked through. Squeeze over the caramelised lime to serve. SERVES 4

herb and mascarpone chicken

150g mascarpone*
2 cloves garlic, crushed
3 tablespoons chopped tarragon leaves
2 tablespoons chopped oregano, plus extra sprigs, for roasting
sea salt and cracked black pepper
1 x 1.8kg chicken, butterflied (see technique, page 130)
olive oil, for brushing

Preheat oven to 200°C (400°F). Place the mascarpone, garlic, tarragon and oregano in a bowl, sprinkle with salt and pepper and mix to combine. Place the chicken on a roasting tray lined with non-stick baking paper. Gently loosen the skin from the breast meat and push the mascarpone mixture under the skin. Brush the chicken with oil and sprinkle with salt and pepper. Top with the extra oregano sprigs and roast for 35–45 minutes or until golden and the juices run clear. SERVES 4

barbecued duck and water chestnut dumplings

char siu chicken dumplings

garlic confit chicken with bread sauce

barbecued duck and water chestnut dumplings

300g shredded Chinese barbecued duck meat[+]
⅓ cup (65g) chopped (canned) water chestnuts
¼ cup (60ml) hoisin sauce*
¼ teaspoon Chinese five-spice powder*
3 cloves garlic, crushed
sesame seeds, for sprinkling
vegetable oil, for shallow frying
glutinous rice dough
⅓ cup (50g) plain (all-purpose) flour
⅓ cup (80ml) boiling water
2 tablespoons caster (superfine) sugar
1⅓ cups (175g) glutinous (sticky) rice flour*
½ cup (125ml) cold water

Place the duck, water chestnut, hoisin sauce, five-spice and garlic in a bowl and mix to combine. Set aside.

To make the glutinous rice dough, place the plain flour and boiling water in a bowl and mix well to combine. Add the sugar, rice flour and water and mix until a soft dough forms. Turn the dough out onto a lightly floured surface and knead for 3–4 minutes. Divide into 24 equal-sized balls. Roll each ball out to form a 9cm round. Place 2 teaspoons of the duck mixture onto one half of each round. Brush the edge with water and fold over to enclose. Press the edge to seal. Brush with water and sprinkle with sesame seeds. Heat the oil in a non-stick frying pan over medium heat. Cook the dumplings, in batches, for 1–2 minutes each side or until golden. Drain on absorbent paper. Serve immediately. MAKES 24
+ You can buy a barbecued duck from Chinese barbecue shops.

SERVE THESE WITH...
soy sauce
hot chilli sauce
Chinese black vinegar

garlic confit chicken with bread sauce

¼ cup (30g) sea salt flakes
¼ cup sage leaves, chopped
1 tablespoon rosemary leaves
1 tablespoon finely grated lemon rind
4 x 250g chicken marylands
1.5 litres olive oil
16 single-clove garlic, skin on
3 bay leaves
1 teaspoon whole black peppercorns
bread sauce
2 cups (500ml) milk
1 brown onion, peeled and quartered
4 cloves garlic, peeled
150g white bread, crusts removed and torn
¼ cup (60g) crème fraîche*
sea salt and cracked black pepper

Place the salt, sage, rosemary and lemon rind in a small food processor and process until combined. Place the chicken on a baking tray and rub with the salt mixture. Cover and refrigerate for 2 hours. Rinse with cold running water to remove the salt and pat dry with absorbent paper.

Preheat oven to 130°C (275°F). Heat the oil in a large ovenproof, heavy-based saucepan over low heat until the temperature reaches 120°C (250°F) on a deep-frying thermometer. Carefully add the chicken, garlic, bay leaves and peppercorns and cover with a lid. Transfer to the oven and cook for 2 hours or until the chicken is cooked through and tender.

While the chicken is cooking, make the bread sauce. Place the milk, onion and garlic in a saucepan over medium heat and cook for 20–25 minutes or until the onion is tender. Discard the onion and garlic and add the bread to the milk. Cook for a further 10 minutes or until the bread is soft and the sauce has thickened. Place the sauce, crème fraîche, salt and pepper in a food processor and process until smooth. Set aside and keep warm.

Gently remove the chicken and garlic from the oil, place on a wire rack and allow to cool slightly. Heat a large, non-stick frying pan over medium heat. Cook the chicken for 2–4 minutes each side or until golden and crispy. Serve the chicken with bread sauce and garlic. SERVES 4
Tip: Confiting offers great flavour and tenderness. You need to make sure the oil is not too hot – you want to poach the chicken, not fry it, so there shouldn't be any bubbles when you place the meat in the oil. Finishing it in the pan gives it a lovely crisp skin to match the succulent meat.

char siu chicken dumplings

⅓ cup (115g) char siu (Chinese barbecue) sauce*
1 tablespoon vegetable oil
2cm piece (10g) fresh ginger, peeled and finely grated
½ teaspoon Chinese five-spice powder*
1 tablespoon honey
2 green onions (scallions), trimmed and sliced
4 x 125g chicken thigh fillets, trimmed
vegetable oil, for deep frying
sambal oelek*, to serve
wonton wrapper dough
1¾ cups (225g) plain (all-purpose) flour, sifted
¾ cup (180ml) warm water

Place the char siu sauce, oil, ginger, five-spice, honey and green
onion in a bowl and mix to combine. Add the chicken and mix to
coat. Cover and refrigerate for 30 minutes.

Preheat oven to 220°C (425°F). Place the chicken, reserving
the marinade, on a baking tray lined with non-stick baking paper
and bake for 18–20 minutes or until cooked through. Allow to cool
to room temperature, chop into small pieces and return to the
reserved marinade. Refrigerate until needed.

To make the wonton wrapper dough, place the flour in a bowl
and gradually add the water, stirring, until a dough begins to form.
Turn the dough out onto a lightly floured surface and knead for
5–6 minutes or until smooth and elastic. Divide the dough into
24 equal portions and roll each piece out to a 10cm round. Place
2 teaspoons of the chicken mixture into the centre of each round,
fold in the edges and twist the top to enclose filling. Heat the oil
in a deep-sided saucepan over high heat until temperature reaches
180°C (350°F) on a kitchen thermometer. Cook the dumplings,
in batches, for 4–5 minutes or until golden brown. Drain on
absorbent paper. Serve with the sambal oelek. MAKES 24
*Tip: You could use 24 store-bought wonton wrappers instead of making
your own dough.*

brandy-roasted chicken
with mushroom pearl barley

1 x 1.8kg whole chicken
4 cloves garlic, crushed
½ cup (125ml) brandy
¼ cup (60ml) olive oil
sea salt and cracked black pepper
50g unsalted butter
1 brown onion, chopped
4 cloves garlic, extra, sliced
30g dried mixed mushrooms, rehydrated in 1 cup (250ml)
    boiling water
500g fresh mixed mushrooms
1 cup (210g) pearl barley
½ cup (125ml) dry white wine
1½ cups (375ml) chicken stock

Preheat oven to 200°C (400°F). Place the chicken, garlic, brandy,
oil, salt and pepper in a bowl and toss to coat. Place in the fridge for
1 hour to marinate.

Secure the chicken legs with kitchen string. Heat a large non-stick
frying pan over high heat and cook the chicken, breast-side down,
for 5 minutes or until golden. Remove from the pan and set aside.
Melt the butter in the pan, add the onion and garlic and cook for
5 minutes or until onion is softened. Strain the dried mushrooms,
reserving the liquid, and add to the pan with the fresh mushrooms.
Cook for 5 minutes. Add the barley and wine and cook for 1 minute
or until the wine is absorbed. Add the reserved mushroom liquid
and stock and stir to combine. Transfer to a baking dish and top
with the chicken. Cover with aluminium foil and roast for 55 minutes.
Remove the foil and roast for a further 10–15 minutes or until the
chicken is golden and cooked through. Serve with the mushroom
pearl barley. SERVES 4–6

brandy-roasted chicken with mushroom pearl barley

HOW TO COOK poached chicken

1
2

lemon-poached chicken

1 litre chicken stock
1 lemon, sliced
4 sprigs lemon thyme
1 clove garlic, halved
4 x 180g chicken breast fillets, trimmed

Place the stock, lemon, thyme and garlic in a deep frying pan over high heat and bring to the boil. Add the chicken and cook for 3 minutes. Remove from the heat, cover with a lid and stand for 10 minutes or until the chicken is cooked through. SERVES 4

RECIPE NOTES
Once you've poached the chicken you can use it in myriad dishes. Shred the meat and use in salads and sandwiches or even in soup. The poached chicken will keep in the refrigerator for up to 2 days.

lemon-poached chicken

orange and juniper roasted duck

harissa chicken with olives

roasted green chicken curry

orange and juniper roasted duck

4 x 230g duck marylands, trimmed
2 teaspoons juniper berries
8 cloves garlic, unpeeled and lightly crushed
peel of 2 oranges, removed with a vegetable peeler
1 tablespoon brown sugar
⅓ cup (80ml) port
10 bay leaves
1kg chat (baby) potatoes, halved
sea salt and cracked black pepper

Preheat oven to 200°C (400°F). Place the duck, juniper berries, garlic, orange peel, sugar, port and bay leaves in bowl and toss to coat. Cover and refrigerate for 1 hour. Place the potatoes in a large baking dish. Place the duck, skin-side down, on the potatoes and sprinkle with salt and pepper. Roast for 20 minutes. Turn the duck and roast for a further 18–20 minutes or until cooked through. SERVES 4

harissa chicken with olives

8 x 220g chicken thigh fillets, bone in, trimmed
8 cloves garlic, unpeeled
1 cup (180g) mixed olives
¼ cup (70g) tomato paste
1 tablespoon harissa paste*
1 tablespoon brown sugar
½ cup (125ml) chicken stock
sea salt and cracked black pepper
400g truss Roma tomatoes
gremolata
½ cup chopped flat-leaf parsley leaves
½ cup chopped coriander (cilantro) leaves
1 tablespoon lemon juice
1 tablespoon shredded lemon zest
2 cloves garlic, crushed

Preheat oven to 180°C (350°F). To make the gremolata, place the parsley, coriander, lemon juice and zest and garlic in a bowl and mix to combine. Set aside.

   Place the chicken, garlic, olives, tomato and harissa pastes, sugar and stock in a large baking dish and sprinkle with salt and pepper. Cover tightly with aluminium foil and roast for 1 hour. Increase temperature to 200°C (400°F). Remove the foil, add the tomatoes and roast for a further 30 minutes or until the chicken is cooked through. Serve with the gremolata. SERVES 4

roasted green chicken curry

½ cup green curry paste (see recipe, below)
400ml coconut milk
2 tablespoons fish sauce*
1 tablespoon finely chopped palm sugar*
4 kaffir lime leaves*
1 stalk lemongrass*, bruised
8 x 220g bone-in chicken thighs, skin on and trimmed
sea salt flakes
2 tablespoons lime juice
sliced baby cucumbers and baby (micro) herbs, to serve

Preheat oven to 180°C (350°F). Place the curry paste, coconut milk, fish sauce, sugar, lime leaves and lemongrass in a deep-sided baking tray and mix to combine. Rub the chicken with salt and place, skin-side up, in the baking tray. Cover with aluminium foil and roast for 1 hour. Increase the temperature to 200°C (400°), remove the foil and roast for a further 35–40 minutes or until the chicken is cooked through and the skin is crispy. Use a metal spoon to skim any fat from the surface of the sauce and stir through the lime juice. Top with the cucumber and baby herbs to serve. SERVES 4

green curry paste

2 tablespoons coriander (cilantro) seeds
1 teaspoon cumin seeds
¼ teaspoon white peppercorns
3 long green chillies*, roughly chopped
2 eschalots* (French shallots), roughly chopped
4 cloves garlic, roughly chopped
2cm piece (10g) fresh turmeric*, peeled and roughly chopped
2 tablespoons coriander (cilantro) root, chopped
6cm piece (30g) fresh galangal*, peeled and roughly chopped
4 kaffir lime leaves*, shredded
1 stalk lemongrass*, white part only, sliced
½ teaspoon shrimp paste*
2 tablespoons peanut oil

Heat a small frying pan over medium heat. Add the coriander seeds, cumin seeds and peppercorns and toast, shaking the pan frequently, for 2–3 minutes or until fragrant and light golden. Place in a small food processor and process until ground. Add the chilli, eschalot, garlic, turmeric, coriander root, galangal, lime leaves, lemongrass, shrimp paste and oil and process, scraping down the sides of the bowl, until smooth. MAKES 1 CUP (250ML)

tamarind duck curry

6 x 250g duck marylands
1¼ cups tamarind curry paste (see recipe, right)
250g apple eggplants* (aubergines), halved
½ tablespoon sea salt flakes, plus extra, for sprinkling
1 tablespoon peanut oil
400ml coconut milk
2½ cups (625ml) chicken stock
2 tablespoons fish sauce*
1 stalk lemongrass*, bruised
2 tablespoons lime juice
shredded green onion (scallion), to serve

Preheat oven to 200°C (400°F). Rub the duck with ¼ cup of the tamarind curry paste and sprinkle with salt. Place, skin-side down, on a lightly greased baking tray and roast for 30 minutes. Turn the duck and cook for a further 15–20 minutes or until golden and cooked through. Set aside.

Place the eggplant in a bowl with the salt and toss to combine. Allow to stand for 15 minutes. Heat the oil in a deep-sided frying pan over high heat. Cook the eggplant, cut-side down, for 2–3 minutes or until golden. Remove from the pan, add the remaining tamarind curry paste and cook for 30–60 seconds or until fragrant. Add the coconut milk, stock, fish sauce and lemongrass and bring to the boil. Reduce the heat to medium, return the eggplants to the pan and cook for 20–25 minutes or until tender and the sauce is reduced. Cut the duck pieces in half, add to sauce and cook for a further 5 minutes. Add the lime juice and stir to combine. Top with the green onion to serve. SERVES 4

SERVE THIS WITH...
steamed rice
baby bok choy
fresh chilli

tamarind curry paste

2 tablespoons coriander (cilantro) seeds
1 teaspoon cumin seeds
3 long red chillies, roughly chopped
2 eschalots* (French shallots), roughly chopped
4 cloves garlic, roughly chopped
2 tablespoons coriander (cilantro) root, chopped
6cm piece (30g) fresh ginger, peeled and roughly chopped
1 stalk lemongrass*, white part only, sliced
¼ cup finely chopped dark palm sugar*
½ cup Thai basil leaves, roughly chopped
1 tablespoon peanut oil
2 tablespoons green peppercorns
⅓ cup (80ml) tamarind pulp*

Heat a small frying pan over medium heat. Add the coriander seeds and cumin seeds and toast, shaking the pan frequently, for 2–3 minutes or until fragrant and light golden. Place in a small food processor and process until ground. Add the chilli, eschalot, garlic, coriander root, ginger, lemongrass, sugar, basil and oil and process, scraping down the sides of the bowl, until smooth. Place in a bowl with the peppercorns and tamarind and mix to combine.
MAKES 1½ CUPS (375ML)

tamarind duck curry

PORK

Here we show off one of the most popular and adaptable meats. Whether it's loin, belly or shoulder, pork is a natural – oven roasted to juicy, crispy perfection, while ribs, tacos, stir-fries and more are proof of its versatility.

sticky barbecue and ginger ribs

lemon-crumbed schnitzel with celeriac remoulade

slow-cooked stout and brown sugar ham

sticky barbecue and ginger ribs

1.5kg American-style pork spare ribs
1 cup (250ml) bourbon whisky
4cm piece (20g) fresh ginger, thinly sliced
2 cloves garlic
1 litre water
barbecue and ginger sauce
½ cup (125ml) bourbon whisky
2 cloves garlic
1 tablespoon finely grated ginger
1 whole dried chilli
½ cup (90g) brown sugar
½ cup (125ml) malt vinegar
1 cup (250ml) tomato sauce (ketchup)

Preheat oven to 200°C (400°F). Place the ribs, whisky, ginger, garlic and water in a large saucepan over high heat and bring to the boil+. Reduce the heat to low and cook for 1 hour.

While the ribs are cooking, make the barbecue and ginger sauce. Place the whisky, garlic, ginger, chilli, sugar, vinegar and tomato sauce in a food processor and process until smooth. Set aside.

Drain ribs and pat dry with absorbent paper. Place on a large baking tray lined with non-stick baking paper and brush with the barbecue and ginger sauce. Roast for 35–40 minutes, brushing every 10 minutes with the sauce, or until sticky and golden. Serve with extra sauce. SERVES 4
+ *Boiling ribs before roasting in the oven will make them tender and succulent.*

SERVE THIS WITH...
barbecued corn
cabbage slaw
sweet potato chips

lemon-crumbed schnitzel with celeriac remoulade

3 cups (210g) fresh breadcrumbs
1½ cups (250g) instant polenta
3 teaspoons finely grated lemon rind
6 x 150g pork schnitzel steaks
6 slices round pancetta*
plain (all-purpose) flour, for dusting
2 eggs, lightly beaten
vegetable oil, for shallow frying
lemon wedges, to serve
celeriac remoulade
1 celeriac (celery root), peeled and thinly sliced
½ cup (150g) whole-egg mayonnaise
2 teaspoons lemon juice
1 teaspoon Dijon mustard

To make the celeriac remoulade, place the celeriac, mayonnaise, lemon juice and mustard in a bowl and combine. Set aside.

Place the breadcrumbs, polenta and lemon rind in a bowl and mix well to combine. Top each steak with a slice of pancetta. Dust with flour, shaking to remove any excess. Dip steaks in the egg and press into the breadcrumb mixture. Heat 1cm of oil in a large frying pan over high heat. Cook the schnitzels, in batches, for 2 minutes each side or until golden and cooked through. Drain on absorbent paper. Serve with celeriac remoulade and lemon wedges. SERVES 6

slow-cooked stout and brown sugar ham

1.5 litres stout beer
3 cups (525g) brown sugar
peel of 1 orange
1 bunch thyme
⅓ cup (80ml) white wine vinegar
1 stick cinnamon
5–6kg ham leg, skin removed and trimmed+

Preheat oven to 180°C (350°F). Place the stout, brown sugar, orange peel, thyme, vinegar and cinnamon in a saucepan over high heat, bring to the boil and cook for 20 minutes. Place the ham, top-side down, in a deep heavy-based baking dish and cover the hock with aluminium foil (this will prevent it from burning). Pour over the stout and brown sugar mixture and roast for 40 minutes. Turn the ham and roast for a further 40 minutes or until golden. Remove ham from the cooking liquid, reserving the liquid, and slice. Strain the liquid and serve with the ham. SERVES 8-10
+ *Use your fingers to gently remove the skin from the ham, before using a knife to trim any excess fat.*

smoky roasted pork loin

chinese-spiced pork loin rack

smoky roasted pork loin

⅔ cup (120g) brown sugar
⅔ cup (240g) treacle*
8 cloves garlic, crushed
2 teaspoons onion salt
1 tablespoon ground coriander (cilantro)
1 tablespoon ground cumin
1 cup (250ml) malt vinegar
4 dried ancho chillies*, chopped
2kg pork loin, skin on and scored at 1cm intervals
sea salt flakes
olive oil, for rubbing

Place the sugar, treacle, garlic, onion salt, coriander, cumin, vinegar
and chilli in a bowl and mix to combine. Transfer to a deep-sided
baking tray and add the pork, skin-side up. Rub the skin with salt
and marinate in the fridge for at least 2 hours.
   Preheat oven to 220°C (425°F). Remove the salt from the rind
and pat dry to remove any excess moisture. Rub the skin with olive oil
and sprinkle with more salt. Roast for 40–45 minutes or until cooked
to your liking and the skin is crisp and golden. Allow to stand for
10 minutes. Strain the cooking liquid into a small saucepan and place
over medium heat. Bring to the boil and cook for 6–8 minutes or
until reduced. Drizzle the pork with the sauce to serve. SERVES 4-6

chinese-spiced pork loin rack

1 x 2.8kg (10-bone) pork loin rack
2 teaspoons Sichuan peppercorns*
1 teaspoon Chinese five-spice powder*
2 whole star anise
1 teaspoon ground cinnamon
1 tablespoon sea salt flakes
1 tablespoon olive oil
250g fresh ginger, sliced

Preheat oven to 220°C (425°F). Using a small, sharp knife score
the pork skin at 1cm intervals. Place the peppercorns, five-spice,
star anise and cinnamon in a non-stick frying pan over high heat
and cook for 1 minute or until fragrant. Place the spices in a mortar
and pestle and pound until well combined. Add the salt and mix to
combine. Rub the pork with the oil and half the spice mix, reserving
remaining mixture. Place the ginger on a baking tray and top with
the pork. Roast for 25–30 minutes. Reduce temperature to 170°C
(325°F) and roast for a further 55–60 minutes or until cooked to
your liking. Slice into cutlets and serve with reserved spice mix.
SERVES 6

spiced pork belly with mint sauce

1 x 1.8kg piece bone-in pork belly
2 tablespoons sea salt flakes
½ teaspoon cumin seeds
½ teaspoon coriander (cilantro) seeds
½ teaspoon fennel seeds
½ teaspoon dried chilli flakes
2 teaspoons thyme leaves
1 tablespoon olive oil
2 bunches rosemary
2 heads garlic, halved
2 lemons, halved
mint sauce
½ cup (110g) caster (superfine) sugar
1 cup (250ml) malt vinegar
1 cup chopped mint leaves

To make the mint sauce, place the sugar and vinegar in a saucepan
over low heat and stir until the sugar is dissolved. Increase the
heat to high and cook for 4–5 minutes or until thickened slightly.
Remove from heat and allow to cool completely. Add the mint,
stir to combine and set aside.
   Preheat oven to 180°C (350°F). Using a small, sharp knife score
the pork skin at 1cm intervals. Place 1 tablespoon salt, the cumin,
coriander, fennel, chilli flakes and thyme in a mortar and pestle and
pound until well combined. Rub the spice mixture into the meat.
Rub the pork skin with the olive oil and remaining salt. Place the
pork, skin-side down, in a baking tray and roast for 2 hours. Increase
temperature to 220°C (425°F). Turn the pork and place the
rosemary, garlic and lemons in the pan under the pork. Roast for a
further 30–45 minutes or until the skin is golden and crispy and the
meat is tender. Serve the pork with the mint sauce, garlic and lemon.
Serve with steamed green beans, if desired. SERVES 6-8
*Tip: For an extra crisp crackle, it's a good idea to rub the skin with salt and
refrigerate, uncovered, overnight. This will help draw the moisture out of
the skin and produce a better crackling. Remove the salt from the rind
and pat dry before continuing with the recipe.*

spiced pork belly with mint sauce

HOW TO COOK pork roast

1

2

rosemary and mustard roasted pork loin

1 x 2.5kg piece boneless loin of pork
1 tablespoon hot English mustard
4 rosemary sprigs, leaves picked
sea salt and cracked black pepper
olive oil, for brushing
3 heads garlic, halved

STEP 1 Using a small, sharp knife, score the pork skin at 1cm intervals.
STEP 2 Turn the loin over and spread the meat with mustard and top with rosemary. Sprinkle with salt and pepper and roll to enclose. Secure with kitchen string, rub the skin with salt and refrigerate, uncovered, overnight.
STEP 3 Preheat oven to 220°C (425°F). Brush the salt from the skin and pat dry with absorbent paper to remove any excess moisture. Brush the skin with oil and rub with salt, making sure to rub into the cuts. Place the pork, skin-side up, in a roasting tray and roast for 30 minutes.
STEP 4 Reduce the oven temperature to 200°C (400°F), add the garlic and roast for a further 15–25 minutes until the skin is golden and crunchy and the meat is tender.
STEP 5 Remove the kitchen string, slice the pork and serve with the caramelised garlic, roasted potatoes and a green salad, if desired.
SERVES 8

RECIPE NOTES
For an extra crisp crackle, rub the skin with salt and refrigerate, uncovered, overnight. This will help draw the moisture out of the skin and produce a better crackling. Remove the salt and pat dry before roasting.

rosemary and mustard roasted pork loin

malt vinegar and bourbon sticky pork belly

malt vinegar and bourbon sticky pork belly

1 cup (250ml) bourbon whisky
1½ cups (375ml) malt vinegar
2 cups (500ml) water
3 cups (525g) brown sugar
10 cloves garlic, bruised and peeled
1 cup (350g) golden syrup
2 sticks cinnamon
4 bay leaves
1 x 2.5kg piece bone-in pork belly

Preheat oven to 180°C (350°F). Place the whisky, 1 cup (250ml) vinegar, water, sugar, garlic, golden syrup, cinnamon and bay leaves in a medium saucepan over high heat and bring to the boil. Cook, stirring occasionally, for 2–3 minutes or until thickened slightly. Place the pork, skin-side down, in a deep-sided, tight-fitting baking dish+. Pour over the sauce, cover with aluminium foil and roast for 3 hours 30 minutes. Carefully turn the pork, add the remaining vinegar and cover with aluminium foil. Roast for a further 30 minutes or until tender. Skim the fat from the surface of the sauce and strain through a sieve. Slice the pork and pour over the sauce to serve. SERVES 6–8
+ *Make sure the pork fits snugly into the baking dish, this will ensure the liquid doesn't evaporate too quickly.*

sage and fennel roasted pork with cider apples

¼ cup (30g) sea salt flakes
1 tablespoon finely chopped sage
1 teaspoon fennel seeds
1 x 4.5kg pork leg
olive oil, for rubbing and brushing
8 baby apples
2 tablespoons apple cider vinegar*
2 tablespoons brown sugar
sea salt and cracked black pepper
4 red onions, peeled and quartered
1 bunch sage, leaves picked

Preheat oven to 220°C (425°F). Using a mortar and pestle, pound the salt, sage and fennel seeds until well combined. Set aside.
Pat the pork dry with absorbent paper and use a sharp knife to score the skin at 1cm intervals. Rub well with oil and the sage and fennel salt and place on a baking tray. Roast for 30 minutes. Reduce heat to 200°C (400°F) and roast for a further 1 hour 30 minutes. While the pork is cooking, use a sharp knife to score around the centre of each apple. Place in a bowl with the vinegar, sugar, salt, pepper and onion and stir to combine. Add to the tray with the pork. Brush the sage leaves with oil and add to the tray with the pork. Roast for a further 20 minutes or until the pork is cooked through and the apples are just tender. SERVES 8

five-spice roasted pork with pumpkin purée and quince glaze

1kg blue kent pumpkin (squash), skin on and chopped
2 tablespoons olive oil
½ teaspoon ground cinnamon
sea salt and cracked black pepper
1 x 1.5kg piece boneless pork belly
1 tablespoon sea salt flakes
1 teaspoon Chinese five-spice powder*
quince glaze
100g quince paste*, chopped
¼ cup (45g) brown sugar
¼ cup (60ml) apple cider vinegar*
½ cup (125ml) chicken stock

Preheat oven to 200°C (400°F). Place the pumpkin on a baking tray, drizzle with 1 tablespoon oil and sprinkle with the cinnamon, salt and pepper. Roast for 1 hour or until golden and tender. Scoop the pumpkin from the skin, place in a food processor and process until smooth. Set aside and keep warm.
Reduce oven temperature to 180°C (350°F). Using a small, sharp knife, score the pork skin at 1cm intervals. Place 1 teaspoon salt and the five-spice in a bowl and mix to combine. Rub the meat with the five-spice salt and rub the skin with the remaining olive oil and salt. Place the pork, skin-side down, in a baking tray and roast for 2 hours 30 minutes. Increase the oven temperature to 220°C (425°F). Turn the pork and roast for a further 25–30 minutes or until the skin is golden and crispy and the meat is tender.
While the pork is cooking, make the quince glaze. Place the quince paste, sugar, vinegar and stock in a small saucepan over medium heat and cook, stirring occasionally, for 3–4 minutes or until the paste is dissolved. Increase the heat to high, bring to the boil and cook for 4–5 minutes or until thickened slightly. Divide the pumpkin purée between plates, top with sliced pork belly and spoon over the quince glaze to serve. SERVES 4

TRY THIS WITH...
roasted cauliflower
steamed green beans
fried Brussels sprouts

sage and fennel roasted pork with cider apples

five-spice roasted pork with pumpkin purée and quince glaze

HOW TO COOK meatloaf

1 2
3 4

basic meatloaf

1 tablespoon olive oil
1 large brown onion, finely chopped
3 cloves garlic, crushed
24 slices flat pancetta*, rind removed
1 cup (70g) fresh breadcrumbs
¼ cup (60ml) milk
2 tablespoons finely chopped rosemary
1 tablespoon Dijon mustard
2 eggs
400g pork mince (ground pork)
400g veal mince (ground veal)
½ cup chopped flat pancetta*, extra
sea salt and cracked black pepper

STEP 1 Preheat oven to 180°C (350°F). Heat the oil in a non-stick frying pan over medium heat. Add the onion and garlic and cook for 5–7 minutes or until softened. Allow to cool completely.
STEP 2 Line a 22cm x 8cm x 7cm tin with the pancetta slices, slightly overlapping. Set aside.
STEP 3 Place the breadcrumbs and milk in a large bowl and set aside for 5 minutes or until the milk is absorbed. Add the onion mixture, rosemary, mustard, egg, pork and veal mince, chopped pancetta, salt and pepper and mix well to combine.
STEP 4 Press the mixture into the tin and fold over any overhanging pancetta. Place the tin on a baking tray and bake for 40–45 minutes or until just cooked. Set aside for 5 minutes before inverting onto a tray lined with non-stick baking paper. Bake for a further 5–10 minutes or until golden. SERVES 6-8

RECIPE NOTES
When spooning the meatloaf mixture into the prepared tin, be sure to use the back of a spoon to press the meat down firmly. This will help your meatloaf to hold its shape and will give it an even texture.

basic meatloaf

salami, ricotta and basil pizza

salami, ricotta and basil pizza

1 x quantity basic pizza dough (see recipe, right)
olive oil, for brushing
1 cup (280g) basic homemade tomato sauce (see recipe, right)
    or store-bought tomato purée (passata)
200g fresh buffalo mozzarella*, torn
200g ricotta
150g salami, thinly sliced
½ cup basil leaves
2 tablespoons olive oil, extra
1 clove garlic, crushed

Preheat oven to 220°C (425°F). Prepare the basic pizza dough.
Place 2 x 30cm-round baking trays in the oven for 5–10 minutes.
Divide the dough into 2 equal-size balls and roll out on a lightly
floured surface to make 2 x 30cm rounds. Brush trays with oil and
top with the dough. Working quickly, spread the bases with the
tomato sauce and top with the mozzarella, ricotta, salami and basil.
Mix the extra olive oil and garlic in a bowl and drizzle over the pizzas.
Bake for 15–20 minutes or until golden and crispy. MAKES 2

———————————

TRY THIS WITH...
spicy salami
anchovies
sun-dried tomatoes

basic pizza dough

1 teaspoon dry yeast
¼ teaspoon caster (superfine) sugar
¾ cup (180ml) lukewarm water
1½ cups (225g) OO (superfine) flour*
1 teaspoon sea salt flakes

Place the yeast, sugar and water in a bowl and mix to combine.
Set aside in a warm place for 5 minutes or until bubbles appear on the
surface. This means the yeast has been activated. Place the flour and
salt in a bowl and make a well in the centre. Add the yeast mixture
and mix together with well-floured hands to form a dough. Knead the
dough on a lightly floured surface for 4–5 minutes or until smooth
and elastic. Place in a lightly greased large bowl under a clean, damp
cloth and set aside in a warm place for 30 minutes or until the dough
has doubled in size. MAKES 2 x 30CM PIZZAS

basic homemade tomato sauce

5kg Roma tomatoes
¼ cup oregano leaves
1 tablespoon sea salt flakes
cracked black pepper

Cut a cross in the top of each tomato, and squeeze to remove the
juice. Remove the white tips with a small sharp knife and discard.
Pass the tomatoes through a mouli+ into a large saucepan. Add
the oregano, salt and pepper and bring to the boil over high heat.
Reduce heat to medium and cook for 1 hour and 30 minutes or
until thickened. Pour into sterilised glass bottles and store for up
to 12 months. MAKES 3 LITRES
+ A mouli is a hand-operated kitchen tool for puréeing and grating,
available from kitchenware stores. As an alternative, you could purée
the tomatoes in a food processor and press through a fine sieve.

pork satay skewers with cucumber and radish salad

crispy pork and chilli mince with snake beans

black bean pork and cabbage pot stickers

pork satay skewers with cucumber and radish salad

400g pork fillet (tenderloin), cut into 1cm-thick strips
peanut oil, for brushing
3 Lebanese cucumbers, peeled, deseeded and sliced
4 radishes, thinly sliced
2 green onions (scallions), thinly sliced
¼ cup (35g) roasted peanuts, roughly chopped
2 tablespoons lime juice
1 tablespoon olive oil
sea salt and cracked black pepper
baby (micro) mint leaves, to serve
satay sauce
¼ cup (60ml) peanut oil
1 long red chilli*, chopped
2 cloves garlic, crushed
1 cup (140g) roasted peanuts
½ teaspoon ground cumin
¼ teaspoon ground turmeric
2 tablespoons kecap manis*
1 tablespoon fish sauce*
½ cup (125ml) coconut milk
½ cup (125ml) boiling water

To make the satay sauce, place the peanut oil, chilli, garlic, peanuts, cumin, turmeric, kecap manis, fish sauce, coconut milk and water in a food processor and process until a thick sauce forms. Divide the sauce into two equal-size portions and set one portion aside. Place the remaining portion in a bowl with the pork and toss to combine. Cover with plastic wrap and refrigerate for 1 hour.

Preheat a char-grill pan or barbecue over medium heat. Thread the pork onto skewers, brush with oil and cook, in batches, for 6 minutes, turning occasionally, or until cooked through. Place the reserved sauce in a saucepan over medium heat and cook for 2 minutes or until heated through. Place the cucumber, radish, green onion, peanuts, lime juice, oil, salt and pepper in a large bowl and toss to combine. Serve the skewers with the cucumber salad, extra satay sauce and sprinkle with the baby mint leaves. MAKES 8

crispy pork and chilli mince with snake beans

400g pork mince (ground pork)
2 cloves garlic, crushed
3cm piece (15g) fresh ginger, peeled and finely grated
¼ cup (80g) chilli jam*
1 teaspoon shrimp paste*
1 tablespoon oyster sauce
1 tablespoon peanut oil
350g snake beans, trimmed
baby (micro) shiso leaves*, to serve

Place the pork, garlic, ginger, chilli jam, shrimp paste and oyster sauce in a bowl and mix well to combine. Cover and refrigerate for 30 minutes. Heat the oil in a large non-stick frying pan over high heat. Add the pork mixture and cook, breaking up any lumps with a wooden spoon, for 12–15 minutes or until crisp and cooked through. Cook the beans in a large saucepan of salted boiling water for 1 minute or until tender. Divide the beans between plates and top with the mince and shiso leaves to serve. SERVES 4

black bean pork and cabbage pot stickers

¼ cup (60ml) vegetable oil
5 cups (230g) thinly sliced Chinese cabbage (wombok)
2 cloves garlic, crushed
400g pork mince (ground pork)
2 tablespoons Chinese black bean paste*
1 eggwhite
⅓ cup chopped chives
24 gow gee wrappers*
Chinese black vinegar* and chilli oil, to serve

Heat 1 tablespoon of oil in a frying pan over medium heat. Add the cabbage and garlic and cook for 2 minutes or until softened. Allow to cool. Place the mince, bean paste, eggwhite and chives in a bowl with the cabbage and mix to combine. Place the gow gee wrappers on a clean benchtop dusted with rice flour and brush the edges with water. Place 1 teaspoon of the pork mixture into the centre of each wrapper, fold over and press the edges to enclose filling. Place the remaining oil and ½ cup (125ml) water in a frying pan over medium heat. Add the dumplings and cook, covered, for 5 minutes. Remove lid and cook for a further 2 minutes or until the water is evaporated and dumplings have a golden crust on one side. Serve with the vinegar and chilli oil. MAKES 24

sichuan pork and ginger soup dumplings

teaspoon gelatine powder
tablespoon water
2 cups (500ml) chicken stock
10cm piece (50g) fresh ginger, peeled and thinly sliced
300g pork mince (ground pork)
3 green onions (scallions), chopped
tablespoon soy sauce
2 teaspoons Chinese cooking wine*
teaspoon caster (superfine) sugar
teaspoon ground Sichuan pepper*
32–34 gow gee wrappers*

Place the gelatine and water in a bowl and stir to combine. Set aside for 5 minutes or until the gelatine is absorbed. Place the stock and ginger in a saucepan over high heat. Reduce heat to medium and cook for 8–10 minutes or until reduced slightly. Add the gelatine and cook, stirring, for 2–3 minutes or until the gelatine is dissolved. Set aside to cool for 20 minutes. Pour the ginger mixture into a bowl and refrigerate for 2 hours or until set.

Place the pork mince, green onion, soy sauce, wine, sugar and pepper in a bowl and mix until well combined. Fold through the ginger jelly until evenly combined with the mince mixture. Place the gow gee wrappers on a clean benchtop dusted with rice flour and brush the edges of the wrappers with water. Place 1½ teaspoons of the mince and jelly mixture onto each wrapper and pinch each side into the centre to enclose filling.

Place the dumplings in a steamer basket lined with non-stick baking paper. Place over a wok or large frying pan of boiling water and steam for 5–6 minutes or until cooked through and jelly is dissolved. Serve immediately. MAKES 32–34

Tip: The ginger jelly will melt as the dumplings are steamed, resulting in a 'soup' forming inside these dumplings. Take care not to lose this delicious broth when you bite into them!

chorizo and capsicum tacos

4 red capsicums (bell peppers), sliced
2 dried chorizo*, sliced
1 clove garlic, sliced
2 tablespoons olive oil
1 tablespoon sherry vinegar*
1 x quantity cornmeal or flour tortillas (see recipes, page 280)
lemon wedges, to serve

Heat a char-grill pan or barbecue over high heat. Char-grill or barbecue the capsicum for 8–10 minutes. Remove from heat and set aside. Char-grill or barbecue the chorizo for 2–3 minutes each side or until golden. Place the capsicum and chorizo in a bowl with the garlic, oil and vinegar and mix well to combine. Place the mixture in a soft tortilla and serve with refried beans (see recipe, below) and lemon wedges. SERVES 8

refried beans

1 cup (200g) black-eyed beans, soaked overnight+
⅓ cup (80ml) olive oil
2 cloves garlic, crushed
1 tablespoon lemon juice
¼ cup chopped flat-leaf parsley leaves
sea salt flakes

Drain the beans, place in a saucepan and cover with cold water. Bring to the boil and cook for 15 minutes or until tender. Drain well. Heat 2 tablespoons of the oil in a non-stick frying pan over high heat. Add the garlic and beans and cook for 1–2 minutes. Remove from heat. Lightly crush with a fork and stir through the lemon juice, parsley, remaining olive oil and salt. MAKES 3 CUPS
+ *You will need to soak the dried beans in a bowl of water overnight.*

sichuan pork and ginger soup dumplings

chorizo and capsicum tacos

pulled pork tacos

pulled pork tacos

850g boneless pork shoulder
3 tablespoons vegetable oil
1 brown onion, chopped
2 teaspoons smoked paprika*
3 cloves garlic, crushed
2 tablespoons apple cider vinegar*
2 teaspoons dried oregano
sea salt and cracked black pepper
2 cups (500ml) water
1 x quantity cornmeal or flour tortillas (see recipes, page 280)
250g smoked or plain mozzarella, sliced
iceberg lettuce, chopped green onions (scallions) and lime wedges,
    to serve

Place the pork, oil, onion, paprika, garlic, vinegar, oregano, salt and pepper in a bowl and mix well to coat. Cover with plastic wrap and refrigerate for 6 hours or overnight to marinate.

Preheat oven to 160°C (325°F). Place pork in a baking dish with the water and cover with aluminium foil. Cook for 4 hours or until meat is tender and falling apart. Shred the meat and discard any fat. Top tortillas with mozzarella and melt under a hot grill (broiler). Top with pork, salsa roja (see recipe, below), lettuce, onion and lime wedges. SERVES 8

SAUCES + CONDIMENTS
salsa roja: Heat 1 tablespoon olive oil in a small saucepan over high heat. Add 1 chopped brown onion and 1 crushed clove garlic, cook for 2–3 minutes or until softened. Add 1 tablespoon red wine vinegar, 1 tablespoon brown sugar, 1 can (400g) chopped tomatoes, sea salt and cracked black pepper, and cook, stirring, for 5–6 minutes or until slightly thickened. MAKES 1½ CUPS

sweet and sour pork

1½ cups (375ml) rice wine vinegar*
⅔ cup (160ml) Chinese cooking wine*
1 cup (220g) caster (superfine) sugar
sea salt flakes
2cm piece (10g) fresh ginger, peeled and thinly sliced
2 cloves garlic, sliced
vegetable oil, for frying
1 cup (200g) rice flour, plus extra, for dusting
1¼ cups (310ml) sparkling mineral water
2 x 380g pork fillets (tenderloins), trimmed and thinly sliced
400g pineapple, peeled and thinly sliced
2 long red chillies*, sliced
2 green onions (scallions), cut into pieces
150g cherry tomatoes, halved
1 cup mint leaves

Place the vinegar, wine, sugar, salt, ginger and garlic in a saucepan over low heat and stir until the sugar is dissolved. Increase heat to high and bring to the boil. Cook for 18–20 minutes or until thickened slightly. Set aside.

Heat the vegetable oil in a saucepan over high heat until the temperature reaches 190°C (375°F) on a deep-frying thermometer. Place the rice flour and mineral water in a bowl and whisk until smooth. Dust the pork and pineapple in the extra rice flour, shaking to remove excess and dip into the batter to lightly coat. Deep-fry, in batches, for 2 minutes or until lightly golden. Drain on absorbent paper. Place the chilli, green onion, tomato and mint in a bowl and mix to combine. Arrange on plates with the pork and pineapple and drizzle with the ginger syrup to serve. SERVES 4

sweet and sour pork

LAMB

We love lamb because it has such a great affinity for fast and slow cooking styles. Grill, roast, fry and braise your way through this collection of simple recipes that showcases this sweet, juicy meat.

slow-cooked lamb with garlic and rosemary

smoky paprika lamb shank parcels

slow-cooked lamb with garlic and rosemary

½ cup (125ml) malt vinegar
½ cup (90g) brown sugar
1 tablespoon olive oil
sea salt and cracked black pepper
1 x 2kg piece lamb shoulder, bone in
18 single-clove garlic*, unpeeled
6 sprigs rosemary
1½ cups (375ml) chicken stock

Preheat oven to 180°C (350°F). Place the vinegar, ¼ cup (45g) sugar, oil, salt and pepper in a large bowl and stir to combine. Add the lamb and set aside to marinate for 20 minutes. Place the lamb, skin-side up, in a large baking dish. Add the garlic, rosemary sprigs, marinade and stock. Sprinkle the lamb with the remaining sugar, cover with aluminium foil and roast for 2 hours 30 minutes. Remove the foil and roast for a further 30 minutes or until the lamb is cooked to your liking. Serve with the garlic. SERVES 4–6

smoky paprika lamb shank parcels

2 teaspoons smoked paprika*
1 teaspoon sea salt flakes
1 tablespoon olive oil
4 x 300g lamb shanks
4 vine-ripened tomatoes, sliced
2 red onions, sliced
1 teaspoon dried chilli flakes
2 cloves garlic, sliced
8 bay leaves
8 sprigs thyme
⅓ cup (80ml) red wine
1 tablespoon brown sugar
purple basil leaves and finely grated lemon rind, to serve

Preheat oven to 180°C (350°F). Place the paprika, salt and oil in a bowl and mix to combine. Rub the lamb shanks with the paprika mixture. Cut 8 x 30cm squares of non-stick baking paper and layer 2 sheets together to make 4 squares. Divide the tomatoes, onion, chilli flakes, garlic, bay leaves and thyme between the centre of each paper square. Top each square with a shank. Place the wine and brown sugar in a bowl and mix to combine. Divide the wine mixture between the squares, bring the ends of the paper together and secure with kitchen string to enclose. Place the parcels on a large baking tray and roast for 2 hours or until tender. Place the parcels in bowls and open

char-grilled capsicum and lamb burger

2 red capsicums (bell peppers)
olive oil, for brushing
400g lamb mince (ground lamb)
sea salt and cracked black pepper
4 burger buns, halved
cucumber raita, jalapeño relish (see recipes, below) and baby
    spinach leaves, to serve

Heat a char-grill pan or barbecue over high heat. Brush the capsicum with oil and char-grill or barbecue, turning occasionally, for 20 minutes or until blackened. Place in a bowl, cover with plastic wrap and allow to cool slightly. Peel off the skins and slice. Set aside.
    Place the mince, salt and pepper in a bowl and mix well to combine. Divide into 4 and shape into thin patties. Brush the patties with oil and char-grill or barbecue for 2–3 minutes each side or until cooked through.
    Brush the bun halves with oil and place on a baking tray. Grill (broil) under a preheated hot grill for 1 minute or until golden. Set aside.
    Spoon the cucumber raita and jalapeño relish onto the buns. Top with patties, capsicum and baby spinach to serve. SERVES 4

cucumber raita

1 cup (280g) thick (natural) Greek-style yoghurt
¼ cup grated Lebanese cucumber
1 tablespoon finely chopped mint leaves
1 clove garlic, crushed
sea salt

Place all the ingredients in a bowl and stir to combine. MAKES 1¼ CUPS

jalapeño relish

1¼ cups pickled jalapeño peppers
1 clove garlic, crushed
¼ cup (55g) caster (superfine) sugar
1 cup (280g) tomato purée (passata)
sea salt

Place all the ingredients in a small saucepan over high heat. Bring to the boil and cook for 5 minutes or until thickened. Set aside to cool. MAKES 1½ CUPS

char-grilled capsicum and lamb burger

HOW TO COOK *roast lamb*

1
2

rosemary and garlic roast lamb

sea salt
1 x 2.4kg lamb leg
3 sprigs rosemary, cut into 2cm lengths
4 cloves garlic, sliced

STEP 1 Sprinkle the lamb with plenty of sea salt and set aside in the refrigerator, uncovered, for 20 minutes.
STEP 2 Preheat oven to 220°C (425°F). Brush the salt from the lamb with absorbent paper. Using a sharp knife, make small incisions in the lamb at even intervals. Insert rosemary sprigs and garlic slices into the slits. Season the lamb with salt and place in a roasting dish lined with non-stick baking paper. Roast for 20 minutes. Reduce the oven temperature to 180°C (350°F) and cook for a further 1 hour for medium or until cooked to your liking. SERVES 4–6

RECIPE NOTES
Salting the lamb in the first step helps to dry the skin, producing a golden, crispier result. As a general rule, allow 18-20 minutes per 500g of lamb.

rosemary and garlic roast lamb

haloumi-crumbed lamb cutlets with tzatziki

red wine and herb lamb shanks

haloumi-crumbed lamb cutlets with tzatziki

9 slices white bread
¼ cup oregano leaves, chopped
½ cup (65g) finely grated haloumi*
sea salt and cracked black pepper
12 x 70g lamb cutlets, trimmed
¼ cup (40g) plain (all-purpose) flour
2 eggs, lightly whisked
⅓ cup (80ml) olive oil
cup (120g) pitted black olives
400g cherry tomatoes, halved
cup flat-leaf parsley leaves
tablespoon lemon juice
tzatziki
2 medium cucumbers, grated
cup (300g) thick (natural) Greek-style yoghurt
2 tablespoons lemon juice
clove garlic, crushed

To make the tzatziki, place the cucumber, yoghurt, lemon juice
and garlic in a small bowl and mix until well combined. Set aside.
    Place the bread in the bowl of a food processor and process
until roughly chopped. Place the breadcrumbs in a bowl with the
oregano, haloumi, salt and pepper and mix until well combined.
    Press the lamb into the flour, dip into the egg and press into
the breadcrumb mixture. Heat half the oil in a large non-stick frying
pan over medium heat. Cook the lamb for 3–4 minutes each side
for medium-rare or until golden and cooked to your liking. Place the
olives, tomatoes, parsley, remaining oil and lemon juice in a bowl
and toss to combine. Serve the lamb with the tomato salad and
tzatziki. SERVES 4–6

TRY THIS WITH...
pork cutlet
veal schnitzel
chicken breast

lamb with moussaka

¼ cup (60ml) olive oil, plus extra, for brushing
2 cloves garlic, crushed
700g tomato purée (passata)
1 teaspoon caster (superfine) sugar
sea salt and cracked black pepper
4 large eggplants (aubergines), thinly sliced
1 cup oregano leaves
300g feta, thinly sliced
1 cup (100g) grated mozzarella
2 x 600g (8-bone) French-trimmed lamb racks
lemon oil
2 tablespoons shredded lemon zest
2 tablespoons oregano leaves
2 tablespoons lemon juice
2 tablespoons olive oil

To make the lemon oil, place the lemon zest, oregano, lemon juice
and olive oil in a bowl and mix to combine. Set aside.
    Preheat oven to 180°C (350°F). Heat 1 tablespoon of oil in a
saucepan over medium heat. Add the garlic and cook for 30 seconds.
Add the tomato passata, sugar, salt and pepper and cook, stirring,
for 3 minutes. Set aside.
    Heat a char-grill pan over medium heat. Brush the eggplant with
oil, sprinkle with salt and pepper and cook for 2 minutes each side.
Layer the eggplant, tomato sauce, oregano and feta in a lightly greased
20cm x 30cm roasting tin, finishing with a layer of eggplant. Top with
mozzarella and bake for 20 minutes or until golden.
    Heat the remaining oil in a large non-stick frying pan over high heat.
Add the lamb and cook for 2–3 minutes each side or until golden.
Place on a baking tray and bake for 12–15 minutes for medium-rare
or until cooked to your liking. Allow to rest before slicing. Serve with
the moussaka and drizzle with the lemon oil. SERVES 4

lamb with moussaka

slow-cooked lamb madras curry

red wine and herb lamb shanks

2 tablespoons olive oil
8 x 250g lamb shanks
2 leeks, trimmed and sliced
1 brown onion, sliced
6 cloves garlic
6 sprigs each thyme and oregano
2 tablespoons plain (all-purpose) flour
2 cups (500ml) red wine
1 litre beef stock

Preheat oven to 180°C (350°F). Heat the oil in a large non-stick pan over high heat. Cook the shanks, in batches, for 1–2 minutes each side or until browned. Remove from pan and place in a baking dish. Set aside. Add the leeks, onion, garlic, thyme and oregano to the pan and cook for 2–3 minutes. Add the flour and stir to combine. Cook for a further 1–2 minutes, add the wine and stock and bring to the boil. Pour over shanks, cover and roast for 2½ hours, turning every 30 minutes. Serve with polenta or mash. To freeze, shred the meat, discarding the bones. Return the meat to pan and combine with sauce before freezing. SERVES 8

slow-cooked lamb madras curry

½ cup madras curry paste (see recipe, right)
¼ cup (70g) tomato paste
2 x 400g cans chopped tomatoes
2 cups (500ml) chicken stock
1 x 2kg piece lamb shoulder, bone in
sea salt and cracked black pepper
4 sprigs curry leaves*
150g pea eggplants* (aubergines)
mint and coriander (cilantro) leaves and cucumber and mint raita
   (see recipe, right), to serve

Preheat oven to 180°C (350°F). Place the curry paste, tomato paste, tomatoes and stock in a large, deep-sided baking tray and stir to combine. Add the lamb, skin-side down, and sprinkle with salt and pepper. Add the curry leaves and cover with aluminium foil. Roast for 2 hours 30 minutes. Increase the temperature to 200°C (400°F). Remove the foil, turn the lamb and roast for a further 30–40 minutes or until the lamb is tender. Add the eggplants and cook for a further 5–7 minutes or until the eggplants are tender. Top with mint and coriander and serve with the cucumber and mint raita. SERVES 4

cucumber and mint raita

1 cup (280g) Greek-style (thick) yoghurt
1 cucumber, grated and drained
½ cup mint leaves, shredded
1 tablespoon lime juice

Place the yoghurt, cucumber, mint and lime juice in a bowl and mix to combine. SERVES 4

madras curry paste

1 tablespoon mustard seeds
2 tablespoons coriander (cilantro) seeds
2 teaspoons cumin seeds
¼ teaspoon black peppercorns
1 tablespoon smoked paprika*
2 long red chillies*, roughly chopped
3 cloves garlic, roughly chopped
6cm piece (30g) fresh ginger, peeled and roughly chopped
2cm piece (10g) fresh turmeric*, peeled and roughly chopped
1 tablespoon malt vinegar
1 tablespoon vegetable oil

Heat a small frying pan over medium heat. Add the mustard, coriander and cumin seeds and peppercorns and toast, shaking the pan frequently, for 2–3 minutes or until fragrant and light golden. Place in a small food processor and process until ground. Add the paprika, chilli, garlic, ginger and turmeric and process until a coarse paste forms. Add the vinegar and oil and process, scraping down the sides of the bowl, until smooth. MAKES ½ CUP (125ML)

TRY THIS WITH…
chicken
beef

SEAFOOD

From simple fish and chips to elegant sashimi and hotpots to share, the ocean's bounty is amply represented in this compilation of recipes that show it off at its best and freshest. These dishes really are the catch of the day.

tempura prawn bites with radish ginger salad

kingfish sashimi with spicy ponzu dressing

crispy-skin salmon with chilli salt

tempura prawn bites with radish ginger salad

1 cup (150g) cornflour (cornstarch)
½ cup (75g) self-raising (self-rising) flour, plus extra, for dusting
1¾ cups (430ml) iced water
vegetable oil, for deep frying
1kg green (raw) prawns (shrimp), peeled, deveined and halved
radish ginger salad
500g radishes, trimmed and thinly sliced
¼ cup (70g) pickled ginger*
¼ cup (60ml) pickled ginger juice
1 tablespoon mirin*
1 tablespoon rice wine vinegar*
¼ teaspoon sesame oil
sesame salt
1 tablespoon sesame seeds, toasted and lightly crushed
2 teaspoons sea salt flakes

To make the radish ginger salad, place the radish, pickled ginger, ginger juice, mirin, vinegar and sesame oil in a bowl and toss to combine. Set aside.

To make the sesame salt, place the sesame seeds and salt in a bowl and mix to combine. Set aside.

Place the cornflour, self-raising flour and water in a bowl and, using a butter knife, mix until just combined. The mixture will be a little lumpy. Set aside for 10 minutes. Heat the oil in a large, deep saucepan over high heat until hot. Dust the prawns in the extra flour and dip in the batter. Deep-fry, in batches, for 3 minutes or until puffed and golden. Drain on absorbent paper. Sprinkle the prawns with the sesame salt and serve with the radish ginger salad. SERVES 4

kingfish sashimi with spicy ponzu dressing

1 x 500g sashimi-grade* kingfish fillet, skin removed
chervil sprigs, to serve
spicy ponzu dressing
¼ cup (60ml) lemon juice
¼ cup (60ml) rice wine vinegar*
⅓ cup (80ml) mirin*
2 tablespoons soy sauce
1 tablespoon chilli oil

To make the dressing, place the lemon juice, vinegar, mirin, soy sauce and chilli oil in a bowl and stir to combine. Set aside.

Place the fish in the freezer for 30 minutes or until firm. Use a sharp knife to thinly slice the fish. Arrange the fish on a plate, spoon over the dressing and top with chervil to serve. SERVES 4

crispy-skin salmon with chilli salt

1 cup (250ml) dashi (see recipe, below)
¼ cup (60ml) mirin*
¼ cup (60ml) soy sauce
2 x 200g salmon fillets, skin on and halved lengthways
vegetable oil, for brushing
sea salt flakes
150g edamame beans*, blanched
chilli salt
1 tablespoon sea salt flakes
1 teaspoon dried chilli flakes

Place the dashi, mirin and soy sauce in a small saucepan over medium heat and cook for 2–3 minutes. Set aside.

To make the chilli salt, place the salt and chilli flakes in a bowl and mix to combine. Set aside.

Using a small, sharp knife, score the skin of the salmon. Brush with the oil and sprinkle with salt. Heat a large non-stick frying pan over high heat. Cook the salmon skin-side down for 3 minutes, turn and cook for a further 3 minutes or until cooked to your liking. Divide the salmon between bowls and spoon over the dashi sauce. Sprinkle with the chilli salt and serve with the edamame beans. SERVES 4

cheat's dashi stock

2 cups (500ml) water
2 tablespoons bonito flakes*

Bring the water to the boil, add the bonito flakes and stir to combine. Remove from the heat and stand for 5 minutes before straining. MAKES 2 CUPS (500ML)

HOW TO COOK beer-battered fish

2
3

beer-battered fish with tartare sauce

1 cup (150g) plain (all-purpose) flour, plus extra, for dusting
½ cup (75g) cornflour (cornstarch)
1 teaspoon baking powder
1 teaspoon caster (superfine) sugar
1 teaspoon sea salt flakes, plus extra, to serve
330ml pale ale beer, chilled
vegetable oil, for deep frying
8 flathead fillets
lemon halves, to serve
tartare sauce
4 cornichons (baby gherkins), chopped
2 teaspoons salted capers, rinsed and dried
½ cup (150g) whole-egg mayonnaise
2 green onions (scallions), sliced
2 tablespoons chives, chopped
¼ cup flat-leaf parsley leaves, chopped
2 tablespoons dill leaves, chopped
2 tablespoons white balsamic vinegar
sea salt and cracked black pepper

STEP 1 To make the tartare sauce, place the cornichons, capers, mayonnaise, green onion, chives, parsley, dill, vinegar, salt and pepper in a bowl and mix to combine. Set aside.
STEP 2 Place the flour, cornflour, baking powder, sugar and salt in a large bowl and mix well to combine.
STEP 3 Gradually add the beer and whisk until smooth.
STEP 4 Heat the vegetable oil in a large saucepan over high heat until the temperature reaches 180°C (350°F) on a kitchen thermometer. Dust the fish with the extra flour and dip into the beer batter, shaking off any excess batter. Deep-fry the fish, in batches, for 2 minutes, turning occasionally, until golden. Drain on absorbent paper and sprinkle with extra salt. Serve with the tartare sauce and lemon.
SERVES 4

RECIPE NOTES
Make sure you use cold beer in your batter as it will help the batter crisp up when it hits the hot oil.

beer-battered fish with tartare sauce

teriyaki tuna

¼ cup (60ml) soy sauce
¼ cup (60ml) mirin*
1 tablespoon caster (superfine) sugar
400g sashimi-grade* tuna
vegetable oil, for deep frying
1 medium eggplant (aubergine), thinly sliced into chips
1 cup (200g) rice flour
baby coriander (cilantro)
5 small sheets nori seaweed*, thinly sliced
1 teaspoon sea salt flakes
1 teaspoon dried chilli flakes

Place the soy sauce, mirin and sugar in a bowl and stir to combine. Add the tuna and set aside for 10 minutes to marinate.

Heat a frying pan over high heat, add the tuna, reserving the marinade, and cook for 30 seconds each side. Remove from the pan, slice and set aside. Add the reserved marinade to the pan and cook for 1 minute or until heated through. Set aside.

Heat the oil in a large, deep saucepan over high heat until hot. Dust the eggplant in the flour and deep-fry, in batches, until golden. Drain on absorbent paper. Top with baby coriander. Combine the seaweed, salt and chilli flakes. Serve the tuna with the seaweed mixture, eggplant chips and marinade. SERVES 4

beetroot and vodka cured kingfish

2 tablespoons black peppercorns, lightly crushed
1 cup chopped flat-leaf parsley leaves
2 cups (600g) rock salt+
1 cup (220g) white sugar
1 large beetroot, peeled and grated
¼ cup (60ml) vodka
1.2kg kingfish fillet, skin on, pin-boned and cut into 3 equal pieces
250g crème fraîche*
1 tablespoon grated horseradish*
2 cups watercress sprigs
toasted rye bread and cracked black pepper, to serve
olive oil, for drizzling

Place the peppercorns, parsley, salt, sugar, beetroot and vodka in a bowl and mix to combine. Layer 2 sheets of plastic wrap on a clean benchtop and spread with half the salt mixture. Top with the kingfish pieces, skin-side down, and cover with remaining salt mixture. Wrap tightly in plastic wrap. Place in a deep-sided tray, top with a smaller tray and weigh down with heavy objects. Refrigerate for 36 hours, turning every 12 hours.

Remove the fish from the plastic wrap and wipe to remove salt mixture. Using a thin, sharp knife, thinly slice and set aside. Place the crème fraîche and horseradish in a bowl and mix to combine. Serve the kingfish with the watercress, rye bread, horseradish cream and extra pepper, and drizzle with olive oil. SERVES 12–14
+ *The type of salt used for curing is important. Use rock salt, rather than a finer salt because its coarseness cures the meat without imparting too much saltiness.*

TRY THE LEFTOVERS...
*tossed through fresh pasta
in a potato and caper salad
on a cream cheese bagel*

teriyaki tuna

beetroot and vodka cured kingfish

citrus and mint cured kingfish with pickled radish

ginger, lemongrass and chilli cured ocean trout

citrus and mint cured kingfish with pickled radish

2⅔ cups (800g) rock salt (see note, page 200)
1¾ cups (385g) white sugar
½ cup (125ml) orange juice
1kg kingfish fillet, skin on, trimmed and pin-boned
½ cup chopped mint leaves
1 lemon, sliced
1 orange, sliced
2 oranges, extra, peeled and thinly sliced
½ cup mint leaves, extra
½ cup coriander (cilantro) leaves
baby coriander (cilantro) leaves (optional), to serve
pickled radish
¼ cup (60ml) white vinegar
¼ cup (60ml) lemon juice
2 tablespoons caster (superfine) sugar
500g radishes, trimmed and thinly sliced

Place the salt, sugar and orange juice in a bowl and mix to combine. Layer 2 sheets of plastic wrap, long enough to completely cover the kingfish, on a clean benchtop and spread with half the salt mixture. Top with the fish, skin-side down, sprinkle with the mint and top with the lemon and orange slices. Cover with remaining salt mixture and wrap tightly in plastic wrap. Place in a deep-sided tray, top with a smaller tray and weigh down with heavy objects. Refrigerate for 48 hours, turning over every 12 hours. Remove the fish from the plastic wrap and wipe with absorbent paper to remove salt mixture. Discard lemon and orange slices. Using a thin, sharp knife, thinly slice and set aside.

To make the pickled radish, place the vinegar, lemon juice and sugar in a bowl and mix until sugar is dissolved. Add the radish and set aside for 5 minutes. Top the fish with the extra orange slices, pickled radish, extra mint, coriander and baby coriander leaves. SERVES 12–14

TRY THE LEFTOVERS…
with steamed rice and broccolini
tossed in a fennel slaw

ginger, lemongrass and chilli cured ocean trout

1kg rock salt (see note, page 200)
2½ cups (550g) white sugar
¼ cup (60ml) white rum
2 long red chillies*, sliced
3 stalks lemongrass*, trimmed and sliced
1.4kg fillet ocean trout, skin on, trimmed and pin-boned
2cm piece (10g) fresh ginger, peeled and finely grated
green papaya and lemongrass salad
1 stalk lemongrass*, trimmed and roughly chopped
½ cup (125ml) lemon juice
1 tablespoon caster (superfine) sugar
1 tablespoon fish sauce*
200g green papaya*, peeled and thinly sliced
1 Lebanese cucumber, peeled, seeded and thinly sliced
¾ cup shaved fresh coconut (optional)
⅓ cup mint leaves

Place the salt, sugar, rum, chilli and lemongrass in a bowl and mix to combine. Layer 2 sheets of plastic wrap, long enough to completely cover the fish, on a clean benchtop and spread with half the salt mixture. Top with the fish, skin-side down, spread with the ginger and cover with remaining salt mixture. Wrap tightly in plastic wrap and place in a deep-sided tray. Top with a smaller tray and weigh down with heavy objects. Refrigerate for 36 hours, turning every 12 hours. Remove the fish from the plastic wrap and wipe with absorbent paper to remove salt mixture. Using a thin, sharp knife, thinly slice and set aside.

To make the green papaya and lemongrass salad, place the lemongrass and lemon juice in a food processor and process for 30 seconds or until finely chopped. Strain the mixture through a fine sieve and discard the lemongrass pulp. Add the sugar and fish sauce to the juice and stir until the sugar is dissolved. Add the papaya, cucumber, coconut and mint and toss to combine. Serve the fish with the papaya salad. SERVES 12–14

TRY THE LEFTOVERS…
on avocado rye bread sandwiches
tossed with noodles, Asian herbs and soy sauce

HOW TO COOK sushi

salmon, avocado and cucumber rolls two-ways

4 sheets nori seaweed*
4 cups cooked basic sushi rice*
1 x 300g salmon fillet, skin off and cut into strips
1 Lebanese cucumber, shredded
1 avocado, peeled and cut into small wedges
pickled ginger*, wasabi* and soy sauce, to serve
basic sushi rice
2½ cups (300g) sushi rice*
3 cups (750ml) water
⅓ cup (80ml) rice wine vinegar
3 tablespoons caster (superfine) sugar
3 teaspoons sea salt flakes

1 2
3 4

STEP 1 To make the basic sushi rice, place the rice in a sieve and rinse under cold running water until the water runs clear. Place the rice and water in a saucepan over high heat and bring to the boil. Cook, uncovered, for 5 minutes. Reduce the heat to low and cook, covered, for a further 10 minutes. Remove from the heat and allow to stand for 5 minutes.

STEP 2 Place the vinegar, sugar and salt in a bowl and stir until the sugar and salt are dissolved. Spread the cooked rice over the base of a non-metallic dish and sprinkle with the vinegar mixture. Stir the rice gently with a spatula until cool to the touch. MAKES 5½ CUPS

TO MAKE INSIDE-OUT SUSHI ROLLS

STEP 3 Wrap a bamboo sushi mat in plastic wrap to prevent the rice from sticking. Using slightly wet fingers, spread ¾ cup of sushi rice evenly over the mat. Top with a nori sheet and press down firmly.

STEP 4 Place another ½ cup of the sushi rice down the middle of the nori sheet and top with 2 strips of salmon, a little shredded cucumber and two wedges of avocado. Roll up from the bottom, using the sushi mat to assist you. Repeat to make 2 rolls. Using a sharp knife, cut each roll into 6 pieces, wiping the knife with a damp cloth between each cut.

TO MAKE REGULAR NORI ROLLS

STEP 3 Place 1 sheet of nori, shiny-side down, on a bamboo sushi mat and top with 1 cup of sushi rice. With slightly wet fingers, spread the rice evenly over the nori sheet leaving a 5cm strip uncovered at the top.

STEP 4 Top with 2 strips of salmon, a little shredded cucumber and two wedges of avocado. Roll up from the bottom, using the sushi mat to assist you. Repeat to make 2 rolls. Using a sharp knife, cut each roll into 6 pieces, wiping the knife with a damp cloth between each cut.
MAKES 24 PIECES

salmon, avocado and cucumber rolls two ways

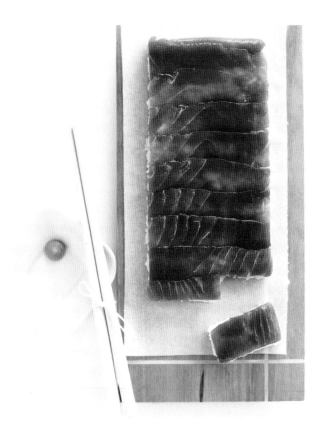

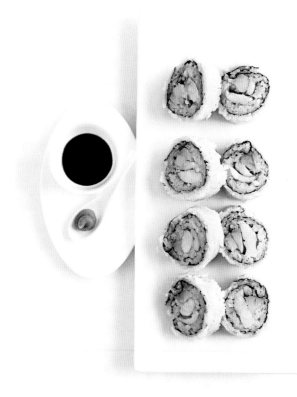

turn-out sushi

300g sashimi-grade* tuna, thinly sliced
1 x quantity basic sushi rice (see recipe, page 206)
wasabi*, soy sauce and pickled ginger*, to serve

Line a 9cm x 19cm cake tin with plastic wrap. Line the base with the
tuna. Top with the sushi rice and press down firmly, folding over the
plastic wrap to enclose. Place a firm piece of cardboard (cut to the
size of the tin) over the rice and weigh down with another tin and
canned vegetables. Place in the fridge for 1 hour to chill. To serve the
sushi, invert the tin and remove the plastic wrap. Slice into rectangles.
Serve with the wasabi, soy sauce and pickled ginger. MAKES 18 PIECES

prawn and avocado sushi

4 sheets nori seaweed*
4 cups basic sushi rice* (see recipe, page 206)
8 cooked prawns (shrimp), peeled, halved and deveined
1 avocado, peeled and cut into small wedges
wasabi* and soy sauce, to serve

Place 1 nori sheet, shiny-side down, on a bamboo sushi mat and top
with 1 cup of sushi rice. With slightly wet fingers, spread the rice
evenly over the nori sheet leaving a 5cm strip uncovered at the top.
Place 4 prawn halves and two wedges of avocado down the centre of
the rice. Roll up from the bottom, using the sushi mat to assist you.
Repeat to make 4 rolls.

Using a sharp knife, cut each roll into 6 pieces, wiping the knife
with a damp cloth between each cut. Serve with the wasabi and soy
sauce. MAKES 24 PIECES

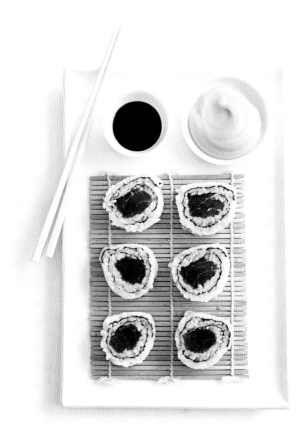

carrot and cucumber sushi

4 sheets nori seaweed*
4 cups basic sushi rice* (see recipe, page 206)
1 carrot, peeled and shredded
1 Lebanese cucumber, shredded
¼ cup pickled ginger*
soy sauce, to serve

Place 1 sheet of nori, shiny-side down, on a bamboo sushi mat and top with 1 cup of sushi rice. With slightly wet fingers, spread the rice evenly over the nori sheet leaving a 5cm strip uncovered at the top. Place a small amount of carrot, cucumber and pickled ginger down the centre of the rice. Roll up from the bottom, using the sushi mat to assist you. Repeat to make 4 rolls. Using a sharp knife, cut each roll into 6 pieces, wiping the knife with a damp cloth between each cut. Serve with the soy sauce. MAKES 24 PIECES

inside-out tuna rolls with wasabi mayonnaise

4 sheets nori seaweed*
4 cups basic sushi rice* (see recipe page 206)
350g fresh tuna loin, cut into strips
wasabi mayonnaise
⅓ cup (100g) Japanese mayonnaise
2 teaspoons wasabi*

To make the wasabi mayonnaise, place the mayonnaise and wasabi in a bowl and mix to combine. Set aside.

Wrap a bamboo sushi mat in plastic wrap to prevent the rice from sticking. Place a nori sheet, shiny-side up, on the mat and top with ¾ cup sushi rice. With slightly wet fingers, spread the rice evenly over the nori sheet to cover. Turn the nori sheet and rice over so the rice is on the bottom. Spread another ½ cup of rice down the middle of the nori sheet and top with 2 strips of tuna. Roll up from the bottom, using the sushi mat to assist you. Repeat to make 4 rolls. Using a sharp knife, cut each roll into 6 pieces, wiping the knife with a damp cloth between each cut. Serve with the wasabi mayonnaise. MAKES 24 PIECES

whole lemongrass snapper with green mango salad

lemon, garlic and parsley grilled lobster

garfish with caper mayonnaise and lemon salt

whole lemongrass snapper with green mango salad

2 stalks lemongrass*, bruised
1 x 700g snapper, scored on each side
olive oil, for drizzling
sea salt and cracked black pepper
1 large red chilli*, thinly sliced
100g bean sprouts
100g green mango*, thinly sliced
½ cup mint leaves
3 green onions (scallions), thinly sliced
lime wedges, to serve
palm sugar dressing
50g dark palm sugar*, finely grated
1 tablespoon fish sauce*
3 tablespoons lime juice
6 kaffir lime leaves*, thinly sliced
1 small red chilli*, chopped

Preheat oven to 200°C (400°F). Layer 2 x 30cm x 40cm pieces of non-stick baking paper on a tray and fold 3 edges in to form an envelope, leaving 1 edge open. Place the lemongrass and fish in the parcel, drizzle with oil and sprinkle with salt and pepper. Fold the remaining edge of the parcel to enclose and bake for 30–35 minutes or until the fish is firm to the touch and cooked through.

Place the chilli, bean sprouts, mango, mint and green onion in a bowl and toss to combine. To make the palm sugar dressing, place the palm sugar, fish sauce, lime juice, lime leaves and chilli in a bowl and mix to combine. Carefully open the parcel, letting the steam escape, and top with the mango salad and spoon over the dressing. Serve with lime wedges. SERVES 2

lemon, garlic and parsley grilled lobster

250g unsalted butter, softened
3 cloves garlic, crushed
1½ tablespoons finely grated lemon rind
½ cup chopped flat-leaf parsley leaves
sea salt and cracked black pepper
4 x 600g raw lobsters, halved and cleaned

Place the butter, garlic, lemon rind, parsley, salt and pepper in a bowl and mix well to combine. Place the lobsters on a baking tray and spread flesh with half the butter mixture. Cook under a preheated hot grill (broiler) for 10 minutes or until the shells are orange and lobster is cooked through. Serve with the remaining butter. SERVES 8

garfish with caper mayonnaise and lemon salt

1 cup (150g) self-raising (self-rising) flour, sifted
1 cup (150g) cornflour (cornstarch)
sea salt flakes
1¾ cups (430ml) iced water
vegetable oil, for deep-frying
16 garfish, cleaned, bones and head removed+
lemon wedges, to serve
caper mayonnaise
1 cup (300g) whole-egg mayonnaise
2 tablespoons lemon juice
2 tablespoons salted capers, rinsed, drained and chopped
1 tablespoon chopped dill
5 gherkins (dill pickles), chopped
lemon salt
2 tablespoons sea salt flakes
2 tablespoons finely grated lemon rind

To make the lemon salt, place the salt and lemon rind in a bowl and stir to combine. Set aside.

To make the caper mayonnaise, place the mayonnaise, lemon juice, capers, dill and gherkin in a bowl and stir to combine. Set aside.

Place the flour, cornflour and salt in a bowl. Make a well in the centre, gradually add the water and mix with a butter knife (the mixture should still be lumpy). Heat the oil in a large, deep saucepan over high heat until hot. Dip the fish in the batter and cook, in batches, for 4–5 minutes or until crisp and cooked through. Drain on absorbent paper. Serve with the caper mayonnaise, lemon salt and lemon wedges. SERVES 8

+ *Get your fishmonger to clean and bone the fish for you.*

garlic and tarragon prawns

lemongrass fish skewers with chilli dressing

garlic and tarragon prawns

1 head garlic, unpeeled
1 tablespoon olive oil
60g unsalted butter, softened
1 bunch tarragon, chopped
1 teaspoon dried chilli flakes
sea salt and cracked black pepper
12 green (raw) prawns (shrimp), butterflied, with tails intact

Preheat oven to 180°C (350°F). Place the garlic on a baking tray, drizzle with oil and roast for 30 minutes. Remove the garlic and increase the oven temperature to 220°C (425°F). Squeeze the garlic cloves from their skins, place in a bowl and mash until smooth. Add the butter, tarragon, chilli flakes, salt and pepper and mix to combine. Place the prawns on a baking tray, top with the garlic butter and cook for 6–8 minutes or until cooked through. SERVES 4

lemongrass fish skewers with chilli dressing

400g firm white fish fillets, skin off, trimmed and chopped
3cm piece (15g) fresh ginger, peeled and chopped
1 clove garlic, crushed
3 coriander (cilantro) roots, chopped
3 kaffir lime leaves*, roughly chopped
2 tablespoons sweet chilli sauce
1 teaspoon fish sauce*
1 eggwhite
sea salt and cracked black pepper
2 stalks lemongrass*, halved lengthways and cut into 12 lengths
2 tablespoons vegetable oil
chilli dressing
1 cup (220g) caster (superfine) sugar
2/3 cup (160ml) white vinegar
6 kaffir lime leaves*
6 long red chillies*, sliced

To make the chilli dressing, place the sugar, vinegar, lime leaves and chilli in a small saucepan over high heat and bring to the boil. Reduce heat to low and cook for a further 4–5 minutes or until thickened slightly. Set aside.

Preheat oven to 200°C (400°F). Place the fish, ginger, garlic, coriander, lime leaves, chilli sauce, fish sauce, eggwhite, salt and pepper in a food processor and process until smooth. Shape tablespoonfuls of the fish mixture around the tops of the lemongrass stalks. Heat the oil in a large non-stick frying pan over medium heat and cook the skewers, in batches, for 3–4 minutes or until browned. Place the skewers on a baking tray lined with non-stick baking paper and bake in the oven for 5–6 minutes or until cooked through. Serve with the chilli dressing. MAKES 12

fish and coleslaw tacos

2 tablespoons olive oil
1 teaspoon chilli flakes
sea salt flakes
4 x 140g snapper fillets, skin on+
1 x quantity cornmeal or flour tortillas (see recipes, page 280)
lime wedges, to serve
coleslaw
¼ cup (75g) whole-egg mayonnaise
2 tablespoons lime juice
1 cup (80g) shredded white cabbage

To make the coleslaw, place the mayonnaise and lime juice in a bowl and stir until well combined. Add the cabbage and toss to coat. Set aside. Combine the oil, chilli flakes and salt and brush over the fish fillets. Heat a non-stick frying pan over high heat. Cook the fish, skin-side down, for 3 minutes. Turn and cook for a further 3 minutes or until cooked through. Serve in tortillas with the coleslaw, pickled onions, salsa cruda, char-grilled chillies, guacamole (see recipes, below) and lime wedges. SERVES 8
+ If snapper is unavailable, you can use other firm white fish, such as flathead, whiting, kingfish and mulloway.

SAUCES + CONDIMENTS

pickled onions: Place 2 thinly sliced red onions, 2 tablespoons white wine vinegar, 1 tablespoon olive oil and sea salt flakes in a non-metallic bowl and toss to coat. Allow to stand for 10 minutes or until the onion begins to soften. MAKES 2 CUPS
salsa cruda: Place 250g halved cherry tomatoes, 250g halved yellow teardrop tomatoes, 1 chopped green onion (scallion), 2 tablespoons lime juice, 2 tablespoons olive oil, 2 crushed cloves garlic, 1 chopped green chilli and sea salt flakes in a bowl and toss to coat. SERVES 8
char-grilled chillies: Place 8 whole jalapeño chillies* in a bowl with 2 teaspoons vegetable oil and toss to coat. Preheat a char-grill pan or barbecue over high heat. Sprinkle the chillies with sea salt flakes and char-grill or barbecue for 3–4 minutes each side or until slightly softened and skins start to blister. MAKES 8
guacamole: Place 2 chopped avocados, 1 long red chilli* (seeds removed) and finely chopped, 2 tablespoons lime juice, ¼ cup chopped coriander (cilantro) leaves, sea salt and cracked black pepper in a bowl and mix until well combined. MAKES 2 CUPS (500ML)

fish and coleslaw taco

prawn and spinach dumplings

crispy crab and ginger dumplings

prawn and spinach dumplings

1 tablespoon sesame oil
2 cloves garlic, crushed
2 tablespoons white sesame seeds
1 long red chilli*, chopped
3 cups chopped water spinach*
12 green (raw) prawns (shrimp), peeled, deveined and chopped
translucent dumpling dough
1¼ cups (185g) potato flour (starch)*, plus extra, for dusting
¼ cup (35g) tapioca flour*
¼ teaspoon table salt
1 cup (250ml) boiling water
1 teaspoon vegetable oil

Heat the sesame oil in a large frying pan over medium heat. Add the garlic, sesame seeds and chilli and cook for 1 minute or until just golden. Add the spinach and cook for a further minute. Allow to cool completely. Add the prawn to the spinach mixture and mix until well combined. Set aside.

To make the translucent dumpling dough, sift the potato flour and tapioca flour into a bowl. Add the salt, boiling water and oil and stir with a wooden spoon until well combined. Turn the dough out onto a clean benchtop lightly dusted with potato flour. While the dough is still warm, knead for 3–4 minutes or until the dough is smooth (if the dough becomes too sticky, you may need to add more potato flour). Divide the dough into 24 equal portions and cover with plastic wrap. Using a rolling pin, roll each portion out to a 9cm round. Place 1½ teaspoons of the spinach and prawn mixture into the centre of each round. Brush the edges with water and fold over to enclose filling. Place the dumplings in a steamer basket lined with non-stick baking paper. Place over a wok or large frying pan of boiling water and steam for 15–20 minutes or until translucent. MAKES 24

crispy crab and ginger dumplings

500g picked cooked crab meat[+], drained
¼ cup (60ml) oyster sauce
2 tablespoons chopped garlic chives
2cm piece (10g) fresh ginger, peeled and finely grated
½ teaspoon ground white pepper
rice flour, for dusting
24 wonton wrappers*
vegetable oil, for deep frying
soy sauce and hot chilli sauce, to serve

Place the crab, oyster sauce, chives, ginger and white pepper in a bowl and mix to combine. Place the wonton wrappers on a clean benchtop dusted with rice flour and brush the edges of the wrappers with water. Place 1½ teaspoons of the crab mixture into the centre of each wonton wrapper and fold in each corner, slightly overlapping, to form an envelope.

Heat the oil in a saucepan over high heat until temperature reaches 180°C (350°F) on a kitchen thermometer. Cook the dumplings, in batches, for 2–3 minutes or until golden. Drain on absorbent paper. Serve with soy and hot chilli sauces. MAKES 24
+ *You can buy fresh or frozen picked crab meat from your fishmonger.*

crispy-skin fish with cauliflower purée and oregano butter

1kg cauliflower, chopped
1 cup (250ml) single (pouring) cream*
3 cups (750ml) chicken stock
20g unsalted butter, chopped
sea salt flakes
4 x 200g firm white fish fillets, skin on
olive oil, for brushing
80g unsalted butter, extra
¼ cup oregano leaves
1 clove garlic, crushed
1 tablespoon white balsamic vinegar

Place the cauliflower, cream and stock in a saucepan over high heat and bring to the boil. Reduce the heat to low, cover with a lid and cook for 20 minutes or until tender. Drain the cauliflower, reserving 2 tablespoons of the liquid. Place the cauliflower and liquid in the bowl of a food processor with the butter and salt and process until smooth. Set aside and keep warm.

Heat a non-stick frying pan over high heat. Brush the fish with oil and cook, skin-side down, for 4–5 minutes or until golden and crisp. Turn and cook for a further 3–4 minutes or until cooked through. Remove from the pan and keep warm. Add the butter and oregano to the pan and cook for 1 minute or until browned. Remove from heat and stir through the garlic and vinegar. Top the purée with the fish and spoon over the oregano butter to serve. SERVES 4

crispy-skin fish with cauliflower purée and oregano butter

fish cakes with garlic and caper mayonnaise

fish cakes with garlic and caper mayonnaise

500g chat (baby) potatoes
500g firm white fish fillets, skin removed, chopped
1 cup (70g) fresh breadcrumbs
2 eggs
1 tablespoon finely grated lemon rind
1 tablespoon store-bought horseradish cream*
½ cup chopped flat-leaf parsley leaves
sea salt and cracked black pepper
40g unsalted butter
3 cups (210g) fresh breadcrumbs, extra
gherkins (dill pickles) and lemon wedges, to serve
garlic and caper mayonnaise
1 cup (300g) whole-egg mayonnaise
1 tablespoon lemon juice
1 clove garlic, crushed
2 tablespoons chopped salted capers, rinsed and drained

Place the potatoes in a saucepan of salted cold water and bring to
the boil. Cook for 15 minutes or until tender. Drain, return to the
saucepan and roughly mash. Allow to cool.

While the potato is cooling, make the garlic and caper mayonnaise.
Place the mayonnaise, lemon juice, garlic and capers in a bowl and
mix well to combine. Set aside.

Add the fish to the potato with the breadcrumbs, eggs, lemon
rind, horseradish, parsley, salt and pepper and mix to combine.

Melt the butter in a non-stick frying pan over medium heat.
Divide the fish cake mixture into 4 patties and press into the extra
breadcrumbs. Cook, in batches, for 3–4 minutes each side or until
golden and cooked through. Serve with the mayonnaise, gherkins
and lemon wedges. SERVES 4

TRY THIS WITH...
cod
snapper
mulloway

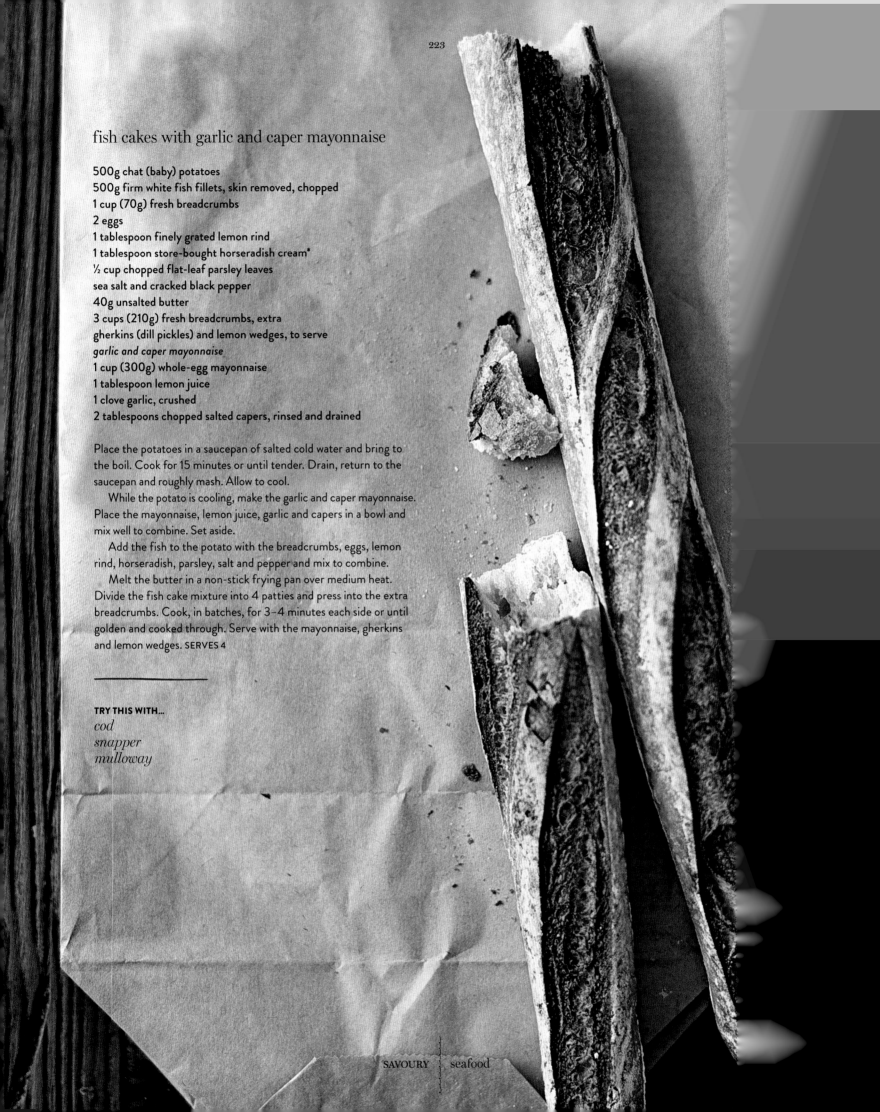

garlic and tarragon seafood hotpot

chorizo and prawn skewers with piri piri sauce

garlic and tarragon seafood hotpot

250g ghee* (clarified butter)
4 raw scampi, butterflied with shells intact+
8 green (raw) tiger prawns, heads removed and tails intact
500g clams (vongole)
6 cloves garlic, crushed
4 sprigs tarragon
2 green onions (scallions), thinly sliced
sea salt and cracked black pepper
herb toast
40g unsalted butter, softened
1 tablespoon finely chopped flat-leaf parsley leaves
1 tablespoon finely chopped tarragon leaves
6 slices baguette

Preheat oven to 180°C (350°F). To make the herb toast, place the butter, parsley and tarragon in a bowl and mix to combine. Spread the baguette slices with the butter and place on a baking tray. Bake for 10–15 minutes or until golden and crisp. Set aside.

Heat the ghee in a heavy-based saucepan over high heat until bubbles appear on the surface. Add the scampi, prawns, clams and garlic and cover with a tight-fitting lid. Cook for 2–4 minutes or until cooked through. Add the tarragon, green onion, salt and pepper and toss to combine. Serve with the herb toasts. SERVES 2
+ To butterfly the scampi, place on a clean chopping board with the underside facing up. Use kitchen scissors to make a cut on either side of the shell. Cut along each side until you reach the head. This will make it easier to remove the meat once cooked.
Tip: Much like a dish of Spanish-style garlic prawns, you will have some molten ghee in the bottom of the saucepan that will have taken on all the garlic and herb flavours. Use it for dipping the toast and seafood into.

TRY THIS WITH...
mussels
lobster tails
firm white fish

spicy fish curry

1 tablespoon peanut oil
800g salmon fillets, skin removed and chopped
sea salt flakes
1 cup red chilli curry paste (see recipe, below)
1 x 400g can chopped tomatoes
1 cup (250ml) store-bought young coconut water*
2 tablespoons fish sauce*
2 tablespoons lime juice
coriander (cilantro) and Vietnamese mint leaves, and store-bought fried eschalots*, to serve

Heat the oil in a large, non-stick frying pan over high heat. Sprinkle the salmon with salt and cook for 1–2 minutes each side or until golden. Set aside. Add the red chilli curry paste and cook, stirring, for 2–3 minutes. Add the tomatoes, coconut water and fish sauce and bring to the boil. Reduce heat to medium and cook for 5–7 minutes or until reduced slightly. Return the fish to the pan and cook for a further 1–2 minutes or until cooked to your liking. Add the lime juice and stir to combine. Top with the coriander and mint leaves and fried eschalots to serve. SERVES 4

red chilli curry paste

3 long red chillies*, roughly chopped
1 teaspoon shrimp paste*
6cm piece (30g) fresh ginger, peeled and roughly chopped
2 eschalots* (French shallots), roughly chopped
4 cloves garlic, roughly chopped
⅓ cup finely chopped dark palm sugar*
4 kaffir lime leaves*, shredded
1 tablespoon peanut oil

Place the chilli, shrimp paste, ginger, eschalot, garlic, sugar, lime leaves and oil in a small food processor and process, scraping down the sides of the bowl, until smooth. MAKES 1 CUP (250ML)

spicy fish curry

green masala curry prawns

chorizo and prawn skewers with piri piri sauce

16 extra large green (raw) prawns (shrimp), peeled with tails intact
16 slices fresh chorizo*
olive oil, for brushing
lemon halves, grilled, to serve
piri piri sauce
1 clove garlic, crushed
2 long red chillies*, deseeded and chopped
¼ cup (60ml) lemon juice
¼ cup (60ml) olive oil
¼ teaspoon cayenne pepper
1 teaspoon smoked paprika*
2 teaspoons caster (superfine) sugar
sea salt and cracked black pepper

To make the piri piri sauce, place the garlic, chilli, lemon juice, oil, cayenne pepper, paprika, sugar, salt and pepper in a small food processor and process until a coarse paste forms. Halve the sauce and set one portion aside.

Preheat a char-grill pan or barbecue over high heat. Wrap each prawn around a slice of chorizo and thread 2 prawns onto each skewer. Brush with one portion piri piri sauce and oil and sprinkle with salt and pepper. Cook the skewers for 3 minutes each side or until the prawns are cooked through. Serve with reserved the piri piri sauce and grilled lemon. MAKES 8

green masala curry prawns

2 tablespoons vegetable oil
24 large green (raw) tiger prawns (shrimp), peeled with tails intact
sea salt flakes
1 teaspoon cardamom pods, lightly crushed
2 sprigs curry leaves*
1 cup green masala curry paste (see recipe, right)
400ml coconut milk
1 cup (250ml) water
2 tablespoons lime juice
baby (micro) herbs and chilli syrup (see recipe, right), to serve

Heat 1 tablespoon oil in a large, deep-sided frying pan over high heat. Add the prawns and cook, in batches, for 2–3 minutes or until golden. Sprinkle with salt and set aside. Add the remaining oil to the pan with the cardamom and curry leaves and cook for 1–2 minutes. Add the masala curry paste and cook, stirring, for 1–2 minutes. Add the coconut milk and water and bring to the boil. Reduce heat to medium and cook for 5–7 minutes or until reduced slightly. Add the prawns and cook for 1–2 minutes or until cooked through. Add the lime juice and stir to combine. Top with baby herbs and the chilli syrup to serve. SERVES 4

chilli syrup

⅓ cup (80ml) water
1 tablespoon fish sauce*
½ cup finely grated palm sugar*
2 long red chillies*, thinly sliced
1 tablespoon lime juice

Place the water, fish sauce, sugar and chilli in a saucepan over medium heat and cook, stirring, until the sugar is dissolved. Increase heat to high and bring to the boil. Cook for 6–8 minutes or until reduced. Stir through the lime juice and allow to cool completely. SERVES 4

green masala curry paste

2 tablespoons coriander (cilantro) seeds
¼ teaspoon white peppercorns
3 long green chillies*, roughly chopped
2 eschalots* (French shallots), roughly chopped
4 cloves garlic, roughly chopped
6cm piece (30g) fresh ginger, peeled and roughly chopped
1 tablespoon chopped coriander (cilantro) root
1 cup coriander (cilantro) leaves
1 teaspoon sea salt flakes
1 cup mint leaves
1 tablespoon finely chopped palm sugar*
1 tablespoon white wine vinegar
1 tablespoon vegetable oil

Heat a small frying pan over medium heat. Add the coriander seeds and peppercorns and toast, shaking the pan frequently, for 2–3 minutes or until fragrant and light golden. Place in a small food processor and process until ground. Add the chilli, eschalot, garlic, ginger, coriander root and leaves, salt, mint, sugar, vinegar and oil and process, scraping down the sides of the bowl, until smooth. MAKES 1 CUP (250ML)

_____

TRY THIS WITH…
fish
lamb
chicken

PIES + TARTS

Pies speak of comfort and generosity, and of warm, rosy cheeks on a cold winter's day. With their warming fillings and golden tops, this selection of classic and updated pastry goods is bound to have you baking in no time at all.

pork, chicken and tarragon pies

beef, guinness and mushroom pie

chicken and leek pie

beef, guinness and mushroom pie

1 tablespoon olive oil
1 x 1.5kg piece beef brisket, chopped into 6cm pieces
1 brown onion, chopped
2 cloves garlic, crushed
1 tablespoon tomato paste
2 teaspoons Worcestershire sauce
1 tablespoon brown sugar
2 cups (500ml) beef stock
1¾ cups (430ml) Guinness ale
2 tablespoons plain (all-purpose) flour
300g Swiss brown mushrooms, halved
2 x quantities hot water pastry (see recipe, page 238)
1 x quantity eggwash (see recipe, page 241)

Heat the oil in a heavy-based saucepan over high heat. Add the beef and cook, in batches, for 4 minutes or until browned. Set aside. Add the onion and garlic and cook for 3 minutes or until softened. Add the tomato paste and Worcestershire sauce and cook for a further 1 minute. Return the beef to the pan with the sugar, stock and beer. Reduce the heat to low and simmer, covered, for 1 hour. Remove the lid and cook for a further 30 minutes or until the beef is tender. Remove the beef and shred with a fork. Add the flour to the pan and cook, stirring, for 2–3 minutes or until thickened. Remove from the heat, add the beef and mushrooms and stir to combine. Refrigerate until cooled.

Preheat oven to 200°C (400°F). Divide the pastry in half and roll each portion out between 2 sheets of non-stick baking paper to 4mm thick. Line a lightly greased 17cm x 35cm pie tin with 1 sheet of the pastry. Spoon the filling into the pastry and place the remaining pastry on top. Press the edges to seal and trim the excess pastry. Brush with the eggwash and bake for 40–45 minutes or until golden. SERVES 4–6

chicken and leek pie

1 tablespoon olive oil
6 x 150g chicken thigh fillets, chopped
40g unsalted butter
2 small leeks, trimmed and sliced
2 cloves garlic, crushed
2 tablespoons thyme leaves
¼ cup (35g) plain (all-purpose) flour
2 cups (500ml) milk
sea salt and cracked black pepper
2 x quantities shortcrust parmesan pastry (see recipe, page 241)
1 x quantity eggwash (see recipe, page 241)

Preheat oven to 180°C (350°F). Heat the oil in a large non-stick frying pan over medium heat. Add the chicken and cook, in batches, for 4–5 minutes or until golden. Remove from pan, set aside and keep warm. Add the butter, leek, garlic and thyme to the pan and cook for 7–8 minutes or until softened. Add the flour and cook for 2 minutes. Add the milk, salt and pepper and cook for a further 3 minutes or until thickened. Return the chicken to the sauce and refrigerate until cooled completely. Divide the pastry in half and roll each portion out between 2 sheets of non-stick baking paper to 3mm thick. Line a 31cm-round lightly greased pie tin with the pastry. Fill with the chicken mixture. Roll the remaining pastry out between 2 sheets of non-stick baking paper to 3mm thick. Place on top of the pie and trim the excess pastry. Brush with the eggwash and bake for 35–40 minutes or until the pastry is golden. MAKES 4

pork, chicken and tarragon pies

20g unsalted butter
1 leek, trimmed and sliced
3 cloves garlic, crushed
2 tablespoons chopped tarragon leaves
500g pork mince (ground pork)
500g chicken mince (ground chicken)
100g ham, chopped
1 x 180g chicken breast fillet, chopped
sea salt and cracked black pepper
2 x quantities hot water pastry (see recipe, page 238)
1 x quantity eggwash (see recipe, page 241)

Preheat oven to 160°C (325°F). Melt the butter in a non-stick frying pan over medium heat. Add the leek, garlic and tarragon and cook for 7–8 minutes or until the leek is softened. Set aside to cool completely.

Place the pork and chicken mince, ham, chicken, leek mixture, salt and pepper in a bowl and mix well to combine. Roll half the pastry out between 2 sheets of non-stick baking paper to 3mm thick. Cut 4 x 21cm rounds from the pastry and use to line 4 x 1½ cup-capacity (375ml) lightly greased pie tins. Spoon the filling into the pastry shells. Roll remaining pastry out between 2 sheets of non-stick baking paper to 3mm thick. Cut 4 x 15cm rounds from the pastry and place on top of the pies. Press the edges to seal and trim excess pastry. Use a 2cm-round cookie cutter to cut small holes from the top of the pies. Brush with eggwash and bake for 1 hour or until golden and the juices run clear. Gently turn pies out to serve. MAKES 4

fish and prawn pies

1 tablespoon olive oil
1 brown onion, chopped
¼ cup (60ml) dry white wine
1½ cups (375ml) single (pouring) cream*
⅓ cup (40g) frozen peas
2 tablespoons chopped flat-leaf parsley leaves
1 tablespoon finely grated lemon rind
¼ teaspoon cayenne pepper
300g ocean trout fillets, skin off and chopped into 4cm pieces
300g snapper fillets, skin off and chopped into 4cm pieces
250g green (raw) prawns (shrimp), peeled and deveined
1 block store-bought puff pastry+, thawed
1 x quantity eggwash (see recipe, page 241)

Preheat oven to 200°C (400°F). Heat the oil in a saucepan over medium heat. Add the onion and cook for 4–5 minutes or until softened. Add the wine and cream and cook for a further 4–5 minutes or until thickened slightly. Remove from heat, add the peas, parsley, lemon rind, cayenne pepper, trout, snapper and prawns and stir to combine. Spoon filling into 4 x 1¼ cup-capacity (310ml) lightly greased pie tins. Roll the pastry out on a lightly floured surface to 5mm thick. Cut 4 x 12cm rounds from pastry and use to top pies. Using a cookie cutter, cut 4 fish shapes from the remaining pastry and place on pies. Trim edges, brush with eggwash and bake for 30–35 minutes or until golden. SERVES 4
+ *If using puff pastry sheets, rather than a block, the cooking time will be less. The pies may be ready within 20–25 minutes.*

fish and prawn pies

HOW TO COOK hot water pastry

1

2

hot water pastry

150g unsalted butter
⅔ cup (180ml) water
½ teaspoon sea salt flakes
2½ cups (375g) plain (all-purpose) flour

STEP 1 Place the butter, water and salt in a saucepan over high heat and bring to the boil. Remove from the heat and set aside.
STEP 2 Sift the flour into a bowl and make a well in the centre. Pour the butter mixture into the flour and using a butter knife, mix to combine until the dough starts to come together. Turn the dough out onto a lightly floured surface and knead until smooth and elastic.

RECIPE NOTES
Hot water pastry is easier to work with and more forgiving than regular pastry made with cold water. It's more pliable and elastic when you roll it out and forms a stronger shell when baked.

hot water pastry

pork, apple and cider pies

shortcrust parmesan pastry

2 cups (300g) plain (all-purpose) flour
1 cup (80g) finely grated parmesan
150g cold unsalted butter, chopped
1 teaspoon sea salt flakes
1 egg
1 tablespoon cold milk

Place the flour, cheese, butter and salt in a food processor
and process for 1–2 minutes or until the mixture resembles fine
breadcrumbs. Add the egg and milk and process for 2 minutes or
until a smooth dough forms. Cover in plastic wrap and refrigerate
for 30 minutes.

eggwash

1 egg, lightly beaten
2 tablespoons single (pouring) cream*

Place the egg and cream in a bowl and mix to combine. Use to glaze
the pastry. The eggwash will add shine and a golden finish to pastry.

beef, chorizo and bean pies

pork, apple and cider pies

2 tablespoons olive oil
1 x 1kg piece pork neck, cut into 2cm pieces
1 brown onion, sliced
2 cloves garlic, sliced
3 cups (750ml) dry apple cider
1 cup (250ml) chicken stock
1 large potato, peeled and chopped
¼ cup chopped sage leaves
sea salt and cracked black pepper
2 Granny Smith apples, peeled and chopped into wedges
2 x 375g blocks store-bought puff pastry*, thawed
1 x quantity eggwash (see recipe, page 241)
2 sage leaves, extra

Heat half the oil in a heavy-based saucepan over high heat. Add the pork and cook, in batches, for 3–4 minutes or until browned. Remove the pork and set aside. Reduce heat to medium. Add the remaining oil, onion and garlic and cook for 3–4 minutes or until softened. Return the pork to the pan with the cider and stock, reduce heat to low and simmer, covered, for 1 hour. Uncover and cook for 15 minutes. Add the potato, sage, salt and pepper and cook for a further 15 minutes or until the potato is just tender. Remove from the heat and stir through the apple.

Preheat oven to 200°C (400°F). Spoon the pork mixture into 2 x 2 cup-capacity (500ml) ovenproof frying pans. Roll the pastry out on a lightly floured surface to 5mm thick. Cut 2 x 18cm rounds from the pastry and use to top the pies. Trim the edges, brush with eggwash and press a sage leaf into the centre of each pie. Bake for 20–25 minutes or until golden. MAKES 2

beef, chorizo and bean pies

1 tablespoon olive oil
1kg beef chuck steak, chopped
1 red onion, chopped
1 fresh chorizo*, sliced
2 x 400g cans cherry tomatoes
¼ cup (60ml) sherry vinegar*
1 tablespoon brown sugar
1 cup (250ml) beef stock
1 x 400g can butter (lima) beans, drained and rinsed
4 sheets store-bought butter puff pastry*, thawed
1 x quantity eggwash (see recipe, page 241)

Preheat oven to 200°C (400°F). Heat the oil in a heavy-based saucepan over high heat. Add the beef and cook, in batches, for 3–4 minutes or until browned. Set aside and keep warm. Add the onion and chorizo and cook for 3–4 minutes or until onion is softened. Return the beef to the pan with the tomatoes, vinegar, sugar and stock and bring to the boil. Reduce the heat to low and simmer, covered, for 30 minutes. Uncover and cook for a further 30 minutes or until thickened. Add the beans and refrigerate until cooled completely. Place 4 x 12cm oval-shaped pie tins on 2 sheets of pastry and cut around the edge of the tin using a small, sharp knife to make 4 ovals. Place the tins on the remaining pastry sheets and cut another 4 ovals, this time leaving a 2cm border. Lightly grease the 4 tins, line with the large pastry ovals and fill with the beef mixture. Top with the remaining pastry ovals and trim the excess. Brush with eggwash and bake for 20 minutes or until golden. MAKES 4

HOW TO COOK shortcrust pastry

basic shortcrust pastry

2 cups (300g) plain (all-purpose) flour
180g unsalted butter, chilled and cut into cubes
½ teaspoon table salt
1 egg yolk
2–3 tablespoons iced water

STEP 1 Place the flour, butter and salt in a food processor and process in short bursts until the mixture resembles fine breadcrumbs.
STEP 2 While the motor is running, add the egg yolk and water until the dough just comes together. Turn the dough out onto a lightly floured surface, gently bring together to form a ball and flatten into a disc shape. Cover in plastic wrap and refrigerate for 1 hour.
STEP 3 Preheat oven to 180°C (350°F). Roll the dough out between 2 sheets of non-stick baking paper to 3mm thick. Line a lightly greased 22cm loose-bottomed tart tin with the pastry. Trim the edges and prick the base with a fork. Refrigerate for 30 minutes.
STEP 4 Line the pastry case with non-stick baking paper and fill with baking weights or rice. Bake for 15 minutes, remove the paper and weights and cook for a further 10 minutes or until the pastry is golden. Allow to cool in the tin. SERVES 6–8

RECIPE NOTES
Shortcrust pastry owes its 'short' crisp texture to butter. The butter can make the pastry quite soft and difficult to roll. If you find your pastry is too soft at any stage, pop it in the fridge for a few minutes to firm up.

basic shortcrust pastry

mushroom and ricotta tarts

1 tablespoon olive oil
6 field mushrooms, sliced
2 cloves garlic, thinly sliced
sea salt and cracked black pepper
1 x quantity shortcrust pastry (see recipe, page 244)
3 eggs, lightly beaten
½ cup (125ml) milk
¾ cup (80g) ricotta
8 sprigs thyme
a mixed green salad, to serve

Preheat oven to 200°C (400°F). Heat the oil in a non-stick frying pan over high heat. Add the mushroom, garlic, salt and pepper and cook for 4–5 minutes or until browned. Set aside.

Roll the pastry out between 2 sheets of non-stick baking paper to 3mm thick. Cut 4 x 15cm rounds from the pastry and use to line 4 x 9.5cm-round lightly greased pie tins. Place the eggs and milk in a bowl and whisk to combine. Divide the mushroom and ricotta between the pie tins and pour over the egg mixture. Top each pie with 2 thyme sprigs and bake for 25–30 minutes or until golden. Serve with a mixed green salad. SERVES 4

roast vegetable pasties

140g carrot, peeled and chopped
170g parsnip, peeled and chopped
500g sweet potato (kumara), peeled and chopped
1 tablespoon olive oil
sea salt and cracked black pepper
½ cup (140g) caramelised onion relish
1 cup (120g) frozen peas
1½ tablespoons chopped rosemary
1½ cups (180g) grated aged cheddar
2 x quantities shortcrust pastry (see recipe, page 244)
1 egg, lightly beaten

Preheat oven to 200°C (400°F). Place the carrot, parsnip and sweet potato on a baking tray. Drizzle with oil and sprinkle with salt and pepper. Roast for 15–17 minutes or until cooked through. Mix the vegetables with the onion relish, peas, rosemary and cheddar. Roll each piece of pastry out between 2 sheets of non-stick baking paper to 3mm thick. Cut 10 x 14cm rounds from the pastry. Place ¼ cup of the filling in the centre of each round and brush edges with egg. Fold over and pinch to seal. Brush with egg and place on a baking tray lined with non-stick paper. Bake for 20–25 minutes or until golden. MAKES 10

tarragon chicken and ham pasties

1 cup (160g) shredded cooked chicken
½ cup (70g) thinly sliced ham
1 cup (120g) grated gruyère
½ cup (120g) sour cream
¼ cup tarragon leaves
2 x quantities shortcrust pastry (see recipe, page 244)
1 egg, lightly beaten

Preheat oven to 200°C (400°F). Place the chicken, ham, cheese, sour cream and tarragon in a bowl and mix well to combine. Roll each piece of pastry out between 2 sheets of non-stick baking paper to 2 x 25cm squares. Cut each pastry sheet into 4 squares. Place ¼ cup of the filling into the centre of each square and brush the edges with egg. Gather the corners into the centre and press together to seal the edges. Brush with egg and place on a baking tray lined with non-stick baking paper. Bake for 20–25 minutes or until golden. MAKES 8

salmon and chive tart

1 shortcrust pastry shell (see recipe, page 244)
400g hot smoked salmon (or trout) fillets, flaked
3 eggs
¾ cup (180ml) single (pouring) cream*
sea salt and cracked black pepper
⅓ cup (80g) crème fraîche*
watercress sprigs and chervil leaves, to serve

Preheat oven to 180°C (350°F). Place the salmon in the base of the cooked pastry shell. Place the eggs and cream in a bowl, sprinkle with salt and pepper and whisk to combine. Pour the egg mixture into the pastry shell and place on a baking tray. Top the tart with spoonfuls of crème fraîche and bake for 25 minutes or until just set. Allow to cool for 5 minutes before serving. SERVES 4–6

beef and ale pies

cauliflower, celeriac and cheese pasties

beef empanadas

beef and ale pies

2 tablespoons olive oil
1 x 1kg piece beef brisket, trimmed and cut into 2cm pieces
sea salt and cracked black pepper
plain (all-purpose) flour, for dusting
1 brown onion, chopped
2 cloves garlic, crushed
2 stalks celery, trimmed and finely chopped
4 bay leaves
1 tablespoon tomato paste
1 tablespoon balsamic vinegar
2⅔ cups (660ml) pale ale
1 cup (250ml) beef stock
1 tablespoon brown sugar
pastry
150g unsalted butter, chopped
⅔ cup (160ml) water
2½ cups (375g) plain (all-purpose) flour
½ teaspoon sea salt flakes
1 egg, lightly beaten

Heat 1 tablespoon of the oil in a large heavy-based saucepan over high heat. Sprinkle the beef with salt and pepper and dust with flour. Cook, in batches, for 3–4 minutes each side or until browned. Remove from the pan and set aside. Heat the remaining oil in the pan. Add the onion, garlic and celery and cook for 5 minutes or until softened. Return the beef to the pan with the bay leaves, tomato paste, vinegar, beer, stock and sugar and bring to the boil. Reduce heat to low, cover with a tight-fitting lid, and cook for 3–3½ hours or until tender. Remove the beef from the cooking liquid and use 2 forks to shred. Discard any fat. Return the beef to the pan and mix with the cooking liquid. Allow to cool completely.

Preheat oven to 200°C (400°F). To make the pastry, place the butter and water in a saucepan over high heat and bring to the boil. Remove from the heat and stir in the flour and salt until a smooth dough forms. Turn the dough out onto a lightly floured surface and knead until smooth and elastic. Roll the pastry out to 2mm thick and cut out 4 x 16cm rounds. Line 4 x 9.5cm-round lightly greased pie dishes with the pastry. Divide the beef mixture between the pastry cases. Cut out 4 x 12.5cm rounds from the remaining pastry and use to top the pies. Press the edges to seal and trim the excess pastry. Use a small, sharp knife to cut a slit in the top of the pies. Brush with the egg and cook for 30–35 minutes or until the pastry is cooked through and golden. MAKES 4

beef empanadas

2 tablespoons olive oil
1 small brown onion, finely chopped
3 cloves garlic, crushed
400g beef mince (ground beef)
1 teaspoon ground cumin
1 teaspoon sweet paprika*
1 teaspoon smoked paprika*
2 teaspoons dried oregano
½ cup (125ml) beef stock
sea salt and cracked black pepper
25g unsalted butter
¼ cup (40g) currants
½ cup flat-leaf parsley leaves, chopped, plus extra, to serve
1 green onion (scallion), thinly sliced
4 sheets store-bought shortcrust pastry
1 egg, lightly beaten
1 tablespoon milk
store-bought tomato relish, to serve

Heat the oil in a large non-stick frying pan over high heat. Add the onion and garlic and cook, stirring frequently, for 2–3 minutes or until light golden. Add the mince, cumin, sweet and smoked paprika and oregano and cook, breaking up any lumps with a wooden spoon, for 5–6 minutes or until golden. Add the stock, salt and pepper and cook for a further 2–3 minutes or until the liquid is reduced. Remove from the heat and stir through the butter, currants, parsley and green onion. Allow to cool completely.

Preheat oven to 200°C (400°F). Using an 11cm-round cookie cutter, cut 4 rounds from each shortcrust pastry sheet. Whisk to combine the egg and milk. Place 2 tablespoonfuls of the beef mixture in the centre of each round, brush the edges with the egg mixture, fold over to enclose and press the edges to seal. Fold and pinch the edges to create a ruffled edge. Repeat with the remaining ingredients. Place on baking trays lined with non-stick baking paper and brush with the remaining egg mixture. Bake for 15–20 minutes or until golden. Sprinkle with extra parsley and serve with tomato relish. MAKES 16

cauliflower, celeriac and cheese pasties

500g cauliflower, chopped
500g celeriac (celery root), peeled and chopped
10 eschalots* (French shallots), peeled
3 sprigs rosemary
1 tablespoon olive oil
40g unsalted butter
¼ cup (35g) plain (all-purpose) flour
2 cups (500ml) milk
1 cup (120g) grated aged cheddar
sea salt and cracked black pepper
2 x quantities shortcrust parmesan pastry, with parmesan omitted
   (see recipe, page 241)
½ cup (100g) grated mozzarella
1 x quantity eggwash (see recipe, page 241)

Preheat oven 180°C (350°F). Place the cauliflower, celeriac, eschalots and rosemary on a baking tray, drizzle with the oil and toss to coat. Roast for 40–45 minutes or until golden. Melt the butter in a saucepan over medium heat, add the flour and cook, stirring, for 1–2 minutes. Gradually add the milk, stirring with a wooden spoon, until smooth. Reduce heat to low and cook, stirring, for a further 4–5 minutes or until thickened. Add the cheddar, salt and pepper and stir until melted and smooth. Add the roasted vegetables and mix to combine. Refrigerate until cooled completely.

Increase oven temperature to 200°C (400°F). Roll the pastry out between 2 sheets of non-stick baking paper to 3mm thick. Cut 12 x 15cm rounds from the pastry. Spoon the filling onto one half of each round and top with the mozzarella. Brush the edges of the rounds with eggwash and fold the pastry over to enclose. Press the edges with a fork to seal and brush with the remaining eggwash. Place the pies on a baking tray lined with non-stick baking paper and bake for 30 minutes or until golden. MAKES 12

lamb shank pies

½ cup (75g) plain (all-purpose) flour
sea salt and cracked black pepper
1 tablespoon olive oil
4 x 250g lamb shanks
1 brown onion, chopped
2 cloves garlic, crushed
1 x 400g can cherry tomatoes
3 cups (750ml) beef stock
½ cup (125ml) red wine
1 tablespoon finely chopped rosemary
1 teaspoon caster (superfine) sugar
lightly crushed cooked peas and mint leaves, to serve
pastry
300g unsalted butter, chopped
1 teaspoon sea salt flakes
1⅓ cups (330ml) water
5 cups (750g) plain (all-purpose) flour
1 egg, lightly beaten

Mix to combine the flour, salt and pepper. Heat the oil in a large heavy-based saucepan over high heat. Dust the lamb shanks in the flour and cook for 3–4 minutes or until well browned. Remove from the pan and set aside. Add the onion, garlic, tomatoes, stock, wine, rosemary and sugar and bring to the boil. Return the lamb shanks to the pan, cover with a tight-fitting lid, reduce heat to medium and cook for 1½ hours or until tender.

Preheat oven to 200°C (400°F). To make the pastry, place the butter, salt and water in a large saucepan over high heat and bring to the boil. Remove from the heat and stir in the flour until a smooth dough forms. Turn out onto a lightly floured surface and knead until smooth and elastic. Roll the pastry out to 2mm thick and cut out 4 x 21cm rounds. Line 4 x 8.5cm-high x 7.5cm-wide lightly greased dariole moulds with the pastry. Divide the shanks, bone-side up, and sauce between the moulds. Roll remaining pastry out to 2mm thick and cut out 4 x 10.5cm rounds. Cut a hole from the centre of each round and place over the pies. Press to seal and trim excess. Brush with egg and bake for 30 minutes or until pastry is golden. Turn out and serve with the peas and mint. SERVES 4

lamb shank pies

SALADS + SIDES

You've chosen the main event, now choose a vibrant side to complement it. There's soft leafy greens for a light touch, and root vegetables perfect with a roast, plus a selection of other irresistible partners to play a supporting role.

mozzarella, lemon and mint salad

crispy parmesan and chilli kale chips

mozzarella, lemon and mint salad

1 head garlic, halved
½ tablespoon olive oil
500g fresh buffalo mozzarella*, torn
½ cup mint leaves
2 tablespoons oregano leaves
1 tablespoon finely grated lemon rind
120g thinly sliced salami, to serve
lemon honey dressing
2 tablespoons lemon juice
1 tablespoon honey
2 tablespoons olive oil
sea salt and cracked black pepper

Preheat oven to 200°C (400°F). Drizzle the garlic with the oil and place, cut-side down, on a baking tray. Roast for 10 minutes or until golden and softened. Set aside.

To make the lemon honey dressing, place the lemon juice, honey, oil, salt and pepper in a bowl and whisk to combine. Place the mozzarella on a dish and top with the mint, oregano and lemon rind. Drizzle with the dressing and serve with the roasted garlic, salami and some crusty bread, if desired. SERVES 4–6

crispy parmesan and chilli kale chips

300g kale, stems removed and roughly torn
1 tablespoon olive oil
½ teaspoon dried chilli flakes
½ cup (40g) finely grated parmesan, plus extra, to serve
sea salt and cracked black pepper

Preheat oven to 180°C (350°F). Place the kale, oil, chilli flakes, parmesan, salt and pepper in a bowl and mix well to combine. Place on a large baking tray and bake for 8–12 minutes or until crispy. Allow to cool and sprinkle with the extra parmesan to serve. SERVES 4

butter lettuce and egg salad with malt vinegar dressing

8 eggs
½ cup (150g) whole-egg mayonnaise
2 tablespoons malt vinegar
2 tablespoons buttermilk
sea salt and cracked black pepper
150g butter lettuce, leaves separated
2 tablespoons chopped chives

Cook the eggs in a saucepan of boiling water for 8–9 minutes. Allow to cool completely. Peel and remove the yolks from 5 eggs, discarding the whites. Cut the remaining eggs into quarters and set aside. Place the egg yolks in a bowl and mash with a fork to form a paste. Add the mayonnaise, vinegar, buttermilk, salt and pepper and whisk to combine. Place the lettuce leaves, reserved eggs and chives on a plate and drizzle with the dressing to serve. SERVES 4

tempura cauliflower

1 cup (150g) cornflour (cornstarch)
½ cup (75g) self-raising (self-rising) flour, plus extra, for dusting
1¾ cups (430ml) iced water
vegetable oil, for deep-frying
1kg cauliflower, thinly sliced
1 teaspoon sea salt flakes
soy sauce and chopped red chilli*, to serve

Place the cornflour, self-raising flour and water in a bowl and mix with a butter knife until just combined (the mixture will be lumpy). Heat the oil in a saucepan over medium heat until hot. Dust the cauliflower in the extra flour, shaking to remove excess, and dip into the batter. Deep-fry, in batches, for 2–3 minutes or until golden. Drain on absorbent paper and sprinkle with salt. Serve with soy sauce and chilli. SERVES 4

butter lettuce and egg salad with malt vinegar dressing

tempura cauliflower

sweet caramelised baby turnips

honey and lemon thyme roasted carrots

sweet caramelised baby turnips

1.6kg baby turnips, peeled and trimmed
1 tablespoon olive oil
20g butter
1 tablespoon brown sugar

Place the turnips in a saucepan of salted cold water and bring
to the boil. Cook for 6–8 minutes or until just tender. Drain well.
Heat the oil and butter in a non-stick frying pan over medium heat.
Add the sugar and stir until dissolved. Add the turnips and cook
for 5–6 minutes or until golden. Serve with roasted meats. SERVES 4

honey and lemon thyme roasted carrots

500g heirloom carrots, peeled and trimmed
2 tablespoons olive oil
¼ cup (60ml) honey
1 tablespoon lemon juice
6 sprigs lemon thyme
sea salt and cracked black pepper

Preheat oven to 200°C (400°F). Place the carrots on a large baking
tray with the oil, honey, lemon juice, thyme, salt and pepper and toss
to combine. Roast for 30 minutes or until the carrots are tender.
Serve with roasted chicken or other meats. SERVES 2

roasted garlic aïoli

4 heads garlic, halved
2 tablespoons olive oil
2 eggs
2 tablespoons lemon juice
1 tablespoon Dijon mustard
sea salt and cracked black pepper
1½ cups (375ml) vegetable oil

Preheat oven to 180°C (350°F). Drizzle the garlic with the oil and
place, cut-side down, on a baking tray lined with non-stick baking
paper. Roast for 30–35 minutes or until softened and golden.
Allow to cool before squeezing the garlic cloves from their skins.
Place in a bowl and mash with a fork until a paste forms. Place the
eggs, lemon juice, mustard, salt and pepper in a food processor or
blender and process until well combined. With the motor running,
gradually pour in the oil in a thin, steady stream and process until
thick and creamy. Fold through the mashed garlic to serve.
MAKES 2 CUPS (500ML)
Tip: The aïoli will keep in the fridge for up to one week.

garlic and thyme bread

6 bread rolls
120g unsalted butter, softened
4 cloves garlic, crushed
sea salt and cracked black pepper
150g fontina*, sliced
12 sprigs thyme

Preheat oven to 200°C (400°F). Using a bread knife, make an
incision through the centre of each roll, making sure not to cut
through. Place the butter, garlic, salt and pepper in a bowl and mix
to combine. Spread the incisions with the butter mixture, reserving
1 tablespoon of mixture. Divide the cheese and thyme between the
rolls and place on a baking tray. Bake for 10–15 minutes or until the
cheese is melted and the bread is golden. While the bread is still
hot, brush with the remaining butter mixture and sprinkle with salt.
Remove thyme before eating. SERVES 4

asparagus and feta salad

⅓ cup (80ml) lemon-flavoured olive oil
2 tablespoons white balsamic vinegar*
1 tablespoon chopped dill
1 tablespoon chopped tarragon
1 tablespoon chopped chives
1 clove garlic, crushed
sea salt and cracked black pepper
800g asparagus, trimmed+
400g feta, sliced

Place the oil, vinegar, dill, tarragon, chives, garlic, salt and pepper in
a bowl and stir to combine. Cook the asparagus in a large saucepan of
salted boiling water for 1 minute or until just tender. Drain and refresh
under cold water. Arrange on a serving plate. Top with feta and spoon
over dressing to serve. SERVES 8
*+ To trim asparagus, either remove the woody end by bending the
stalk at the base until it snaps, or shave off the tough outer skin using
a vegetable peeler. Cut with a knife to make a neat edge.*

roasted garlic aïoli

garlic and thyme bread

asparagus and feta salad

apple and fennel salad with salted caramel pecans

apple and fennel salad with salted caramel pecans

12 slices prosciutto
¼ cup (60ml) maple syrup
1 cup (120g) pecans
½ cup (110g) caster (superfine) sugar
1 tablespoon water
1 teaspoon sea salt flakes
2 tablespoons white balsamic vinegar*
2 tablespoons olive oil
4 small red apples, thinly sliced
4 bulbs baby fennel, thinly sliced

Preheat oven to 160°C (325°F). Place the prosciutto on a baking tray lined with non-stick baking paper, brush with maple syrup and bake for 10 minutes or until crisp and golden. Set aside.
   Place the pecans, sugar, water and salt in a bowl and toss to coat. Heat a large non-stick frying pan over medium heat. Add the pecans and cook for 6–8 minutes, stirring occasionally, or until caramelised. Set aside to cool. Place the vinegar and oil in a bowl and whisk to combine. Place the apple, fennel, prosciutto and pecans in a bowl, drizzle with the dressing and toss to coat. SERVES 6

coriander pesto potato salad

1kg chat (baby) potatoes
340g apple (white) cucumbers, peeled, deseeded and thinly sliced
6 marinated artichoke hearts, quartered
baby (micro) shiso leaves*, to serve
coriander pesto
1 cup coriander (cilantro) leaves
¼ cup (40g) blanched almonds, toasted
1 clove garlic, crushed
⅓ cup (25g) finely grated parmesan
2 tablespoons white balsamic vinegar*
½ cup (125ml) olive oil
sea salt and cracked black pepper

Place the potatoes in a large saucepan of salted cold water over high heat. Bring to the boil and cook for 18–20 minutes or until tender. Drain, allow to cool slightly and remove the skins with a small knife.
   While the potatoes are cooking, make the coriander pesto. Place the coriander, almonds, garlic, parmesan, vinegar, oil, salt and pepper in a small food processor and process until a smooth paste forms. Place in a large bowl and set aside. Add the cooled potatoes, cucumber, artichokes, salt and pepper to the pesto and toss to coat. Top with the shiso leaves to serve. SERVES 4

polenta-crusted potatoes

1kg starchy potatoes, peeled and quartered
½ cup (85g) instant polenta
3 tablespoons olive oil
1 teaspoon sea salt flakes

Preheat oven to 220°C (425°F). Place the potato in a large saucepan of salted cold water and bring to the boil. Cook for 10–12 minutes or until just tender. Drain and return to the pan with the polenta, oil and salt. Shake the pan to fluff the potato and coat in the polenta. Place the potato on a baking tray and roast for 30 minutes or until crisp and golden. SERVES 4

zucchini and mozzarella salad with lemon vinaigrette

1 green zucchini (courgette), thinly sliced+
1 yellow zucchini (courgette), thinly sliced
½ cup each mint and basil leaves
360g fresh buffalo mozzarella*, torn
lemon vinaigrette
1 tablespoon lemon juice
2 tablespoons olive oil
½ teaspoon Dijon mustard
sea salt and cracked black pepper

To make the lemon vinaigrette, place the lemon juice, oil, mustard, salt and pepper in a bowl and whisk to combine. Place the zucchini, mint, basil and mozzarella in a bowl and toss gently to combine. Spoon over the lemon vinaigrette to serve. SERVES 4
+ Use a vegetable peeler to slice the zucchini into ribbons.

coriander pesto potato salad

polenta-crusted potatoes

zucchini and mozzarella salad with lemon vinaigrette

HOW TO COOK *salsa verde*

salsa verde

2 cups flat-leaf parsley leaves
2 cups mint leaves
2 tablespoons capers, rinsed and drained
2 teaspoons Dijon mustard
1 teaspoon shredded lemon zest
2 tablespoons lemon juice
¼ cup (60ml) olive oil
sea salt and freshly cracked black pepper

STEP 1 Place the parsley, mint, capers, mustard, lemon zest, lemon juice and oil in a small food processor and process until a rough paste forms.
STEP 2 Season with salt and pepper. MAKES 1 CUP (250ML)

RECIPE NOTES
Salsa verde loses its freshness very quickly when exposed to the air as the chopped herbs start to oxidise, so it's important to make salsa verde shortly before serving. You can serve this with roasted chicken, steak or grilled fish.

salsa verde

choy sum with black bean sauce

ginger gai larn

sweet potato, leek and sage gratin

sweet potato, leek and sage gratin

40g unsalted butter
4 leeks, trimmed and sliced
2 cloves garlic, crushed
sea salt and cracked black pepper
800g sweet potato (kumara), peeled and thinly sliced
800g waxy potatoes, peeled and thinly sliced
2 tablespoons olive oil
1 cup sage leaves
300g fontina*, sliced

Preheat oven to 200°C (400°F). Melt the butter in a non-stick frying pan over medium heat. Add the leek and garlic, salt and pepper and cook for 5 minutes or until softened. Place the sweet potato, potato, oil and salt and pepper in a bowl and toss to combine. Layer the sweet potato, potato, leek, sage and cheese in a 26cm x 34cm baking tray lined with non-stick baking paper, finishing with a layer of cheese. Cover loosely with aluminium foil and bake for 30 minutes. Remove foil and bake for a further 30 minutes or until golden and cooked through. SERVES 6–8

choy sum with black bean sauce

1 tablespoon sesame oil
2 bunches choy sum*, cut into 10cm lengths
2 cloves garlic, sliced
¼ cup (60ml) Chinese black bean sauce*
½ cup (125ml) chicken stock

Heat the oil in a wok over high heat. Add the choy sum and garlic and cook for 4–5 minutes, stirring, or until tender. Add the black bean sauce and stock and cook for a further 2–3 minutes or until sauce has thickened slightly. SERVES 4–6

ginger gai larn

¼ cup (60ml) oyster sauce
½ teaspoon sesame oil
1 cup (250ml) water
5cm piece (20g) fresh ginger, sliced
1 bunch gai larn* (Chinese broccoli), trimmed

Place the oyster sauce, sesame oil, water and ginger in a small saucepan over high heat and bring to the boil. Add the gai larn, cover and cook for 1–2 minutes. Drain, discarding the ginger, and transfer to a serving dish. Spoon over the oyster sauce to serve. SERVES 4

caramelised onion hummus dip

1 x 400g can chickpeas (garbanzos), rinsed and drained
1 tablespoon tahini*
1 clove garlic, crushed
2 tablespoons lemon juice
sea salt flakes
⅓ cup (80ml) olive oil
olive oil, extra, sumac* and toasted pita bread, to serve
caramelised onion
1½ tablespoons olive oil
1 brown onion, sliced
2 tablespoons brown sugar
1½ tablespoons balsamic vinegar

To make the caramelised onion, heat the oil in a non-stick frying pan over medium heat. Add the onion and cook for 8 minutes or until softened. Add the sugar and vinegar and cook for 1–2 minutes or until caramelised. Set aside to cool.

Place the chickpeas, tahini, garlic, lemon juice, salt and oil in a food processor and process until smooth. Top with caramelised onion, drizzle with oil and sprinkle with sumac. Serve with toasted pita bread. MAKES 2½ CUPS (625ML)

crushed broad bean, feta and mint dip

600g fresh or frozen broad (fava) beans
1½ cups chopped mint leaves
200g marinated feta, crumbled
1 clove garlic, crushed
¼ cup (20g) finely grated parmesan
2 tablespoons white balsamic vinegar*
¼ cup (60ml) olive oil
sea salt and cracked black pepper
char-grilled Turkish bread, to serve

Cook the broad beans in boiling water for 3–5 minutes or until tender. Peel and roughly chop. Place in a bowl with the mint, feta, garlic, parmesan, vinegar, oil, salt and pepper. Lightly crush with a spoon and mix well to combine. Serve with char-grilled Turkish bread. MAKES 2 CUPS (500ML)

caramelised onion hummus dip

crushed broad bean, feta and mint dip

garlic yoghurt dip

2½ cups (700g) plain Greek-style (thick) yoghurt
1 teaspoon sea salt flakes
1 clove garlic, crushed
¼ teaspoon cracked white pepper
sea salt flakes, extra
lemon-flavoured olive oil, for drizzling

Place the yoghurt and salt in a bowl and stir to combine. Line a sieve
with fine muslin and place over a deep bowl. Pour the yoghurt
mixture into the sieve. Cover and refrigerate overnight⁺. Place the
drained yoghurt mixture in a bowl with the garlic, pepper and extra
salt and mix well to combine. Drizzle with lemon-flavoured oil to
serve. MAKES 2 CUPS
+ The excess liquid from the yoghurt will drain through the muslin and into
the bowl during the night, leaving a type of yoghurt cream cheese called
labna in Middle Eastern cuisine. Discard the drained liquid. You can find
muslin at specialty kitchenware stores or fabric stores.

cornmeal tortillas

2 cups (340g) white cornmeal*
2 cups (300g) plain (all-purpose) flour
1 tablespoon sea salt flakes
60g cold lard, chopped
2½ cups (625ml) hot water

Place the cornmeal, flour and salt in a bowl and mix well to combine.
Add the lard and, using your fingertips, rub into the flour mixture
until it resembles fine breadcrumbs. Add the water and, using a
butter knife, mix until the dough comes together. Knead dough on a
lightly floured surface until smooth. Preheat a heavy-based non-stick
frying pan over high heat. Divide dough into 18 pieces. Roll each
piece out to a 20cm round and cook for 1–2 minutes each side or
until lightly browned. MAKES 18
Tip: Cornmeal tortillas have a slightly different flavour from flour tortillas.

flour tortillas

4 cups (600g) plain (all-purpose) flour
1 tablespoon sea salt flakes
50g cold unsalted butter, chopped
2½ cups (625ml) hot water

Place the flour and salt in a bowl and mix well to combine. Add the
butter and, using your fingertips, rub into the flour until mixture
resembles fine breadcrumbs. Add the water and, using a butter knife,
mix until the dough comes together. Knead dough on a lightly floured
surface until smooth. Heat a non-stick frying pan over high heat.
Divide the dough into 18 pieces. Roll each piece out to a 20cm round
and cook for 1–2 minutes each side or until lightly browned. MAKES 18
Tip: You can keep your tortillas warm by stacking them and covering
with a tea towel until you are ready to fill them.

garlic yoghurt dip

SWEET

cookies, biscuits + slices

small cakes

cakes

puddings

pies + tarts

desserts

COOKIES, BISCUITS + SLICES

Whether your vice is a molten brownie, a warm choc-chip cookie straight from the oven, or a golden caramel slice, treat-time never looked better than this compilation of portable, hand-held sweet delights.

jam and coconut slice

lemon curd squares

jam and coconut slice

1 cup (220g) caster (superfine) sugar
1 cup (80g) desiccated coconut
2 cups (300g) plain (all-purpose) flour
200g unsalted butter, melted
1 cup (320g) raspberry jam
coconut topping
3 cups (225g) shredded coconut
2 eggwhites, lightly beaten

Preheat oven to 180°C (350°F). Place the sugar, coconut, flour and butter in a bowl and mix until combined. Press into the base of a lightly greased 20cm x 30cm slice tin lined with non-stick baking paper. Bake for 20 minutes or until golden. Allow to cool slightly. Spread the base with the jam.

To make the coconut topping, place the coconut and eggwhites in a bowl and mix well to combine. Spread over the jam and bake for 25 minutes or until golden. Allow to cool completely in the tin before serving. MAKES 18

TRY THIS WITH...
strawberry jam
apricot jam
plum jam

lemon curd squares

2 cups (300g) plain (all-purpose) flour, sifted
½ cup (110g) caster (superfine) sugar
1 teaspoon vanilla extract
125g cold unsalted butter, chopped
icing (confectioner's) sugar, for dusting
lemon filling
4 eggs
2 egg yolks, extra
2 cups (440g) caster (superfine) sugar
⅓ cup (50g) plain (all-purpose) flour, sifted
1 tablespoon finely grated lemon rind
1 cup (250ml) lemon juice

Preheat oven to 180°C (350°F). Place the flour, sugar, vanilla and butter in the bowl of a food processor and process until dough comes together⁺. Press into the base of a lightly greased 20cm x 30cm slice tin lined with non-stick baking paper. Bake for 20–25 minutes or until golden. Set aside.

Reduce the oven temperature to 160°C (325°F). To make the lemon filling, place the eggs and extra egg yolks in a bowl and whisk to combine. Add the sugar, flour, lemon rind and juice and whisk until smooth. Pour over the cooked base and cook for 30 minutes or until just set. Refrigerate for 2 hours or until firm. Dust with icing sugar to serve. MAKES 18
+ *Don't worry if the dough appears dry and crumbly rather than smooth, it will come together as you press it into the tin.*

gingernut cookies

150g unsalted butter, softened
1 teaspoon vanilla extract
1¼ cups (225g) brown sugar
1 egg
1¼ cups (185g) plain (all-purpose) flour, sifted
1 tablespoon ground ginger, sifted
¼ teaspoon bicarbonate of (baking) soda, sifted
1 cup (220g) Demerara sugar*, for rolling

Preheat oven to 180°C (350°F). Place the butter, vanilla and sugar in an electric mixer and beat for 8–10 minutes or until combined. Add the egg and beat for 2–3 minutes or until pale and fluffy. Add the flour, ginger and bicarbonate of soda and beat until a smooth dough forms. Roll tablespoonfuls of the dough into balls and roll in the Demerara sugar. Place on baking trays lined with non-stick baking paper, leaving room to spread. Bake for 10–12 minutes or until edges are golden. Cool on wire racks. MAKES 24

gingernut cookies

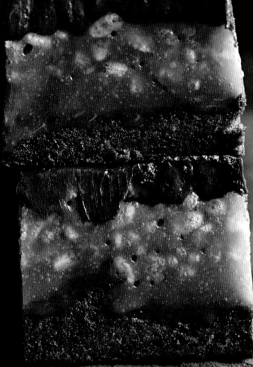

caramel crunch brownie

brownie cookies with peanut butter frosting

caramel crunch brownie

100g dark chocolate, chopped
125g unsalted butter
1 cup (175g) brown sugar
2 eggs
⅔ cup (100g) plain (all-purpose) flour, sifted
1 tablespoon cocoa
caramel crunch
2 cups (440g) caster (superfine) sugar
½ cup (125ml) water
½ cup (125ml) single (pouring) cream*
50g unsalted butter
2 cups (70g) puffed rice cereal
chocolate ganache
300g dark chocolate, chopped
½ cup (125ml) single (pouring) cream*

Preheat oven to 180°C (350°F). Place the chocolate and butter in a small saucepan over low heat and stir until melted and smooth. Set aside. Place the sugar, eggs, flour and cocoa in a bowl with the chocolate mixture and mix until well combined. Pour into a lightly greased 20cm-square cake tin lined with non-stick baking paper and bake for 30–35 minutes or until set. Allow to cool in the tin.

To make the caramel crunch, place the sugar and water in a small saucepan over low heat and stir, brushing any sugar crystals from the sides of the pan with a wet pastry brush. When the sugar is dissolved, increase heat to high, bring to the boil and cook (do not stir) for 8–10 minutes until golden and the mixture reaches 160°C (325°F) on a sugar thermometer. Add the cream and butter and stir until well combined. Stir through the rice cereal and pour the caramel mixture over the brownie, smoothing the top. Set aside for 30 minutes at room temperature or until almost set.

To make the chocolate ganache, place the chocolate and cream in a saucepan over low heat and stir until melted and smooth. Pour over the caramel and allow to cool at room temperature for 3 hours or until set. Slice to serve. SERVES 12
+ *This brownie is best eaten within 2 days. Do not refrigerate.*

brownie cookies with peanut butter frosting

350g dark chocolate, chopped
40g unsalted butter
2 eggs
⅔ cup (150g) caster (superfine) sugar
1 teaspoon vanilla extract
¼ cup (35g) plain (all-purpose) flour, sifted
¼ teaspoon baking powder, sifted
peanut butter frosting
1 cup (160g) icing (confectioner's) sugar mixture
1 cup (280g) smooth peanut butter
80g unsalted butter
1 teaspoon vanilla extract
⅓ cup (80ml) single (pouring) cream*

Preheat oven to 180°C (350°F). Place 200g of the chocolate and the butter in a small saucepan over low heat and stir until melted and smooth. Set aside. Place the eggs, sugar and vanilla in the bowl of an electric mixer and whisk for 15 minutes or until pale and creamy. Stir through the flour, baking powder, chocolate mixture and remaining chocolate and allow to stand for 10 minutes. Spoon tablespoonfuls of the mixture, at a time, onto baking trays lined with non-stick baking paper. Bake for 8–10 minutes or until puffed and cracked. Allow to cool completely on trays.

To make the peanut butter frosting, place the sugar, peanut butter, butter and vanilla in an electric mixer and beat for 6 minutes or until light and fluffy. Add the cream and beat for a further 2 minutes. Spread half the cookies with the peanut butter frosting and sandwich with the remaining cookies. MAKES 12

classic brownie

400g dark chocolate, chopped
280g unsalted butter
2 cups (350g) brown sugar
6 eggs
1 cup (150g) plain (all-purpose) flour

Preheat oven to 180°C (350°F). Place half the chocolate and butter in a small saucepan over low heat and stir until melted and smooth. Allow to cool slightly. Place the sugar, eggs and flour in a bowl with the chocolate mixture and mix to combine. Stir through the remaining chocolate pieces and pour the mixture into a lightly greased 20cm x 30cm slice tin lined with non-stick baking paper. Bake for 30–35 minutes or until cooked when tested with a skewer. Cool in the tin and cut into squares. SERVES 8
+ *These brownies will keep in an air-tight container at room temperature for 3–4 days.*

classic brownie

HOW TO COOK shortbread

1

3

basic shortbread

250g cold unsalted butter, chopped
1 cup (160g) icing (confectioner's) sugar, sifted
1½ cups (225g) plain (all-purpose) flour, sifted
½ cup (100g) rice flour+, sifted
1 teaspoon vanilla extract
icing (confectioner's) sugar, extra, for dusting

STEP 1 Preheat oven to 180°C (350°F). Place the butter, icing sugar, plain flour, rice flour and vanilla in the bowl of a food processor and process until the dough just comes together.
STEP 2 Lightly grease a 24cm round loose-bottomed fluted tin. Press dough into the tin using the back of a spoon. Refrigerate for 15 minutes or until firm.
STEP 3 Use a 6cm round cookie cutter to cut a round from the centre of the dough. Discard the round and place the cutter back in the centre. Use a sharp knife to score the dough into 8 wedges and prick with a skewer.
STEP 4 Bake for 35–40 minutes or until light golden. Remove from the tin and allow to cool on a wire rack. Dust with icing sugar and cut into wedges to serve. MAKES 8
+ *Rice flour gives shortbread its classic crisp, crumbly texture.*

RECIPE NOTES
Pressing the dough into the tin with the back of a spoon will help to give your shortbread a smooth, even surface. Removing a round from the centre creates a more traditional shortbread shape. It also prevents the end of the biscuit from breaking off, removing the fragile point.

basic shortbread

jam drops

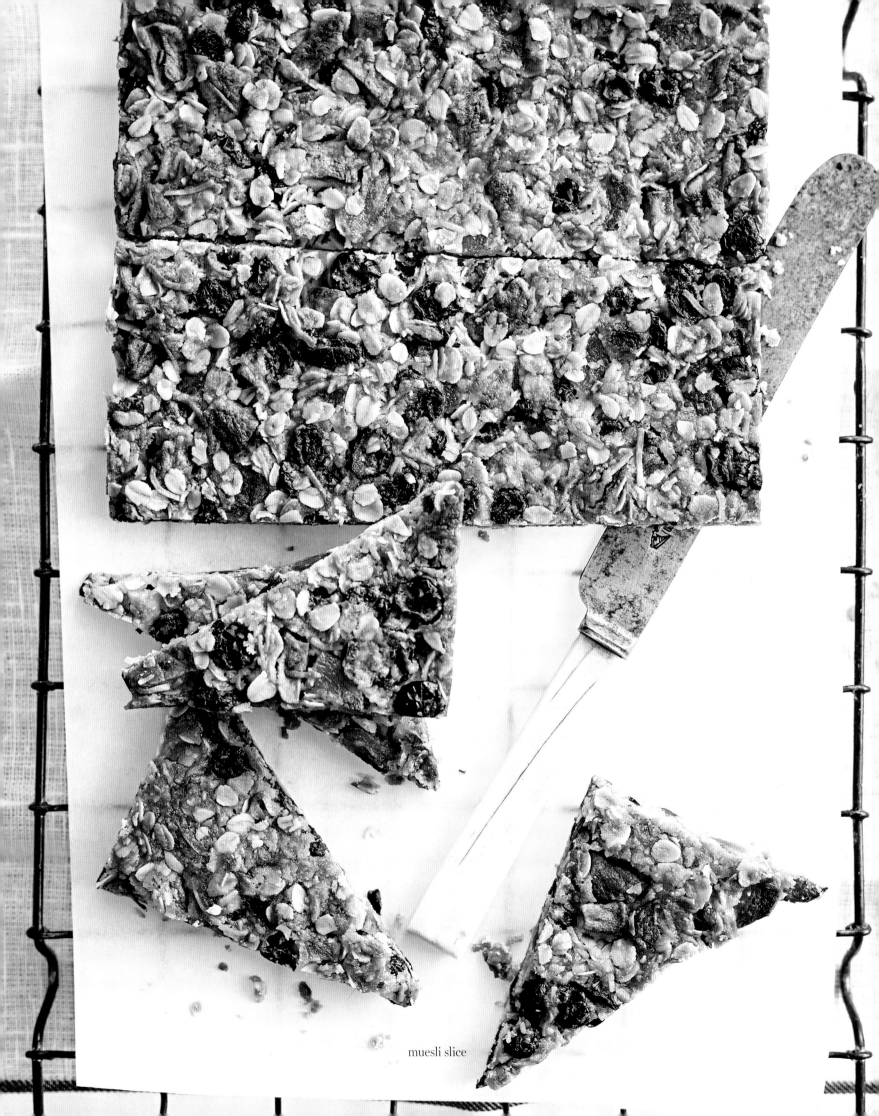

muesli slice

anzac biscuits

jam drops

250g unsalted butter, softened
¾ cup (165g) caster (superfine) sugar
2 teaspoons vanilla extract
1 egg yolk
1 tablespoon finely grated lemon rind
2¼ cups (335g) plain (all-purpose) flour, sifted
½ cup (160g) strawberry jam

Preheat oven to 160°C (325°F). Place the butter and sugar in an electric mixer and beat for 8–10 minutes or until pale and creamy. Add the vanilla, egg yolk and lemon rind and beat to combine. Add the flour and beat until a smooth dough forms. Cover the dough with plastic wrap and refrigerate for 30 minutes or until firm. Roll tablespoonfuls of dough into balls and place on baking trays lined with non-stick baking paper. Flatten slightly and press a finger into the centre of each biscuit to make an indent. Fill the indent with ½ teaspoon of jam. Bake for 15–20 minutes or until light golden. Allow to cool on baking trays for 5 minutes before transferring to wire racks to cool completely. MAKES 38
Tip: To ensure the biscuits don't crack, make the indent in the dough quickly before it dries out.

muesli slice

125g unsalted butter, chopped
¼ cup (90g) golden syrup
1 cup (100g) rolled oats
½ cup (95g) sultanas
½ cup (85g) dried cranberries
½ cup (75g) chopped dried apricots
½ cup (40g) shredded coconut
½ cup (30g) chopped dried apples
½ cup (75g) self-raising (self-rising) flour
½ cup (90g) brown sugar

Preheat oven to 180°C (350°F). Place the butter and golden syrup in a small saucepan over low heat and cook, stirring, until the butter is melted. Place the oats, sultanas, cranberries, apricot, coconut, apple, flour and sugar in a bowl and mix to combine. Add the butter mixture and mix to combine. Using the back of a spoon, press the mixture into the base of a lightly greased 20cm x 30cm slice tin lined with non-stick baking paper. Bake for 20–25 minutes or until golden. Allow to cool completely in the tin before cutting into triangles to serve. MAKES 14

anzac biscuits

2 cups (180g) rolled oats
1 cup (150g) plain (all-purpose) flour
⅔ cup (150g) caster (superfine) sugar
¾ cup (60g) desiccated coconut
⅓ cup (115g) golden syrup
125g unsalted butter
1 teaspoon bicarbonate of (baking) soda
2 tablespoons hot water

Preheat oven to 160°C (325°F). Place the oats, flour, sugar and coconut in a bowl and mix to combine. Place the golden syrup and butter in a saucepan over low heat and cook, stirring, until melted. Combine the bicarbonate of soda with the water and add to the butter mixture. Pour into the oat mixture and mix well to combine. Spoon tablespoonfuls of the mixture onto baking trays lined with non-stick baking paper and flatten to 7cm rounds, allowing room to spread. Bake for 8–10 minutes or until deep golden. Allow to cool on baking trays for 5 minutes before transferring to wire racks to cool completely. MAKES 35

choc-peppermint slice

⅔ cup (100g) self-raising (self-rising) flour, sifted
¼ cup (25g) cocoa, sifted
½ cup (40g) desiccated coconut
¼ cup (55g) caster (superfine) sugar
140g unsalted butter, melted
1 egg, lightly beaten
peppermint filling
3½ cups (480g) icing (confectioner's) sugar, sifted
2½ tablespoons boiling water
½ teaspoon peppermint essence
chocolate topping
200g dark chocolate, chopped
1 tablespoon vegetable oil

Preheat oven to 180°C (350°F). Place the flour, cocoa, coconut, sugar, butter and egg in a bowl and mix well to combine. Press into the base of a lightly greased 20cm x 30cm slice tin lined with non-stick baking paper and bake for 12–15 minutes or until soft to the touch and cooked through. Set aside to cool completely.

To make the peppermint filling, place the icing sugar, water and peppermint essence in a bowl and stir to combine. Working quickly, spread over the cooled base and refrigerate for 1 hour or until firm.

To make the chocolate topping, place the chocolate and oil in a heatproof bowl over a saucepan of simmering water and stir until melted and smooth. Pour the chocolate over the filling and swirl the tin to coat. Refrigerate for 30 minutes or until firm. Cut into squares and keep refrigerated until ready to serve. MAKES 20

choc-peppermint slice

caramel slice

vanilla custard slice

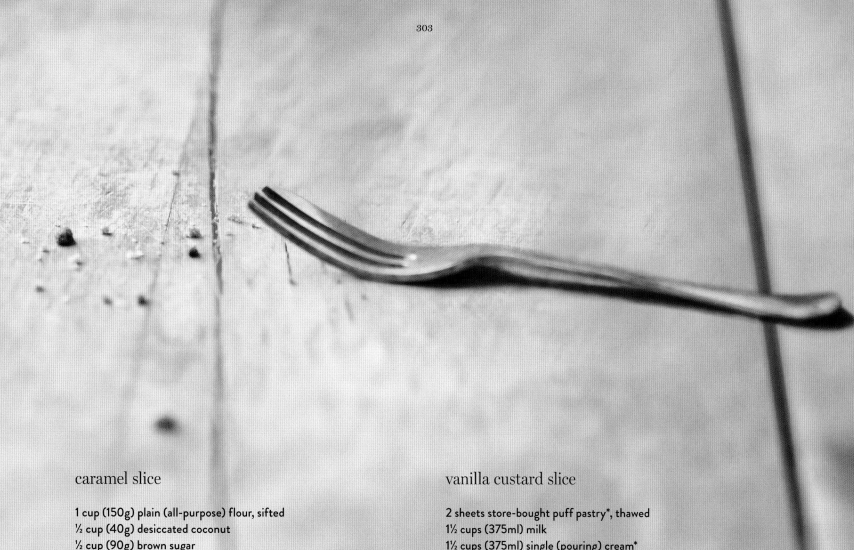

caramel slice

1 cup (150g) plain (all-purpose) flour, sifted
½ cup (40g) desiccated coconut
½ cup (90g) brown sugar
125g unsalted butter, melted
caramel filling
⅓ cup (115g) golden syrup
125g unsalted butter, chopped
2 x 395g cans sweetened condensed milk
chocolate topping
200g dark chocolate, chopped
1 tablespoon vegetable oil

Preheat oven to 180°C (350°F). Place the flour, coconut, sugar and butter in a bowl and mix well to combine. Using the back of a spoon, press the mixture into the base of a lightly greased 20cm x 30cm slice tin lined with non-stick baking paper and bake for 15–20 minutes or until golden.

While the base is cooking, make the caramel filling. Place the golden syrup, butter and condensed milk in a saucepan over low heat and cook, stirring continuously, for 6–7 minutes or until the butter is melted and the caramel has thickened slightly. Pour the caramel over the cooked base and bake for 15–20 minutes or until golden. Cool slightly before refrigerating until cold.

To make the chocolate topping, place the chocolate and oil in a heatproof bowl over a saucepan of simmering water and stir until melted and smooth. Pour the chocolate over the caramel mixture and swirl the tin to coat the caramel. Refrigerate for 30 minutes or until firm. Cut into slices to serve. MAKES 20

vanilla custard slice

2 sheets store-bought puff pastry*, thawed
1½ cups (375ml) milk
1½ cups (375ml) single (pouring) cream*
60g unsalted butter, chopped
2 teaspoons vanilla extract
⅔ cup (150g) caster (superfine) sugar
⅓ cup (50g) cornflour (cornstarch)
½ cup (125ml) water
6 egg yolks
icing (confectioner's) sugar, for dusting

Preheat oven to 180°C (350°F). Place the pastry sheets on baking trays lined with non-stick baking paper. Top each pastry sheet with non-stick baking paper and place an additional baking tray on each pastry sheet as a weight. Bake for 20–25 minutes or until golden. Cool completely on wire racks. Using a serrated knife, trim the pastry sheets to 22cm square. Set aside.

Place the milk, cream, butter, vanilla and sugar in a saucepan over medium heat and cook until just boiling. Remove from the heat. Combine the cornflour and water and whisk into the hot milk mixture with the egg yolks. Return to the heat, whisking, and bring to the boil. Cook, whisking, for 30 seconds–1 minute or until thickened. Place 1 pastry sheet in the base of a lightly greased 22cm-square cake tin lined with non-stick baking paper[+]. Top with the custard and the remaining pastry sheet and press down gently. Refrigerate for 3–4 hours or until set. Dust with icing sugar and slice into squares to serve. MAKES 12

+ *Ensure you have enough baking paper hanging over the sides of the tin so you can lift the slice out after it has chilled.*

HOW TO COOK *macarons*

1 2

3 4

basic macarons with vanilla butter cream

1¼ cups (200g) icing (confectioner's) sugar
1 cup (120g) almond meal (ground almonds)
3 eggwhites, at room temperature
1 tablespoon caster (superfine) sugar
vanilla butter cream
125g unsalted butter, softened
1 vanilla bean, split and seeds scraped
1 cup (160g) icing (confectioner's) sugar

STEP 1 Preheat oven to 150°C (300°F). Sift the icing sugar and almond meal into a bowl and mix to combine. Set aside. Place the eggwhites in an electric mixer and whisk on high for 30 seconds. Add the caster sugar and whisk for 10 minutes until stiff peaks form.
STEP 2 Fold through the almond meal mixture in 2 batches until smooth.
STEP 3 Place the mixture in a piping bag fitted with a 1.5cm plain nozzle and pipe 4cm rounds onto baking trays lined with non-stick baking paper. Lightly tap the trays (see recipe notes, below).
STEP 4 Allow to stand for 20 minutes or until a 'skin' forms on the top of the macarons. Reduce temperature to 130°C (275°F) and bake macarons for 17–18 minutes or until crisp on the outside and moist in the centre. Allow to cool completely on trays.
STEP 5 To make the vanilla butter cream, place the butter and vanilla seeds in an electric mixer and beat for 6–8 minutes or until pale and creamy. Add the icing sugar and beat for a further 10 minutes or until light and fluffy. Spread the vanilla butter cream onto half the cooled macarons and sandwich with remaining macarons. **MAKES 24**

RECIPE NOTES
Lightly tap the trays on the benchtop by gently lifting and releasing before allowing the macarons to rest for 20 minutes. This will help to remove any air bubbles from the mixture and ensure a smooth macaron.

basic macarons with vanilla butter cream

raspberry and ginger cheesecake slice

cheesecake swirl chocolate brownies

raspberry and ginger cheesecake slice

375g store-bought gingernut biscuits
115g unsalted butter, melted
3 teaspoons gelatine powder
¼ cup (60ml) water
375g cream cheese
1 teaspoon vanilla extract
1 cup (220g) caster (superfine) sugar
1 cup (250ml) single (pouring) cream*
375g raspberries

Place the biscuits in the bowl of a food processor and process until the mixture resembles fine breadcrumbs. Place in a bowl with the melted butter and mix well to combine. Using the back of a spoon, press the mixture into the base of a lightly greased 20cm x 30cm slice tin lined with non-stick baking paper. Refrigerate for 30 minutes or until firm. Combine the gelatine and the water and set aside for 5 minutes or until water is absorbed. Place the cream cheese, vanilla and sugar in an electric mixer and beat for 4–5 minutes or until smooth. Add the cream and beat for 2–3 minutes or until thickened. Gently fold through the gelatine and pour the mixture over the biscuit base. Smooth with a spatula and top with raspberries. Refrigerate for 2 hours or until set. Slice to serve. SERVES 6–8

cheesecake swirl chocolate brownies

200g dark chocolate, chopped
250g unsalted butter, chopped
1¾ cups (300g) brown sugar
4 eggs
1⅓ cups (200g) plain (all-purpose) flour, sifted
¼ teaspoon baking powder, sifted
⅓ cup (35g) cocoa, sifted
cheesecake swirl
250g cream cheese, softened
⅓ cup (75g) caster (superfine) sugar
2 eggs

Preheat oven to 180°C (350°F). Place the chocolate and butter in a saucepan over low heat and stir until smooth. Place in a bowl with the sugar and eggs, and whisk to combine. Add the flour, baking powder and cocoa and whisk until smooth. Pour into a lightly greased 22cm tin lined with non-stick baking paper and set aside.

To make the cheesecake swirl, place the cream cheese, sugar and eggs in the bowl of a food processor and process until smooth. Place large spoonfuls of the cheesecake mixture on top of the chocolate mixture and, using a butter knife, swirl to partially combine. Bake for 50 minutes or until set. MAKES 12

chocolate chip cookies

1 cup (175g) brown sugar
¾ cup (165g) white sugar
150g unsalted butter, softened
2 teaspoons vanilla extract
1 egg
1½ cups (225g) plain (all-purpose) flour, sifted
½ teaspoon table salt
½ teaspoon baking powder, sifted
400g dark chocolate, chopped

Preheat oven to 160°C (325°F). Place the brown and white sugars, butter and vanilla in an electric mixer and beat for 8–10 minutes or until pale and creamy. Scrape down the sides of the bowl and add the egg, beating well to combine. Add the flour, salt and baking powder and beat, on low speed, until a dough forms. Fold through the chocolate. Roll 2 tablespoonfuls of the dough at a time into balls, and flatten slightly. Place on lightly greased baking trays lined with non-stick baking paper, allowing room to spread. Bake for 17–20 minutes or until golden. Allow to cool on trays. MAKES 22
Tip: Although the cookies will still be soft to the touch when baked, you can tell they're ready to remove from the oven when the edges are golden.

VARIATIONS

white chocolate and macadamia chip cookies: Simply substitute the dark chocolate for 250g chopped white chocolate and 150g chopped macadamia nuts.
triple chocolate chip cookies: Reduce the dark chocolate quantity to 150g and add 150g chopped white chocolate and 100g chopped milk chocolate to the cookie dough.

chocolate chip cookies + triple chocolate chip cookies
+ white chocolate and macadamia chip cookies

SMALL CAKES

Though small in size, these dainty cupcakes, fruit-studded muffins, indulgent doughnuts and more are big on flavour. Package them up for a sweet gift, put on an afternoon tea spread or offer up a sweet little lunchbox surprise.

coffee meringue brownie

dark chocolate and raspberry brownie tarts

chocolate bourbon cupcakes with peanut butter icing

Chocolate bourbon cupcakes with peanut butter icing

2 tablespoons bourbon whisky
40g unsalted butter, chopped
½ cup (50g) Dutch cocoa, sifted
2 eggs
⅓ cup (80g) sour cream
1⅓ cups (200g) plain (all-purpose) flour, sifted
1 teaspoon bicarbonate of (baking) soda, sifted
1¼ cups (275g) caster (superfine) sugar
bourbon caramel sauce
½ cup (110g) caster (superfine) sugar
2 tablespoons water
2 tablespoons single (pouring) cream*
1 tablespoon bourbon whisky
peanut butter icing
1 cup (160g) icing (confectioner's) sugar mixture, sifted
1 cup (260g) smooth peanut butter
80g unsalted butter, softened
1 teaspoon vanilla extract
⅓ cup (80ml) single (pouring) cream*

Preheat oven to 160°C (325°F). Place the bourbon and butter in a small saucepan over medium heat and stir until the butter is melted. Remove from the heat and whisk in the cocoa. Place the eggs and sour cream in a separate bowl and whisk to combine. Add the bourbon mixture, flour, bicarbonate of soda and sugar and whisk to combine. Divide the mixture between 12 x ½ cup-capacity (125ml) cupcake tins lined with cupcake cases and bake for 25–30 minutes or until cooked when tested with a skewer. Remove from the tins and place on a wire rack to cool completely.

To make the bourbon caramel sauce, place the sugar and water in a small saucepan over medium heat and stir until just combined. Bring to the boil and cook, without stirring, for 7–8 minutes or until lightly caramelised+. Remove from the heat and carefully add the cream and bourbon. Return the saucepan to the heat and stir until combined. Set aside and allow to cool completely.

To make the peanut butter icing, place the sugar, peanut butter, butter and vanilla in an electric mixer and beat for 6–8 minutes or until pale and fluffy. Scrape down the sides of the bowl, add the cream and beat for a further 1 minute. Spread the cooled cupcakes with the icing and drizzle with the bourbon caramel sauce to serve. MAKES 12

+ Once the sugar syrup begins to caramelise, gently swirl the pan to ensure the sauce caramelises evenly.

Coffee meringue brownie

200g dark chocolate, chopped
250g unsalted butter
⅔ cup (150g) caster (superfine) sugar
1 cup (175g) brown sugar
4 eggs
1⅓ cups (200g) plain (all-purpose) flour
2 tablespoons cocoa
1 tablespoon coffee liqueur
coffee meringue
4 eggwhites
1 cup (220g) caster (superfine) sugar
1 tablespoon cornflour (cornstarch)
2 teaspoons white vinegar
1 teaspoon coffee liqueur, plus extra, to serve

Preheat oven to 160°C (325°F). Place the chocolate and butter in a small saucepan over low heat and stir until smooth. Allow to cool slightly. Place the caster sugar, brown sugar, eggs, flour, cocoa and liqueur in a bowl with the chocolate mixture and mix until well combined. Pour into a lightly greased 11cm x 34cm loose-bottomed tart tin and bake for 25–30 minutes or until set. Allow to cool in tin.

Preheat a grill (broiler) to high. To make the coffee meringue, place the eggwhites in an electric mixer and whisk until soft peaks form. Gradually add the sugar and whisk until thick and glossy. Add the cornflour, vinegar and coffee liqueur and whisk until well combined. Spoon the meringue over the brownie and grill (broil) for 1 minute or until golden. Slice and drizzle with the extra coffee liqueur to serve. SERVES 8
Tip: You could also use a small kitchen blowtorch, available from specialty kitchenware stores, to toast the meringue.

TRY THIS WITH…
sweet sherry
marsala
hazelnut liqueur

dark chocolate and raspberry brownie tarts

200g dark (70%) chocolate, chopped
60g unsalted butter
½ cup (90g) brown sugar
¼ cup (60ml) single (pouring) cream*
3 eggs
¼ cup (35g) plain (all-purpose) flour
250g raspberries
chocolate ganache
300g dark chocolate, chopped
1 cup (250ml) single (pouring) cream*

Preheat oven to 150°C (300°F). Place the chocolate, butter, sugar and cream in a saucepan over low heat and stir until melted and smooth. Place the eggs and flour in a bowl and whisk until well combined. Whisk in the chocolate mixture until combined. Pour into 4 x 10cm round lightly greased springform cake tins lined with non-stick baking paper and top with the raspberries. Bake for 35–40 minutes or until cooked when tested with a skewer.

To make the chocolate ganache, place the chocolate and cream in a small saucepan over low heat and stir until melted and smooth. Serve the tarts with the chocolate ganache. MAKES 4

vanilla cupcakes with vanilla butter icing

1¼ cups (185g) self-raising (self-rising) flour, sifted
½ cup (110g) caster (superfine) sugar
100g unsalted butter, softened
2 eggs
2 tablespoons milk
1½ teaspoons vanilla extract
vanilla butter icing
185g unsalted butter, softened
1½ cups (240g) icing (confectioner's) sugar, sifted
1½ tablespoons milk
1½ teaspoons vanilla extract

Preheat oven to 160°C (325°F). Place the flour, sugar, butter, eggs, milk and vanilla in an electric mixer and beat on medium speed for 2 minutes or until pale and smooth. Spoon the mixture into 12 x ½ cup-capacity (125ml) tins lined with cupcake cases. Bake for 20–24 minutes or until cooked when tested with a skewer. Place on a wire rack to cool completely.

To make the vanilla butter icing, place the butter in an electric mixer and beat for 6–8 minutes or until pale and creamy. Add the sugar, milk and vanilla and beat for a further 10–15 minutes or until pale and fluffy. Spread the cupcakes with the icing to serve. MAKES 12

VARIATION

vanilla and lemon curd cupcakes: Use a cutter to remove a round from the top of each cupcake and scoop out some cake. Fill with whipped cream and store-bought lemon curd, and replace the rounds. Dust with icing (confectioner's) sugar to serve.

(clockwise from above) vanilla cupcakes with vanilla butter icing + chocolate and caramel cupcakes + chocolate cupcakes with chocolate butter icing + vanilla and lemon curd cupcakes

(*clockwise from left*) blueberry muffins + banana and coconut muffins
+ raspberry and white chocolate muffins

chocolate cupcakes with chocolate butter icing

1 cup (150g) self-raising (self-rising) flour, sifted
¼ cup (25g) cocoa, sifted
¾ cup (135g) brown sugar
100g unsalted butter, softened
2 eggs
2 tablespoons milk
1½ teaspoons vanilla extract
chocolate butter icing
185g unsalted butter, softened
1½ cups (240g) icing (confectioner's) sugar, sifted
½ cup (50g) cocoa, sifted
1½ tablespoons milk
1½ teaspoons vanilla extract

Preheat oven to 160°C (325°F). Place the flour, cocoa, sugar, butter, eggs, milk and vanilla in an electric mixer and beat on medium speed for 2 minutes or until pale and smooth. Spoon the mixture into 12 x ½ cup-capacity (125ml) tins lined with cupcake cases. Bake for 20–24 minutes or until cooked when tested with a skewer. Place on a wire rack to cool completely.

To make the icing, place the butter in an electric mixer and beat for 6–8 minutes or until pale and creamy. Add the icing sugar, cocoa, milk and vanilla and beat for a further 10–15 minutes or until pale and fluffy. Spread the cooled cupcakes with the icing to serve. MAKES 12

VARIATION

chocolate and caramel cupcakes: Use a cutter to remove a round from the top of each cupcake and scoop out some cake. Fill with store-bought caramel and replace the rounds. Dust with cocoa to serve.

blueberry muffins

2 cups (300g) plain (all-purpose) flour, sifted
2 teaspoons baking powder, sifted
¾ cup (165g) caster (superfine) sugar
1 cup (240g) sour cream
2 eggs
1 teaspoon finely grated lemon rind
1 teaspoon vanilla extract
⅓ cup (80ml) vegetable oil
1¼ cups (150g) fresh or frozen (not thawed) blueberries

Preheat oven to 180°C (350°F). Place the flour, baking powder and sugar in a bowl and stir to combine. Place the sour cream, eggs, lemon rind, vanilla and oil in a separate bowl and whisk until smooth. Stir the sour cream mixture through the flour mixture until just combined. Stir through the blueberries. Spoon the mixture into 12 x ½ cup-capacity (125ml) tins lined with non-stick baking paper. Bake for 25–30 minutes or until cooked when tested with a skewer. MAKES 12

banana and coconut muffins

2 cups (300g) plain (all-purpose) flour, sifted
2 teaspoons baking powder, sifted
¾ cup (165g) caster (superfine) sugar
1 cup (240g) sour cream
2 eggs
1 teaspoon finely grated lemon rind
1 teaspoon vanilla extract
⅓ cup (80ml) vegetable oil
½ cup mashed banana
½ cup (40g) shredded coconut, plus extra, for sprinkling

Preheat oven to 180°C (350°F). Place the flour, baking powder and sugar in a bowl and stir to combine. Place the sour cream, eggs, lemon rind, vanilla and oil in a separate bowl and whisk until smooth. Stir the sour cream mixture through the flour mixture until just combined. Stir through the banana and coconut. Spoon the mixture into 12 x ½ cup-capacity (125ml) tins lined with non-stick baking paper. Sprinkle with extra coconut and bake for 25–30 minutes or until cooked when tested with a skewer. MAKES 12

raspberry and white chocolate muffins

2 cups (300g) plain (all-purpose) flour, sifted
2 teaspoons baking powder, sifted
¾ cup (165g) caster (superfine) sugar
1 cup (240g) sour cream
2 eggs
1 teaspoon finely grated lemon rind
1 teaspoon vanilla extract
⅓ cup (80ml) vegetable oil
1½ cups (240g) frozen raspberries
1 cup (175) white chocolate, chopped

Preheat oven to 180°C (350°F). Place the flour, baking powder and sugar in a bowl and stir to combine. Place the sour cream, eggs, lemon rind, vanilla and oil in a separate bowl and whisk until smooth. Stir the sour cream mixture through the flour mixture until just combined. Stir through the raspberries and chocolate. Spoon the mixture into 12 x ½ cup-capacity (125ml) tins lined with non-stick baking paper. Bake for 25–30 minutes or until cooked when tested with a skewer. MAKES 12

HOW TO COOK brioche

1 2
3 4

basic brioche

1 x 8g sachet dry yeast
1 tablespoon lukewarm water
¼ cup (55g) caster (superfine) sugar
¼ teaspoon sea salt flakes
2 tablespoons lukewarm milk
1⅔ cups (250g) OO flour*
2 eggs, lightly beaten
225g unsalted butter, chopped and softened
1 egg, extra, lightly beaten

STEP 1 Place the yeast and water in a bowl and mix to combine. Set aside in a warm place for 5 minutes or until bubbles appear on the surface. Combine the sugar, salt and milk in a separate bowl. Place the flour, yeast mixture and egg in the bowl of an electric mixer and, using a dough hook, beat on low for 1 minute. Increase speed to high, add the milk mixture and beat for 10 minutes or until dough comes away from the sides of the bowl.
STEP 2 While the motor is running, gradually add the butter and beat for 6–7 minutes or until glossy and elastic.
STEP 3 Place the dough in a bowl and cover with plastic wrap. Set aside in a warm place for 2–3 hours or until the dough has doubled in size.
STEP 4 Preheat oven to 180°C (350°F). Divide the dough into 4 equal-sized balls and knead on a lightly floured surface until smooth. Place in a 22cm x 8cm lightly greased loaf tin, cover with a clean, damp cloth and set aside for 1 hour or until doubled in size. Make a cut in the centre of each ball, brush with the extra egg and bake for 35–40 minutes or until golden. Allow to stand for 10 minutes. SERVES 8

RECIPE NOTES
The amount of butter in the dough results in a rich, golden brioche, but it can make the dough very sticky. To avoid it becoming difficult to work with, it's a good idea to roll it out on a cool, lightly floured benchtop.

basic brioche

orange brioche muffins with lemon icing

1 x quantity basic brioche dough (see recipe, page 320)
1 tablespoon finely grated orange rind
1 egg, lightly beaten
orange zest, to serve
lemon icing
2 cups (320g) icing (confectioner's) sugar mixture, sifted
2 tablespoons boiling water
2 teaspoons lemon juice

Make the basic brioche dough, following steps 1, 2 and 3, adding the orange rind with the milk at step 1. Divide dough into 6 equal-sized balls and knead on a lightly floured surface until smooth. Place in a 6 x 1 cup-capacity (250ml) lightly greased muffin tin. Cover with a clean, damp cloth and set aside for 1 hour.

Preheat oven to 200°C (400°F). Brush the dough with egg and bake for 15–17 minutes or until golden. Cool on a wire rack.

To make the lemon icing, place the icing sugar, water and lemon juice in a bowl and mix to combine. Place the rack of brioche over a baking tray lined with non-stick baking paper and spoon over the icing. Allow to set and top with orange zest to serve. MAKES 6

chocolate-swirl brioche

1 x quantity basic brioche dough (see recipe, page 320)
75g dark chocolate, chopped
¼ cup (60ml) single (pouring) cream*
1 egg, lightly beaten

Make the basic brioche dough, following steps 1, 2 and 3. Place the chocolate and cream in a small saucepan over low heat and stir for 2–3 minutes or until melted and smooth. Set aside to cool completely. Roll the dough out on a lightly floured surface to a 45cm x 30cm rectangle. Spread with the chocolate mixture and, starting from the longest edge, roll to enclose the filling. Place in a 22cm lightly greased Bundt tin. Cover with a clean, damp cloth and set aside for 1 hour or until doubled in size.

Preheat oven to 180°C (350°F). Brush the dough with egg and bake for 35–40 minutes or until golden. SERVES 8-10

cinnamon brioche scrolls

1 x quantity basic brioche dough (see recipe, page 320)
¼ cup (55g) caster (superfine) sugar
½ tablespoon ground cinnamon
1 egg, lightly beaten
1½ tablespoons Demerara sugar*

Make the basic brioche dough, following steps 1, 2 and 3 (page 320).
Place the caster sugar and cinnamon in a bowl and mix well to combine.
Roll the dough out on a lightly floured surface to a 45cm x 25cm
rectangle. Sprinkle with the cinnamon mixture and starting from the
longest edge, roll to enclose filling. Using a sharp knife, trim the
edges and cut into 14 pieces. Place the scrolls side by side in a 20cm
round lightly greased tin, cover with a clean, damp cloth and set
aside for 1 hour or until dough has doubled in size.

Preheat oven to 180°C (350°F). Brush the dough with egg and
sprinkle with the Demerara sugar. Bake for 15 minutes, loosely cover
with aluminium foil and bake for a further 15–20 minutes or until
golden. Turn out onto a wire rack to cool. MAKES 14

raspberry and almond brioche tarts

1 x quantity basic brioche dough (see recipe, page 320)
50g unsalted butter, melted
¼ cup (55g) caster (superfine) sugar
1 egg, lightly beaten
½ cup (60g) almond meal (ground almonds)
1 tablespoon plain (all-purpose) flour
125g raspberries
1 egg, extra, lightly beaten

Make the basic brioche dough, following steps 1, 2 and 3. Roll the
dough out on a lightly floured surface to 1cm thick. Using a 10cm
round cookie cutter, cut 6 x 10cm rounds from the dough. Using a
7cm round cookie cutter, press lightly into the dough rounds to create
a border. Place rounds on a baking tray lined with non-stick baking
paper. Place the butter, sugar, egg, almond meal and flour in a bowl
and mix to combine. Add the raspberries and spoon mixture into
the centre of the rounds. Cover with a clean, damp cloth and set
aside for 1 hour or until doubled in size.

Preheat oven to 180°C (350°F). Brush the edges of the tarts
with extra egg and bake for 17–19 minutes or until golden. MAKES 6

molten peanut butter and chocolate fondant cakes

200g dark chocolate, chopped
100g unsalted butter, chopped
2 eggs
2 egg yolks, extra
½ cup (110g) caster (superfine) sugar
¼ cup (35g) plain (all-purpose) flour, sifted
8 tablespoons smooth peanut butter
cocoa, for dusting

Preheat oven to 200°C (400°F). Place the chocolate and butter in a saucepan over low heat and stir until the chocolate is melted and smooth. Place the eggs, extra yolks and sugar in a bowl and whisk until well combined. Add the chocolate mixture and flour and whisk until well combined. Spoon two-thirds of the mixture into 4 x 1 cup-capacity (250ml) well-greased dariole moulds. Spoon 2 tablespoons of peanut butter into the centre of each mould and spoon over the remaining chocolate mixture. Place the moulds on a baking tray and bake for 16–18 minutes or until puffed. Gently turn out the cakes immediately and dust with cocoa to serve. MAKES 4
+ *Serve immediately to ensure they have a lovely, molten centre.*

classic jam doughnuts

2 teaspoons active dry yeast
1½ tablespoons lukewarm water
½ cup (125ml) lukewarm milk
2 tablespoons caster (superfine) sugar
50g unsalted butter, melted
2¼ cups (335g) plain (all-purpose) flour
2 eggs
vegetable oil, for deep-frying
1¾ cups (560g) store-bought raspberry jam
lavender sugar, for dusting+

Place the yeast, water, milk and 1 tablespoon of sugar in a large bowl and set aside in a warm place for 10 minutes or until bubbles appear on the surface. Add the butter, flour, eggs and remaining sugar to the yeast mixture and use a butter knife to mix until a sticky dough forms. Turn out onto a lightly floured surface and knead until smooth. Place the dough in a lightly oiled bowl, cover with a clean, damp cloth and set aside in a warm place for 45 minutes or until doubled in size.

Knead the dough on a lightly floured surface for 5 minutes or until smooth and elastic. Roll out to 1cm thick and use an 8cm round cutter to cut 10 rounds from the dough. Place the rounds on a baking tray lined with non-stick baking paper and set aside for 30 minutes or until risen.

Place the oil and a kitchen thermometer in a large, deep saucepan over medium heat until temperature reaches 180°C (350°F). Cook doughnuts, in batches, for 1–2 minutes each side or until golden. Drain on absorbent paper. Place the jam in a piping bag. Carefully pierce doughnuts with a knife and fill with the jam. Dust with lavender sugar and serve immediately. MAKES 10
+ *You can make lavender sugar by placing dried or fresh (pesticide-free) lavender flowers in a jar with caster (superfine) sugar. Set aside for 1–2 days to infuse. You can buy dried lavender from specialty grocery stores. Or try dusting your doughnuts with vanilla sugar; simply place a vanilla bean in a jar of sugar for a delicate vanilla flavour.*

molten peanut butter and chocolate fondant cake

classic jam doughnuts

little custard doughnuts

little custard doughnuts

2 teaspoons active dry yeast
1½ tablespoons lukewarm water
½ cup (125ml) lukewarm milk
2 cups (440g) caster (superfine) sugar
50g unsalted butter, melted
2¼ cups (335g) plain (all-purpose) flour
2 eggs
vegetable oil, for deep-frying
1 cup (250ml) thick store-bought custard

Place the yeast, water, milk and 1 tablespoon of sugar in a large bowl and set aside in a warm place for 10 minutes or until bubbles appear on the surface. Add the butter, flour, eggs and remaining sugar to the yeast mixture and use a butter knife to mix until a sticky dough forms. Turn out onto a lightly floured surface and knead until smooth. Place the dough in a lightly oiled bowl, cover with a clean, damp cloth and set aside in a warm place for 45 minutes or until doubled in size.

Knead the dough on a lightly floured surface for 5 minutes or until smooth and elastic. Roll 1 tablespoonful of dough into balls at a time and place on a baking tray lined with non-stick baking paper and set aside for 30 minutes or until risen.

Place the oil and a kitchen thermometer in a large, deep saucepan over medium heat until temperature reaches 180°C (350°F). Cook the doughnuts, in batches, for 1 minute each side or until golden. Drain on absorbent paper. Place the custard in a piping bag. Carefully pierce doughnuts with a knife and fill with the custard. Serve immediately. MAKES 30

TRY FILLING WITH...
lemon curd
raspberry jam
chocolate-hazelnut spread

italian doughnuts

2 teaspoons active dry yeast
1½ tablespoons lukewarm water
½ cup (125ml) lukewarm milk
2 tablespoons caster (superfine) sugar
50g unsalted butter, melted
2¼ cups (335g) plain (all-purpose) flour
2 eggs
½ cup (80g) sultanas
vegetable oil, for deep-frying
icing (confectioner's) sugar, for dusting
ricotta filling
300g ricotta
1 teaspoon finely grated lemon rind
1 tablespoon caster (superfine) sugar

To make the ricotta filling, place the ricotta, lemon rind and sugar in a bowl and mix to combine. Place in the refrigerator.

Place the yeast, water, milk and 1 tablespoon of sugar in a large bowl and set aside in a warm place for 10 minutes or until bubbles appear on the surface. Add the butter, flour, eggs, remaining sugar and sultanas to the yeast mixture and use a butter knife to mix until a sticky dough forms. Turn out onto a lightly floured surface and knead until smooth. Place the dough in a lightly oiled bowl, cover with a clean, damp cloth and set aside in a warm place for 45 minutes or until doubled in size.

Knead the dough on a lightly floured surface for 5 minutes or until smooth and elastic. Divide into 2 equal portions and roll each piece out to 1cm thick. Top 1 piece of dough with spoonfuls of the ricotta filling and sandwich with remaining dough. Use a 6cm round cutter to cut around the ricotta. Place the pillows on a baking tray lined with non-stick baking paper and set aside for 30 minutes or until risen. Place the oil and a kitchen thermometer in a large, deep saucepan over medium heat until temperature reaches 170°C (340°F). Cook the doughnuts, in batches, for 3–4 minutes each side or until golden. Drain on absorbent paper. Allow to cool slightly and dust with icing sugar to serve. MAKES 18

italian doughnuts

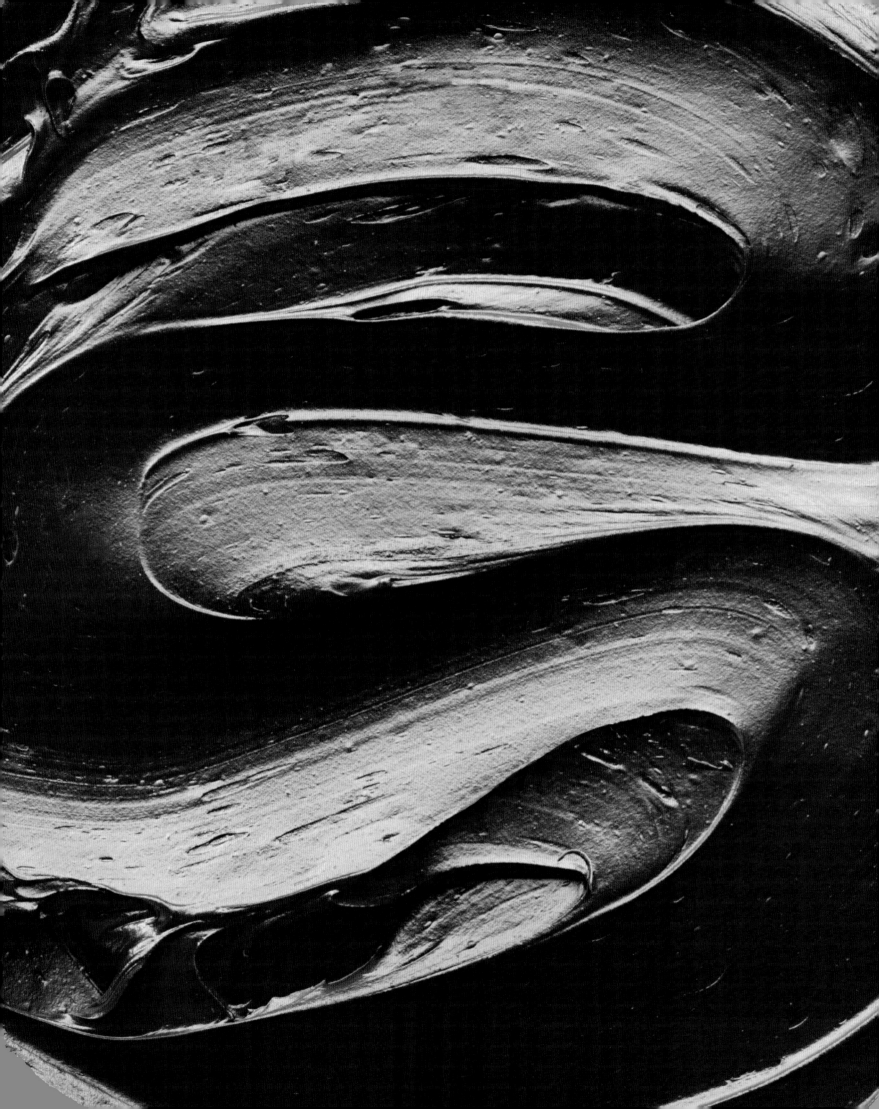

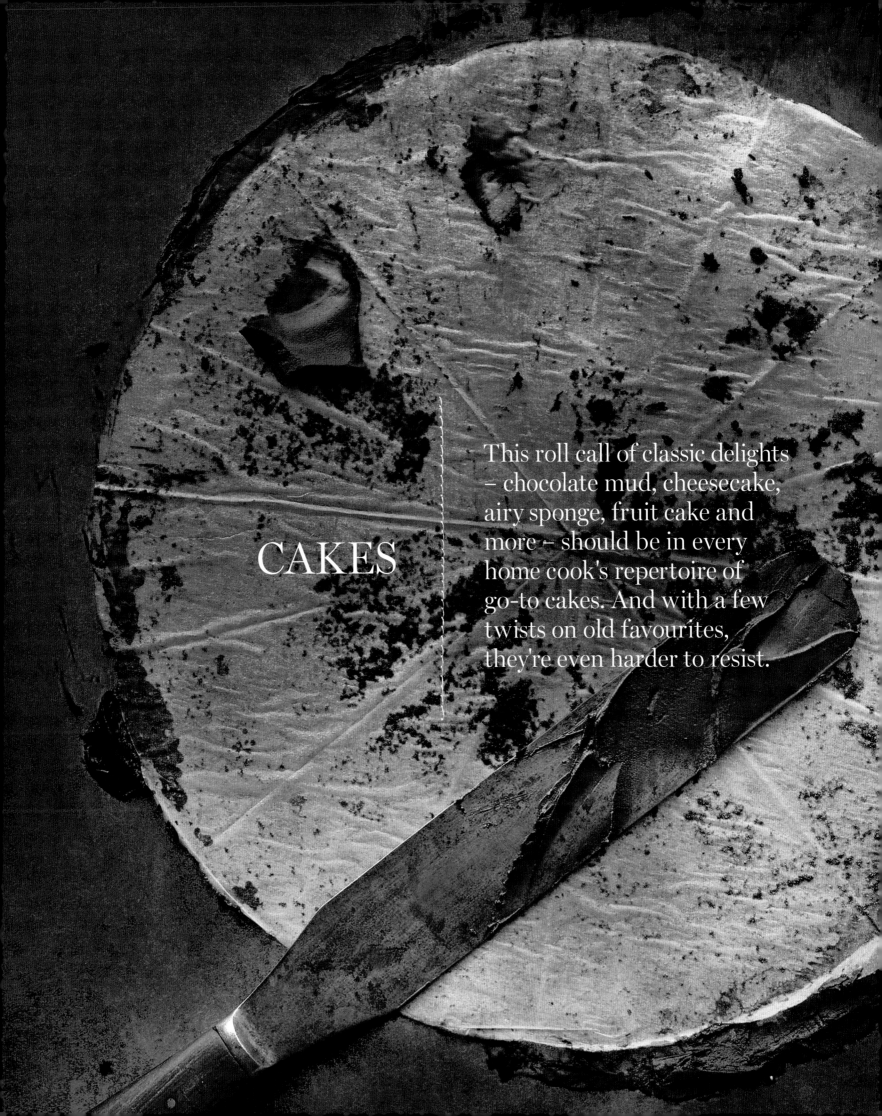

CAKES

This roll call of classic delights – chocolate mud, cheesecake, airy sponge, fruit cake and more – should be in every home cook's repertoire of go-to cakes. And with a few twists on old favourites, they're even harder to resist.

chocolate buttermilk layer cake

chocolate mud cake

chocolate buttermilk layer cake

1 cup (250ml) water
125g unsalted butter, chopped
⅓ cup (35g) cocoa, sifted
2 cups (300g) plain (all-purpose) flour, sifted
1 teaspoon bicarbonate of (baking) soda, sifted
2 cups (440g) caster (superfine) sugar
2 eggs
½ cup (125ml) buttermilk
1 teaspoon vanilla extract
chocolate cream cheese frosting
100g unsalted butter, softened
500g cream cheese
2 cups (320g) icing (confectioner's) sugar mixture, sifted
½ cup (50g) cocoa, sifted

Preheat oven to 160°C (325°F). Place the water, butter and cocoa in a saucepan over medium heat and stir until the butter has melted. Place the flour, bicarbonate of soda and sugar in a bowl, add the cocoa mixture and whisk to combine. Add the eggs, buttermilk and vanilla and whisk to combine. Divide the mixture between 2 lightly greased 18cm round cake tins lined with non-stick baking paper. Bake for 40–45 minutes or until cooked when tested with a skewer. Allow to cool in the tins for 10 minutes. Turn out onto wire racks to cool completely.

While the cake is baking, make the chocolate cream cheese frosting. Place the butter and cheese in the bowl of an electric mixer and beat for 6–8 minutes or until pale and creamy. Add the icing sugar and cocoa and beat for a further 6–8 minutes or until light and fluffy. To assemble, slice the cakes in half horizontally using a bread knife. Place one cake layer on a plate and spread with one quarter of the frosting. Repeat with remaining layers and frosting, finishing with a layer of frosting. SERVES 6–8

rum and date cake with caramel sauce

1½ cups (210g) fresh pitted dates, chopped
½ cup (90g) prunes, chopped
½ cup (75g) raisins
¾ cup (180ml) boiling water
½ cup (125ml) dark rum
1½ teaspoons bicarbonate of (baking) soda, sifted
1½ cups (225g) self-raising (self-rising) flour, sifted
1⅓ cups (235g) brown sugar
225g unsalted butter, melted
1½ teaspoons vanilla extract
6 eggs
caramel sauce
100g unsalted butter
¾ cup (135g) brown sugar
½ cup (175g) golden syrup
1 cup (250ml) single (pouring) cream*
¼ cup (60ml) dark rum

Preheat oven to 160°C (325°F). Place the dates, prunes, raisins, boiling water, rum and bicarbonate of soda in a small food processor and set aside for 10 minutes. Process the date mixture until smooth and set aside.

Place the flour and sugar in a bowl and mix to combine. Add the butter, vanilla, eggs and date mixture and mix well to combine. Spoon into a well-greased 3.5 litre-capacity Bundt tin and bake for 55–60 minutes or until cooked when tested with a skewer. Allow to cool in the tin for 10 minutes. Turn out onto a wire rack to cool completely.

To make the caramel sauce, place the butter, sugar, golden syrup, cream and rum in a saucepan over medium heat and stir until the sugar is dissolved. Bring to the boil and cook for 10–12 minutes or until thickened. Allow sauce to cool for 10 minutes before pouring over the cake to serve. SERVES 8–10

rum and date cake with caramel sauce

maple and date syrup cake

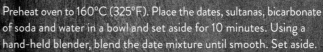

chocolate mud cake

400g unsalted butter, chopped
400g dark chocolate, chopped
⅓ cup (15g) instant coffee granules
2 teaspoons vanilla extract
¼ cup (60ml) water
6 eggs
2 cups (440g) caster (superfine) sugar
1½ cups (225g) self-raising (self-rising) flour, sifted
½ cup (25g) cocoa, sifted
chocolate ganache
1 cup (250ml) single (pouring) cream*
300g dark chocolate, chopped

Preheat oven to 160°C (325°F). Place the butter, chocolate, coffee, vanilla and water in a saucepan over low heat and stir until melted. Set aside and allow to cool to room temperature.

Place the eggs and sugar in the bowl of an electric mixer and beat for 6 minutes or until pale and thick. Add the chocolate mixture and beat until combined. Fold through the flour and cocoa. Pour into a lightly greased 24cm round cake tin lined with non-stick baking paper. Bake for 1 hour 30 minutes or until cooked when tested with a skewer. Allow to cool in the tin for 10 minutes. Turn out onto a wire rack to cool completely.

To make the chocolate ganache, place the cream and chocolate in a saucepan over low heat and stir until melted and smooth. Set aside and allow to cool to room temperature. Spread ganache over the cooled cake to serve. SERVES 6–8

maple and date syrup cake

1 cup (230g) fresh pitted dates, chopped
½ cup (80g) chopped sultanas
1 teaspoon bicarbonate of (baking) soda
¾ cup (180ml) boiling water
1⅓ cups (225g) self-raising (self-rising) flour, sifted
¾ cup (130g) brown sugar
150g unsalted butter, melted
2 tablespoons maple syrup
1 teaspoon vanilla extract
4 eggs
2 cups (500ml) maple syrup, extra

Preheat oven to 160°C (325°F). Place the dates, sultanas, bicarbonate of soda and water in a bowl and set aside for 10 minutes. Using a hand-held blender, blend the date mixture until smooth. Set aside.

Place the flour and sugar in a bowl and mix to combine. Add the butter, maple syrup, vanilla, eggs and date mixture and mix well to combine. Spoon the mixture into a lightly greased 20cm round tin lined with non-stick baking paper and bake for 50 minutes or until cooked when tested with a skewer. Allow to cool in the tin for 10 minutes. Turn out onto a wire rack to cool completely.

Place the extra maple syrup in a saucepan over high heat and cook for 10 minutes or until slightly thickened. Allow to cool slightly. Pour the warm syrup over the cake to serve. SERVES 8-10

lemon pound cake

1½ cups (225g) plain (all-purpose) flour
1 teaspoon baking powder
120g unsalted butter, softened
1 tablespoon finely grated lemon rind
1 cup (220g) caster (superfine) sugar
2 eggs
½ cup (125ml) milk
icing (confectioner's) sugar, for dusting

Preheat oven to 160°C (325°F). Sift the flour and baking powder into a bowl and set aside. Place the butter and lemon rind in an electric mixer and beat on medium speed for 3–4 minutes or until smooth. Gradually add the sugar, scraping down the sides of the bowl with a spatula and continue beating for 5–6 minutes or until pale and creamy. Add the eggs, one at a time, beating well after each addition. Reduce speed to low and gradually add the flour mixture and milk, alternating, and occasionally scraping down the bowl, until smooth. Spoon into a lightly greased 8.5cm x 26.5cm x 9cm loaf tin (2-litre capacity) double-lined with non-stick baking paper and bake for 60–65 minutes or until cooked when tested with a skewer. Allow to cool in the tin for 10 minutes before turning out onto a wire rack to cool completely. Dust with icing sugar to serve. SERVES 8-10

coconut, palm sugar and banana upside-down cake

fruit loaf

½ cup (125ml) orange juice
1 cup (130g) sweetened dried cranberries
½ cup (80g) currants
½ cup (80g) raisins
200g unsalted butter, softened
⅔ cup (150g) caster (superfine) sugar
1 vanilla bean, split and seeds scraped
1 tablespoon finely grated orange rind
3 eggs
1 cup (150g) plain (all-purpose) flour, sifted
1 teaspoon baking powder, sifted
½ cup (60g) almond meal (ground almonds)
¼ teaspoon ground cardamom
icing (confectioner's) sugar, for dusting

Preheat oven to 160°C (325°F). Place the juice in a small saucepan over medium heat and bring to a simmer. Place the cranberries, currants and raisins in a bowl, pour over the orange juice and set aside for 15 minutes. Place the butter, sugar, vanilla seeds and orange rind in an electric mixer and beat for 6–8 minutes or until pale and creamy. Scrape down the sides of the bowl and add the eggs, one at a time, beating well after each addition. Drain the fruit, reserving the liquid. Add the liquid to the bowl in a thin, steady stream and beat to combine. Add the flour, baking powder, almond meal and cardamom and beat until just combined. Stir through the fruit and spoon into a lightly greased 8.5cm x 26.5cm x 9cm loaf tin (2-litre capacity) double-lined with non-stick baking paper. Bake for 1 hour 10 minutes–1 hour 20 minutes or until cooked when tested with a skewer. Cool the cake in the tin for 10 minutes before turning out onto a wire rack to cool completely. Dust with the icing sugar to serve. SERVES 8–10

TRY THIS WITH...
sultanas
chopped dried figs
chopped dried apricots

carrot cake with cream cheese icing and caramelised pecans

2 cups (300g) self-raising (self-rising) flour, sifted
1 teaspoon baking powder, sifted
1 teaspoon ground cinnamon
1 teaspoon ground ginger
¼ teaspoon ground nutmeg
1½ cups (265g) dark brown sugar
4 eggs
1 cup (250ml) sunflower oil
1 teaspoon vanilla extract
360g carrots, peeled and grated
⅔ cup (110g) sultanas
½ cup (60g) chopped pecans
cream cheese icing
100g unsalted butter, softened
500g cream cheese, softened
2 cups (320g) icing (confectioner's) sugar mixture, sifted
2 tablespoons lemon juice
caramelised pecans
1 cup (120g) pecans
½ cup (110g) caster (superfine) sugar
1 tablespoon water

To make the caramelised pecans, place the pecans, sugar and water in a bowl and toss to coat. Place the pecans in a large non-stick frying pan over medium heat and cook, stirring occasionally, for 6–8 minutes or until caramelised. Place on a baking tray lined with non-stick baking paper and allow to cool. Roughly chop and set aside.

Preheat oven to 180°C (350°F). Place the flour, baking powder, cinnamon, ginger, nutmeg and sugar in a bowl and mix to combine. Place the eggs, oil and vanilla in a separate bowl and whisk to combine. Add to the flour mixture and stir until smooth. Add the carrot, sultanas and chopped pecans and mix to combine. Divide mixture between 2 x 20cm round lightly greased cake tins lined with non-stick baking paper. Bake for 30–35 minutes or until cooked when tested with a skewer. Allow to cool in tins for 5 minutes before turning onto a wire rack to cool completely.

To make the cream cheese icing, place the butter and cream cheese in an electric mixer and beat for 8–10 minutes or until pale and creamy. Add the icing sugar and beat for a further 6–8 minutes or until pale and fluffy. Add the lemon juice and beat for a further 2 minutes. Spread one cake with half the icing and sandwich with remaining cake. Spread with the remaining icing and top with the caramelised pecans to serve. SERVES 8–10

carrot cake with cream cheese icing and caramelised pecans

jam and cream sponge cake

coconut, palm sugar and banana upside-down cake

75g unsalted butter, softened
½ cup (135g) finely grated light palm sugar
¼ cup (45g) brown sugar
2 teaspoons vanilla extract
1 egg
¾ cup (115g) plain (all-purpose) flour, sifted
½ teaspoon baking powder, sifted
¼ cup (20g) desiccated coconut
¼ cup (60ml) milk
banana caramel
100g unsalted butter, chopped
½ cup (90g) brown sugar
3–4 medium ladyfinger (sugar) bananas, halved lengthways

Preheat oven to 180°C (350°F). To make the banana caramel, place the butter and brown sugar in a small saucepan over medium heat and stir until the butter is melted. Bring to the boil and stir for a further 1 minute or until the mixture has thickened. Pour the caramel into a lightly greased 16cm x 26cm deep baking tray. Arrange the banana halves, cut-side down, over the caramel and set aside.

Place the butter, palm sugar and brown sugar in an electric mixer and beat for 10 minutes or until pale and creamy. Scrape down the sides of the bowl, add the vanilla and egg and beat well until combined. Add the flour, baking powder and coconut and beat until just combined. Add the milk and beat to combine. Spoon the mixture carefully over the bananas and spread with a palette knife to smooth the top. Place on a baking tray lined with non-stick baking paper+ and bake for 30–35 minutes or until cooked when tested with a skewer. Loosen the edges with a knife and carefully turn out the cake to serve. Serve with double (thick) cream or ice-cream, if desired. SERVES 6–8
+ *Place your banana upside-down cake on a baking tray lined with non-stick baking paper before baking to ensure any caramel that overflows from the tin doesn't stick to the bottom of the oven and burn.*

jam and cream sponge cake

⅔ cup (100g) plain (all-purpose) flour
¼ teaspoon baking powder
4 eggs
½ cup (110g) caster (superfine) sugar
50g unsalted butter, melted and cooled
½ cup (125ml) single (pouring) cream*
1 cup (320g) strawberry jam
fresh raspberries, to decorate
icing (confectioner's) sugar, for dusting

Preheat oven to 180°C (350°F). Sift the flour and baking powder three times and set aside. Place the eggs and sugar in an electric mixer and whisk on high speed for 10–12 minutes or until pale, thick and tripled in volume. Sift half the flour mixture over the egg mixture and using a large metal spoon, gently fold to combine. Repeat with the remaining flour. Add the butter and gently fold to combine. Divide the mixture between 2 x 20cm round lightly greased shallow cake tins lined with non-stick baking paper. Bake for 16–18 minutes or until sponges are springy to the touch and come away from the sides of the tins. Remove from the tins and cool completely on wire racks. Whisk the cream until soft peaks form. Spread one cake with the jam, top with the cream and berries and sandwich with the remaining cake. Dust with icing sugar to serve. SERVES 6–8

TRY THIS WITH...
strawberries
lemon curd
passionfruit pulp

HOW TO COOK *banana bread*

1 2
3 4

basic banana bread

125g unsalted butter, softened
1 cup (175g) brown sugar
1 teaspoon vanilla extract
2 eggs
2 cups mashed banana
1¾ cups (255g) plain (all-purpose) flour, sifted
1 teaspoon baking powder, sifted
1 teaspoon bicarbonate of (baking) soda
1 teaspoon ground cinnamon
⅓ cup (115g) golden syrup
unsalted butter, extra, to serve

STEP 1 Preheat oven to 160°C (325°F). Place the butter, sugar and vanilla in an electric mixer and beat for 8–10 minutes or until pale and creamy.
STEP 2 Scrape down the sides of the bowl, add the eggs and beat well to combine.
STEP 3 Add the banana, flour, baking powder, bicarbonate of soda, cinnamon and golden syrup and stir to combine.
STEP 4 Spoon the mixture into a 26cm x 11cm lightly greased loaf tin lined with baking paper. Bake for 60–65 minutes or until cooked when tested with a skewer. Cool in the tin for 20 minutes before turning out onto a wire rack to cool completely. Slice and serve with the extra butter. SERVES 6-8

RECIPE NOTES
It's important to use ripe or even overripe bananas when making banana bread. This will give your bread a sweeter banana flavour and extremely moist texture.

basic banana bread

banana and date bread
with maple cream cheese icing

1 x quantity basic banana bread (see recipe, page 344)
1 cup (140g) chopped pitted dates
⅓ cup (80ml) maple syrup
maple cream cheese icing
500g cream cheese, softened
½ cup (80g) icing (confectioner's) sugar, sifted
½ cup (125ml) maple syrup

To make the maple cream cheese icing, place the cream cheese, icing sugar and maple syrup in a food processor and process until smooth. Refrigerate until needed.

Preheat oven to 160°C (325°F). Follow steps 1 and 2 of the basic recipe. At step 3, add the dates with the banana and substitute the golden syrup for maple syrup. Spoon the mixture into a 26cm x 11cm lightly greased loaf tin lined with baking paper. Bake for 65–70 minutes or until cooked when tested with a skewer. Cool in the tin for 20 minutes before turning out onto a wire rack to cool completely. Using a palette knife, spread the bread with the icing. Refrigerate for 30 minutes or until the icing is set. SERVES 6–8

banana, raspberry and coconut bread

1 x quantity basic banana bread (see recipe, page 344)
1 cup (160g) frozen raspberries
½ cup (25g) sweetened coconut flakes, plus extra, for sprinkling

Preheat oven to 160°C (325°F). Follow steps 1 and 2 of the basic recipe. At step 3, add the raspberries and coconut with the banana. Spoon the mixture into a 26cm x 11cm (2.5 litre-capacity) lightly greased loaf tin lined with baking paper and sprinkle with the extra coconut flakes. Bake for 80–85 minutes or until cooked when tested with a skewer. Cool in the tin for 20 minutes before turning out onto a wire rack to cool completely. SERVES 6–8

banana and peanut butter bread

1 x quantity basic banana bread (see recipe, page 344)
½ cup (140g) crunchy peanut butter
⅓ cup (80ml) maple syrup
icing (confectioner's) sugar, for dusting

Preheat oven to 160°C (325°F). Follow steps 1 and 2 of the basic recipe. At step 3, add the peanut butter with the banana and substitute the golden syrup for maple syrup. Spoon the mixture into a 26cm x 11cm (2.5 litre-capacity) lightly greased loaf tin lined with baking paper. Bake for 85–90 minutes or until cooked when tested with a skewer. Cool in the tin for 20 minutes before turning out onto a wire rack to cool completely. Dust with icing sugar to serve. SERVES 6–8

banana, hazelnut and chocolate bread

1 x quantity basic banana bread (see recipe, page 344)
½ cup (70g) toasted hazelnuts, chopped
1 cup (90g) chopped dark chocolate

Preheat oven to 160°C (325°F). Follow steps 1 and 2 of the basic recipe. At step 3, add the hazelnuts and chocolate with the banana. Spoon the mixture into a 26cm x 11cm (2.5 litre- capacity) lightly greased loaf tin lined with baking paper. Bake for 70–75 minutes or until cooked when tested with a skewer. Cool in the tin for 20 minutes before turning out onto a wire rack to cool completely. SERVES 6–8

classic lemon cheesecake

1 cup (150g) plain (all-purpose) flour
¼ cup (55g) caster (superfine) sugar
100g unsalted butter, chopped
filling
330g cream cheese, softened
500g ricotta
4 eggs
1⅓ cups (295g) caster (superfine) sugar
¼ cup (60ml) lemon juice
2 tablespoons finely grated lemon rind
½ teaspoon vanilla extract
1½ tablespoons cornflour (cornstarch)
1½ tablespoons water
1 cup (250ml) single (pouring) cream, whipped

Preheat oven to 150°C (300°F). Place the flour, sugar and butter in a bowl and rub with your fingertips to form a rough dough. Using the back of a spoon, press the mixture into the base of a lightly greased 20cm round springform tin lined with non-stick baking paper. Bake the base for 30 minutes or until golden and just cooked. Set aside.

To make the filling, place the cream cheese, ricotta, eggs, sugar, lemon juice and rind, and vanilla in a food processor and process until smooth. Place the cornflour and water in a bowl and mix until smooth. Add the cornflour mixture to the cheese mixture and mix to combine. Pour the mixture over the base and bake for 1 hour 10 minutes or until light golden and just set. Turn the oven off and allow to cool in the oven with the door closed. Refrigerate for 1 hour or until chilled. Top with the cream to serve. SERVES 8–10

blueberry almond cake

4 eggs
1 cup (220g) caster (superfine) sugar
1 teaspoon vanilla extract
1 cup (150g) self-raising (self-rising) flour
150g unsalted butter, melted
1 cup (120g) almond meal (ground almonds)
250g blueberries

Preheat oven to 160°C (325°F). Place the eggs, sugar and vanilla in the bowl of an electric mixer and whisk for 8–10 minutes or until thick, pale and tripled in volume. Sift the flour over the egg mixture and fold through. Fold through the butter and almond meal. Pour the mixture into a 20cm x 30cm slice tin lined with non-stick baking paper and top with the blueberries. Bake for 30–35 minutes or until cooked when tested with a skewer. Turn out onto a wire rack to cool. SERVES 8

TRY THIS WITH...
raspberries
ground hazelnuts
ground walnuts

classic lemon cheesecake

blueberry almond cake

madeira cake

mexican three-milk cake

madeira cake

170g unsalted butter, softened
¾ cup (165g) caster (superfine) sugar
1 teaspoon vanilla extract
3 eggs
1 cup (150g) plain (all-purpose) flour
¾ teaspoons baking powder
⅔ cup (80g) almond meal (ground almonds)

Preheat oven to 170°C (350°F). Place the butter, sugar and vanilla in the bowl of an electric mixer and beat until light and creamy. Gradually add the eggs, beating well after each addition. Sift the flour and baking powder over the butter mixture and gently fold through with the almond meal.

Spoon the mixture into a lightly greased 22cm x 8cm loaf tin lined with non-stick baking paper and bake for 50 minutes or until cooked when tested with a skewer. Leave in the tin for 5 minutes before turning out onto a wire rack to cool. SERVES 8-10

SERVE THIS WITH...
sweet sherry
espresso coffee
jam and cream

mexican three-milk cake

180g unsalted butter, softened
1 cup (220g) caster (superfine) sugar
2 tablespoons vanilla extract
5 eggs
1½ cups (225g) self-raising (self-rising) flour, sifted
2 cups (250ml) milk
1 cup (250ml) sweetened condensed milk
1 cup (250ml) buttermilk
2 cups (500ml) single (pouring) cream*
fresh passionfruit pulp, to serve

Preheat oven to 180°C (350°F). Place the butter and sugar in an electric mixer and beat for 8–10 minutes or until pale and creamy. Add 1 tablespoon vanilla extract and beat to combine. Gradually add the eggs, one at a time, beating well after each addition. Gradually add the flour and beat until just combined. Spoon the mixture into a lightly greased 20cm x 30cm slice tin lined with non-stick baking paper and bake for 30–35 minutes or until cooked when tested with a skewer. Using a skewer, pierce holes all over the top of the cake and place in the refrigerator to cool completely.

While the cake is cooling, place the milk, condensed milk, buttermilk and remaining vanilla in a jug and mix well to combine. Pour the milk mixture over the cake and return to the refrigerator for a further 2 hours or until the milk mixture is absorbed. Place the cream in a bowl and whisk until soft peaks form. Top the cake with the cream and drizzle with passionfruit pulp to serve. SERVES 6-8

PUDDINGS

Warm and comforting, like a hug from your mum, these tempting puddings have all the bases covered. Whether it's a generous and creamy rice pud or a version rich with chocolate, indulgence is only a spoonful away.

baked brûlée rice custard

burnt caramel rice pudding

baked brûlée rice custard

1 litre single (pouring) cream*
2 teaspoons vanilla extract
2 teaspoons ground nutmeg
8 egg yolks
¾ cup (165g) caster (superfine) sugar
1½ cups cooked arborio rice* (see recipe, below)

Preheat oven to 160°C (325°F). Place the cream, vanilla and nutmeg in a saucepan over high heat and bring just to the boil. Remove from heat and allow to cool slightly.

Place the egg yolks and ½ cup (110g) of the sugar in a bowl and whisk until thick and pale. Pour the warm cream mixture into the egg mixture and whisk to combine. Return the mixture to the saucepan and stir over low heat for 6–8 minutes or until thickened. Add the rice and stir to combine. Spoon mixture into 2 x 1½ cup-capacity (375ml) ovenproof ramekins. Place the ramekins in a baking dish and pour in enough boiling water to come halfway up the sides of the ramekins. Bake for 55–60 minutes or until just set. Remove from tray and refrigerate for 2–3 hours or until set.

Sprinkle the remaining sugar over each custard and place on a baking tray under a preheated hot grill (broiler) for 30 seconds or until the top is caramelised. SERVES 4

cooked arborio rice

½ cup arborio rice*
¾ cup (180ml) water

Place the rice and water in a heavy-based saucepan over high heat and bring to the boil. Reduce heat to low, cover and simmer for 15-20 minutes or until water is absorbed and rice is tender. MAKES 1½ CUPS

classic baked rice pudding

1½ cups cooked arborio rice* (see recipe, below left)
1 vanilla bean, split and seeds scraped
½ cup (80g) sultanas
4 sticks cinnamon
4 strips lemon rind
3 cups (750ml) milk
3 eggs, lightly beaten
⅓ cup (75g) caster (superfine) sugar

Preheat oven to 160°C (325°F). Place the cooked rice, vanilla seeds and sultanas in a bowl and mix to combine. Place 1 cinnamon stick and 1 piece of lemon rind in the base of each 4 x 2 cup-capacity (500ml) ovenproof dishes and divide the rice mixture evenly between the dishes. Place the milk, eggs and sugar in a large jug and mix well to combine. Divide the milk mixture evenly between the dishes. Bake for 35–40 minutes or until set. SERVES 4

basic rice pudding

1 cup (200g) arborio rice*
1 litre milk
½ cup (110g) caster (superfine) sugar
1 vanilla bean, split and seeds scraped

Place the rice, milk, sugar and vanilla seeds in a saucepan over high heat and bring to the boil. Reduce heat to low, cover and cook, stirring occasionally, for 25–30 minutes or until rice is tender. SERVES 4

burnt caramel rice pudding

1 x quantity basic rice pudding (see recipe, above)
½ cup (110g) caster (superfine) sugar, extra
½ cup (125ml) double (thick) cream*

Follow the basic rice pudding recipe. Place the extra sugar in a small saucepan over low heat and cook for 8–10 minutes, swirling the pan occasionally, or until sugar is dissolved and golden. Stir the cream through the pudding and drizzle with the caramel to serve. SERVES 4

classic baked rice pudding

HOW TO COOK baked custard

1 2
3 4

classic baked vanilla custard

2 cups (500ml) single (pouring) cream*
1 cup (250ml) milk
1 vanilla bean, split and seeds scraped
2 eggs
3 egg yolks, extra
½ cup (110g) caster (superfine) sugar

STEP 1 Preheat oven to 150°C (300°F). Place the cream, milk, vanilla bean and seeds in a saucepan over high heat until the mixture just comes to the boil. Remove from heat and set aside.
STEP 2 Place the eggs, extra yolks and sugar in a bowl and whisk until well combined. Gradually add the hot cream mixture to the egg mixture, whisking well to combine.
STEP 3 Strain custard into a 1.5 litre-capacity ovenproof dish.
STEP 4 Place the dish in a water bath. Bake for 1 hour 25 minutes or until just set.
STEP 5 Remove from the water bath and allow to stand for 15 minutes before serving. SERVES 4–6

RECIPE NOTES
To make a water bath, place the custard dish in a deep-sided baking dish and pour in enough boiling water to come halfway up the sides of the custard dish. This will ensure an evenly cooked and velvety custard.

classic baked vanilla custard

marmalade brioche baked custard

360g brioche*, sliced
unsalted butter, softened, for spreading
1 cup (340g) orange marmalade
1 litre single (pouring) cream*
2 cups (500ml) milk
1 vanilla bean, split and seeds scraped
4 eggs
6 egg yolks, extra
1 cup (220g) caster (superfine) sugar
Demerara sugar*, for sprinkling

Preheat oven to 150°C (300°F). Spread the brioche with butter and marmalade and arrange, upright, in a 3 litre-capacity ovenproof dish. Place the cream, milk and vanilla in a saucepan over high heat until the mixture just comes to the boil. Set aside.

Place the eggs, extra yolks and sugar in a bowl and whisk until well combined. Gradually add the hot cream mixture to the egg mixture, whisking well to combine. Strain the custard over the brioche and sprinkle with the Demerara sugar. Place the dish in a water bath (see recipe notes, page 360). Bake for 1 hour 5 minutes–1 hour 10 minutes or until just set. Remove from the water bath and allow to stand for 15 minutes before serving. SERVES 6–8

sugar and spice baked custards

2 cups (500ml) single (pouring) cream*
1 cup (250ml) milk
1 vanilla bean, split and seeds scraped
2 sticks cinnamon
2 star anise
¼ teaspoon mixed spice
2 eggs
3 egg yolks, extra
½ cup (90g) brown sugar

Preheat oven to 150°C (300°F). Place the cream, milk, vanilla, cinnamon, star anise and mixed spice in a saucepan over high heat until the mixture just comes to the boil. Remove from the heat and set aside.

Place the eggs, extra yolks and sugar in a bowl and whisk until well combined. Gradually add the hot cream mixture to the egg mixture, whisking well to combine. Strain into 4 x 1½ cup-capacity (375ml) ovenproof dishes. Place the dishes in a water bath (see recipe notes, page 360). Bake for 55 minutes–1 hour or until just set. Remove from the water bath and allow to stand for 15 minutes before serving. SERVES 4

baked lemon rice custard

2 cups (500ml) single (pouring) cream*
1 cup (250ml) milk
1 vanilla bean, split and seeds scraped
1 tablespoon lemon zest
2 eggs
3 egg yolks, extra
½ cup (110g) caster (superfine) sugar
1 cup cooked arborio rice* (see recipe, page 358)
¼ cup (40g) currants
finely grated nutmeg, to serve

Preheat oven to 150°C (300°F). Place the cream, milk, vanilla and lemon zest in a saucepan over high heat until the mixture just comes to the boil. Remove from the heat and set aside.

Place the eggs, extra yolks and sugar in a bowl and whisk until well combined. Gradually add the hot cream mixture to the egg mixture, whisking well to combine. Spread the rice and currants over the base of a 1.5 litre-capacity ovenproof dish. Strain the custard over the rice and place in a water bath (see recipe notes, page 360). Bake for 50 minutes–1 hour or until just set. Remove from the water bath, sprinkle with nutmeg and allow to stand for 15 minutes before serving. SERVES 4–6

baked chocolate custard cups

2 cups (500ml) single (pouring) cream*
1 cup (250ml) milk
1 vanilla bean, split and seeds scraped
150g dark chocolate, finely chopped
2 eggs
3 egg yolks, extra
½ cup (110g) caster (superfine) sugar

Preheat oven to 150°C (300°F). Place the cream, milk, vanilla and chocolate in a saucepan over high heat and stir to melt the chocolate. Cook until the mixture just comes to the boil. Remove from the heat and set aside.

Place the eggs, extra yolks and sugar in a bowl and whisk until well combined. Gradually add the hot cream mixture to the egg mixture, whisking well to combine. Strain into 6 x 1 cup-capacity (250ml) teacups. Place the teacups in a water bath (see recipe notes, page 360). Bake for 45 minutes or until just set. Remove from the water bath and allow to stand for 15 minutes before serving. SERVES 6
Tip: This recipe is also delicious served chilled. Simply refrigerate until cold before serving.

chocolate soufflés with chocolate sauce

dark chocolate and caramel puddings

rhubarb, pomegranate and vanilla cobblers

chocolate soufflés with chocolate sauce

2 egg yolks
⅓ cup (80ml) milk
1 tablespoon cornflour (cornstarch)
1 tablespoon Dutch cocoa, plus extra, for dusting
¼ cup (55g) caster (superfine) sugar
40g dark chocolate, finely chopped
3 eggwhites
¼ teaspoon cream of tartar
40g unsalted butter, melted, for brushing
1 tablespoon caster (superfine) sugar, extra, for dusting
chocolate sauce
75g dark chocolate, finely chopped
¼ cup (60ml) single (pouring) cream*
1 teaspoon vanilla extract

Preheat oven to 180°C (350°F). Place the egg yolks, milk, cornflour, cocoa and sugar in a small saucepan over medium heat and cook, whisking, for 3 minutes or until the mixture just begins to thicken. Add the chocolate and cook, whisking, for a further 1 minute or until very thick. Transfer to a large bowl and refrigerate for 5 minutes. Place the eggwhites and cream of tartar in a bowl and whisk until stiff peaks form. Remove the chocolate mixture from the fridge and beat until smooth. Fold the eggwhite mixture into the chocolate mixture in three batches. Brush 2 x 1 cup-capacity (250ml) ramekins with the melted butter+ and dust with the extra sugar. Spoon the chocolate mixture into the ramekins and run your finger 5mm around the inner edge of each ramekin++. Place the ramekins on a tray and bake for 15–17 minutes or until risen and golden.

While the soufflés are cooking, make the chocolate sauce. Place the chocolate, cream and vanilla in a small saucepan over low heat and cook, stirring, for 5–6 minutes or until melted and smooth. Dust the soufflés with extra cocoa and spoon over the sauce. Serve immediately. SERVES 2
+ Use a pastry brush to coat the ramekins with the butter in an upwards motion, this will help the soufflés to rise.
++ Removing some of the excess sugar from the edge of the ramekin will also help the soufflés to rise.

dark chocolate and caramel puddings

1 x 380g can store-bought caramel filling or dulce de leche*
⅓ cup (80ml) double (thick) cream*
200g dark chocolate, chopped
60g unsalted butter
3 eggs
½ cup (90g) brown sugar
1 teaspoon vanilla extract
½ cup (60g) almond meal (ground almonds)
cocoa, for dusting

Preheat oven to 200°C (400°F). Place the caramel in a bowl and whisk until smooth. Add the cream and mix well to combine. Place ⅓ cup (80ml) of the caramel mixture in the base of each of 4 x 1½ cup-capacity (375ml) ovenproof dishes. Place the chocolate and butter in a heatproof bowl over a saucepan of simmering water and stir until the chocolate is melted and smooth. Place the eggs, sugar and vanilla in an electric mixer and beat for 8–10 minutes or until doubled in size. Fold the chocolate mixture and almond meal through the egg mixture and divide between the dishes. Place on a baking tray and bake for 18–20 minutes or until risen and the centres are soft. Stand for 5 minutes. Dust with cocoa to serve. MAKES 4

rhubarb, pomegranate and vanilla cobblers

2 cups (300g) self-raising (self-rising) flour, sifted
200g unsalted butter
½ cup (110g) caster (superfine) sugar
⅔ cup (160ml) buttermilk
2 teaspoons vanilla extract
3 pomegranates, seeds removed
750g rhubarb, trimmed and chopped into 5cm lengths
⅔ cup (150g) caster (superfine) sugar, extra
2 vanilla beans, split and seeds scraped
⅓ cup (25g) flaked almonds
icing (confectioner's) sugar and double (thick) cream*, to serve

Preheat oven to 180°C (350°F). Place the flour, butter and sugar in a food processor and process until the mixture resembles fine breadcrumbs. Gradually add the buttermilk and vanilla extract and process until the mixture just comes together. Add ⅓ of the pomegranate seeds and stir to combine. Set aside.

Place the rhubarb, extra sugar, remaining pomegranate seeds and vanilla in a bowl and toss to coat. Divide between 4 x 1½ cup-capacity (375ml) skillets. Top with the cobbler mixture and sprinkle with the almonds. Bake for 35–40 minutes or until golden and cooked through. Dust with icing sugar and serve with cream, if desired. SERVES 4

HOW TO COOK steamed puddings

1 2
3 4

basic steamed maple puddings

1 cup (250ml) maple syrup
vanilla ice-cream or single (pouring) cream*, to serve
basic pudding mixture
150g unsalted butter, softened
⅔ cup (150g) caster (superfine) sugar
2 eggs
1 teaspoon vanilla extract
2 cups (300g) plain (all-purpose) flour
2 teaspoons baking powder
1 cup (250ml) milk

STEP 1 Preheat oven to 170°C (350°F). Place the maple syrup in a saucepan over medium heat and bring to the boil for 7–9 minutes or until thickened. Pour into 6 x 1 cup-capacity (250ml) lightly greased ramekins and refrigerate.
STEP 2 Place the butter, sugar, eggs, vanilla, flour, baking powder and milk in an electric mixer and beat until well combined. Divide the mixture between the ramekins.
STEP 3 Place the puddings in a water bath.
STEP 4 Cover tightly with 2 sheets aluminium foil+ and bake for 45–50 minutes or until the puddings are springy to the touch. Remove puddings from the water bath and invert onto plates. Serve warm with vanilla ice-cream or cream, if desired. MAKES 6
+ *Lightly grease the foil before securing tightly around the tray to ensure your puddings don't stick to it as they bake.*

RECIPE NOTES
To make a water bath, place the puddings in a deep-sided baking dish and pour in enough boiling water to come halfway up the sides of the ramekins. This will ensure the puddings are cooked evenly.

basic steamed maple pudding

lemon syrup and almond puddings

150g unsalted butter, softened
⅔ cup (150g) caster (superfine) sugar
2 eggs
1 teaspoon vanilla extract
1 cup (150g) plain (all-purpose) flour
1 cup (120g) almond meal (ground almonds)
2 teaspoons baking powder
1 cup (250ml) milk
lemon syrup
⅔ cup (160ml) lemon juice
300ml water
1½ cups (330g) caster (superfine) sugar
1 small lemon, thinly sliced

Preheat oven to 170°C (350°F). To make the syrup, place the lemon juice, water and sugar in a saucepan over low heat and stir until sugar is dissolved. Bring to the boil and cook for 6–8 minutes or until thickened. Divide half the syrup between 6 x 1 cup-capacity (250ml) baking dishes and refrigerate. Add the lemon slices to the remaining syrup and simmer over low heat for 4–6 minutes or until the lemon is transparent. Set aside to cool.

Follow steps 2–4 of the basic recipe (see page 368), adding almond meal at step 2 and baking for 45–50 minutes. Top the puddings with the lemon slices and extra syrup to serve. MAKES 6

butterscotch and hazelnut pudding

150g unsalted butter, softened
⅔ cup (115g) brown sugar
2 eggs
1 teaspoon vanilla extract
1½ cups (225g) plain (all-purpose) flour
½ cup (50g) hazelnut meal (ground hazelnuts)
2 teaspoons baking powder
1 cup (250ml) milk
icing (confectioner's) sugar, for dusting
butterscotch sauce
1 cup (175g) brown sugar
60g unsalted butter
1 cup (250ml) single (pouring) cream*

Preheat oven to 170°C (350°F). To make the butterscotch sauce, place the sugar, butter and cream in a saucepan over low heat and stir until the sugar is dissolved. Increase heat to high and bring to the boil, stirring occasionally, for 5–7 minutes or until thickened. Pour into a 1.75 litre-capacity baking dish and refrigerate.

Follow steps 2–4 of the basic recipe (see page 368), using brown sugar instead of caster, adding the hazelnut meal at step 2 and adjusting the baking time to 1 hour 5 minutes–1 hour 10 minutes. Dust with icing sugar to serve. SERVES 6

coconut and jam puddings

¾ cup (240g) strawberry jam
1 tablespoon warm water
150g unsalted butter, softened
⅔ cup (150g) caster (superfine) sugar
2 eggs
1 teaspoon vanilla extract
1½ cups (225g) plain (all-purpose) flour
½ cup (40g) desiccated coconut
2 teaspoons baking powder
1 cup (250ml) milk

Preheat oven to 170°C (350°F). Place the strawberry jam and water in a bowl and mix well to combine. Spoon into 6 x 1 cup-capacity (250ml) baking dishes and refrigerate.

    Follow steps 2–4 of the basic recipe (see page 368), adding the coconut at step 2 and baking for 45–50 minutes. MAKES 6

date and ginger puddings with fudge sauce

1 teaspoon bicarbonate of (baking) soda
¾ cup (105g) chopped dates
½ cup (125ml) boiling water
150g unsalted butter, softened
⅔ cup (115g) brown sugar
2 eggs
1 teaspoon vanilla extract
2 cups (300g) plain (all-purpose) flour
2 teaspoons baking powder
1 cup (250ml) milk
2 teaspoons ground ginger
fudge sauce
100g dark chocolate, chopped
¼ cup (60ml) single (pouring) cream*
25g unsalted butter

Preheat oven to 170°C (350°F). Place the bicarbonate of soda, dates and water in a bowl and set aside for 5 minutes. Place in a food processor and process until smooth. Follow steps 2–4 of the basic recipe (see page 368), using brown sugar and adding the date mixture and ginger at step 2. Pour the mixture into 4 x 2 cup-capacity (500ml) dishes and adjust baking time to 40–45 minutes.

    Melt the chocolate, cream and butter over low heat, stirring, for 4–5 minutes until smooth. Top the puddings with sauce. SERVES 6-8

strawberry brioche bread and butter pudding

plum clafoutis

strawberry brioche bread and butter pudding

2 cups (500ml) milk
2½ cups (625ml) single (pouring) cream*
8 egg yolks
½ cup (110g) caster (superfine) sugar
2 teaspoons vanilla extract
200g brioche* loaf, sliced
¼ cup (40g) currants
750g strawberries, hulled and halved
¼ cup (55g) raw sugar

Preheat oven to 200°C (400°F). Place the milk and cream in a
saucepan over medium heat and cook until just boiling. Remove from
the heat and set aside. Place the egg yolks, sugar and vanilla in a bowl
and whisk to combine. Gradually whisk the warm milk mixture into
the egg mixture to combine. Arrange the brioche slices in the base
of a lightly greased 2 litre-capacity baking dish. Pour the custard over
the brioche and top with the currants and strawberries. Sprinkle with
the sugar and bake for 20–25 minutes or until golden. SERVES 6

plum clafoutis

unsalted butter, for greasing
⅓ cup (75g) caster (superfine) sugar, plus extra, for dusting
400g plums, stones removed and halved
⅓ cup (50g) plain (all-purpose) flour
1 teaspoon vanilla extract
1 cup (250ml) single (pouring) cream*
3 eggs

Preheat oven to 180°C (350°F). Grease a 2 litre-capacity ovenproof
dish with the butter and dust with sugar. Place the plums, cut-side up,
in the dish. Place the flour, sugar, vanilla and cream in a bowl and
whisk to combine. Add the eggs and whisk until smooth. Pour the
mixture over the plums and bake for 35–40 minutes or until puffed
and golden. Serve warm with vanilla ice-cream, if desired. SERVES 6
*Tip: Clafoutis is a baked French pudding traditionally made with cherries
and easily adaptable to other stone fruit.*

blueberry, apple and coconut crumble

½ cup (110g) caster (superfine) sugar
1 vanilla bean, split and seeds scraped
4 Granny Smith (green) apples, peeled and chopped
500g blueberries
coconut crumble
⅓ cup (75g) caster (superfine) sugar
⅔ cup (50g) shredded coconut
120g unsalted butter, melted
1 cup (150g) plain (all-purpose) flour, sifted

Preheat oven to 180°C (350°F). To make the coconut crumble,
place the sugar, coconut, butter and flour in a bowl and rub with
your fingertips until the mixture resembles course breadcrumbs.
Place the sugar, vanilla seeds, apple and blueberries in a bowl and
mix well to combine. Spoon into a 27cm round shallow tray. Sprinkle
over the crumble mixture and bake for 20–25 minutes
or until golden. SERVES 6

TRY THIS WITH...
raspberries
peaches
pears

blueberry, apple and coconut crumble

PIES + TARTS

From sunny tarts bursting with juicy summer fruit to generous wintry pies paired with creamy custard, there's nothing sweeter or more comforting than the perfect combination of golden pastry with a delicious filling.

apple, rhurbarb and cinnamon pan pie

maple brûlée tart

plum and coconut galette

apple, rhubarb and cinnamon pan pies

8 large Granny Smith (green) apples, peeled, cored and chopped
4 stalks rhubarb, trimmed and chopped
1 tablespoon lemon juice
½ cup (110g) caster (superfine) sugar
1 teaspoon ground cinnamon
1 teaspoon vanilla extract
2 tablespoons cornflour (cornstarch)
1 tablespoon water
2 sheets store-bought puff pastry
1 egg, lightly beaten
2 tablespoons white sugar
¼ teaspoon ground cinnamon, extra
store-bought vanilla custard, to serve

Preheat oven to 200°C (400°F). Place the apple, rhubarb, lemon juice, caster sugar, cinnamon and vanilla in a bowl and toss to combine. Divide the mixture between 2 x 14cm frying pans with a heatproof handle and cover with aluminium foil. Place over medium heat and cook for 6–8 minutes or until just tender. Remove from the heat. Combine the cornflour and water, divide between pans, and stir through the apple mixture. Cut 2 x 20cm rounds from the pastry and make a small cut in the centre of each round. Place on top of the apple mixture and pinch the edges to seal. Brush the pastry with egg. Combine the white sugar and extra cinnamon and sprinkle over the pastry. Bake for 25–30 minutes or until golden and crisp. Serve with custard. SERVES 4–6

TRY THIS WITH...
pears
plums
poached quince

plum and coconut galette

1 cup (80g) desiccated coconut
¼ cup (55g) caster (superfine) sugar
2 eggwhites
500g blood plums, stones removed and thinly sliced
1 eggwhite, for brushing
white sugar, for sprinkling
pastry
1⅔ cups (250g) plain (all-purpose) flour
1 tablespoon caster (superfine) sugar
¼ teaspoon baking powder
180g unsalted butter, chopped
⅓ cup (80ml) iced water
1 teaspoon vanilla extract

Preheat oven to 180°C (350°F). To make the pastry, place the flour, sugar and baking powder in a food processor and process to combine. Add the butter and process until the mixture resembles fine breadcrumbs. While the motor is running, gradually add the water and vanilla and process until the mixture comes together to form a smooth dough. Flatten into a disc shape, cover in plastic wrap and refrigerate for 30 minutes.

Roll out the pastry between 2 sheets of non-stick baking paper to 5mm thick and 30cm round. Place on a baking tray lined with non-stick baking paper. Place the coconut, caster sugar and eggwhites in a bowl and mix well to combine. Top the pastry with the coconut filling, leaving a 4cm border. Top with the plums and fold over the pastry edges. Brush with the eggwhite and sprinkle with the sugar. Bake for 25–30 minutes or until the pastry is cooked through and golden. SERVES 6–8

maple brûlée tart

1 cup (250ml) milk
1 cup (250ml) single (pouring) cream*
2 eggs, plus 2 egg yolks, extra
½ cup (110g) caster (superfine) sugar
¼ cup (60ml) maple syrup
white sugar, for sprinkling
vanilla pastry
1⅔ cups (250g) plain (all-purpose) flour
1 tablespoon caster (superfine) sugar
¼ teaspoon baking powder
180g cold unsalted butter, chopped
⅓ cup (80ml) iced water
1 teaspoon vanilla extract

Preheat oven to 160°C (325°F). To make the vanilla pastry, place the flour, sugar and baking powder in a food processor and process to combine. Add the butter and process until the mixture resembles fine breadcrumbs. While the motor is running, gradually add the water and vanilla and process until the mixture comes together to form a smooth dough. Flatten into a disc shape, cover with plastic wrap and refrigerate for 30 minutes.

Roll out the pastry on a lightly floured surface to 3mm thick. Line a lightly greased 28cm pie tin with the pastry. Prick with a fork and blind bake for 10–15 minutes.

Pour the milk and cream into a small saucepan over low heat until just boiling. Place the eggs, extra yolks, caster sugar and maple syrup in a bowl and whisk to combine. Gradually whisk in the milk mixture. Allow to cool. Pour the mixture into the pastry case and bake for 15–20 minutes or until just set. Allow to cool in the tin.

Sprinkle the tart with sugar just before serving and caramelise with a small kitchen blowtorch until a golden crust forms+. SERVES 4
+ *You can buy a small kitchen blowtorch from specialty kitchenware stores and online. They make easy work of a tart this size.*

blueberry pies

1½ cups (225g) plain (all-purpose) flour, sifted
125g cold unsalted butter, chopped
½ cup (80g) icing (confectioner's) sugar, sifted
3 egg yolks
2 teaspoons vanilla extract
1 tablespoon iced water
250g blueberries
1 tablespoon cornflour (cornstarch)
2 tablespoons caster (superfine) sugar
40g unsalted butter, extra, melted
1 egg yolk, extra, lightly beaten
raw sugar, for sprinkling
double (thick) cream*, to serve

Place the flour, butter and icing sugar in a food processor and process in short bursts until the mixture resembles fine breadcrumbs. While the motor is running, add the egg yolks and vanilla. Add the iced water and process until the dough just comes together. Turn out onto a lightly floured surface, bring the dough together and flatten into a disc shape. Cover in plastic wrap and refrigerate for 1 hour.

Preheat oven to 190°C (375°F). Roll out the pastry between 2 sheets of non-stick baking paper to 3mm thick. Use an 11cm round cookie cutter to cut out 6 rounds from the pastry. Use a small, sharp knife to make a slit in the side of the pastry rounds. Line 6 x ½ cup-capacity (125ml) lightly greased muffin tins with the pastry. Place the blueberries, cornflour, caster sugar and extra butter in a bowl, toss to combine and divide between the pies. Using a 9cm round cookie cutter, cut 6 rounds from the remaining pastry. Make 3 small holes in the centre of each round and place on top of the pie cases, pressing the edges to seal and trimming any excess pastry. Brush the tops with the extra yolk, sprinkle with raw sugar and bake for 18 minutes or until the tops are golden. Serve with cream. MAKES 6

blueberry pies

HOW TO COOK tarte tartin

basic apple tarte tatin

1 x 375g block puff pastry*, thawed
¾ cup (165g) caster (superfine) sugar
¼ cup (60ml) water
50g unsalted butter, chopped
4 Granny Smith (green) apples, peeled, cored and quartered
single (pouring) cream, to serve

STEP 1 Preheat oven to 190°C (375°F). Using a rolling pin, roll the pastry out on a lightly floured surface to 5mm thick. Using a plate as a guide, cut a 23cm round from the pastry and set aside.
STEP 2 Place the sugar and water in a 20cm round oven-proof non-stick frying pan over low heat and cook, stirring, until the sugar is dissolved. Increase heat to medium and bring to the boil. Cook, without stirring, for 7–9 minutes or until light golden. Add the butter and stir until melted and well combined.
STEP 3 Remove the pan from the heat and carefully arrange the apples, cut-side up and slightly overlapping, in the caramel.
STEP 4 Top with the pastry round and fold the edges under to tuck in the apples. Using a sharp knife, make 3 small cuts in the centre of the pastry.
STEP 5 Place the pan on a baking tray and bake for 35–40 minutes or until the pastry is puffed and golden. Allow to stand for 2–3 minutes. Loosen the edges with a knife. Carefully turn out the tarte to serve Serve with cream. SERVES 4

RECIPE NOTES
To turn out your tarte Tatin, it's a good idea to firstly loosen the edges of the pastry with a palette knife. Place a serving plate over the frying pan and, using a tea towel if the pan is hot, carefully invert the tart.

basic apple tarte tartin

fig, honey and vanilla tarte tatins

1 x 375g block puff pastry*, thawed
½ cup (110g) caster (superfine) sugar
¼ cup (60ml) water
1 vanilla bean, split and seeds scraped
¼ cup (90g) honey
50g unsalted butter, chopped
6 figs, halved

Preheat oven to 190°C (375°F). Using a rolling pin, roll the pastry out on a lightly floured surface to 5mm thick. Using an 11.5cm round cookie cutter, cut 4 rounds from the pastry and set aside.

Place the sugar, water, vanilla bean and seeds in a small non-stick frying pan over low heat and cook, stirring, until dissolved. Increase heat to medium and bring to the boil. Cook for 7–9 minutes, without stirring, or until light golden. Remove the vanilla bean and discard. Add the honey and butter and stir until melted and combined.

Divide the caramel between 4 x 9.5cm round lightly greased pie tins. Divide figs, cut-side down, between tins. Top with the pastry rounds and fold the edges under to tuck in the figs. Make a small cut in the pastry. Place the tins on a baking tray and bake for 25–27 minutes or until the pastry is puffed and golden. Allow to stand for 2–3 minutes. Loosen edges with a knife. Carefully turn out the tartes to serve. MAKES 4

rhubarb and cinnamon tarte tatin

1 x 375g block puff pastry*, thawed
¾ cup (165g) caster (superfine) sugar
¼ cup (60ml) water
50g unsalted butter, chopped
2 sticks cinnamon
850g rhubarb, trimmed and cut into 19cm lengths

Preheat oven to 190°C (375°F). Using a rolling pin, roll the pastry out on a lightly floured surface to 5mm thick. Cut out a 22cm x 32cm rectangle from the pastry and set aside.

Place the sugar and water in a small non-stick frying pan over low heat and cook, stirring, until the sugar is dissolved. Increase heat to medium and bring to the boil. Cook for 7–9 minutes, without stirring, or until light golden. Add the butter and cinnamon and stir until the butter is melted and well combined.

Pour the caramel into a lightly greased 20cm x 30cm slice tin and arrange the rhubarb pieces in the caramel. Top with the pastry and fold the edges under to tuck in the rhubarb. Make 3 small cuts in the pastry. Place on a larger baking tray and bake for 30–35 minutes or until the pastry is puffed and golden. Allow to stand for 2–3 minutes. Loosen the edges with a knife. Carefully turn out the tarte to serve. SERVES 4

pear, maple and ginger tarte tatin

1 x 375g block puff pastry*, thawed
½ cup (110g) caster (superfine) sugar
¼ cup (60ml) water
¼ cup (60ml) maple syrup
50g unsalted butter, chopped
2 tablespoons (45g) chopped glacé ginger*
3 firm pears, peeled, halved and cored

Preheat oven to 190°C (375°F). Using a rolling pin, roll the pastry out on a lightly floured surface to 5mm thick. Using a plate as a guide, cut a 23cm round from the pastry and set aside.

Place the sugar and water in a 20cm round ovenproof non-stick frying pan over low heat and cook, stirring, until the sugar is dissolved. Increase heat to medium and bring to the boil. Cook, without stirring, for 7–9 minutes or until light golden. Add the maple syrup and butter and stir until melted and combined.

Remove the pan from the heat, add the ginger and carefully arrange the pears, cut-side-up, in the caramel. Top with the pastry and fold the edges under to tuck in the pears. Using a sharp knife, make 3 small cuts in the pastry. Place the pan on a baking tray and bake for 35–40 minutes or until the pastry is puffed and golden. Allow to stand for 2–3 minutes. Loosen the edges with a knife. Carefully turn out the tarte to serve. SERVES 4

plum and cardamom tarte tatins

1 x 375g block puff pastry*, thawed
¾ cup (165g) caster (superfine) sugar
¼ cup (60ml) water
12 cardamom pods, bruised with the back of a knife
50g unsalted butter, chopped
3 plums, halved and stones removed
single (pouring) cream*, to serve

Preheat oven to 190°C (375°F). Using a rolling pin, roll the pastry out on a lightly floured surface to 5mm thick. Using a 9cm round cookie cutter, cut 6 rounds from the pastry and set aside.

Place the sugar, water and cardamon in a small non-stick frying pan over low heat and cook, stirring, until the sugar is dissolved. Increase heat to medium and bring to the boil. Cook for 7–9 minutes, without stirring, or until light golden. Remove the cardamom pods, add the butter and stir until melted and well combined.

Divide the caramel between 6 x ½ cup-capacity (125ml) non-stick muffin tins. Place the plums, cut-side down, in the caramel. Top with the pastry rounds and fold the edges under to tuck in the plums. Make a small cut in the pastry. Place tins on a baking tray and bake for 22–24 minutes or until puffed and golden. Stand for 2–3 minutes. Loosen the edges and carefully turn out the tartes. Serve with cream. MAKES 6

blueberry and lemon mascarpone tart

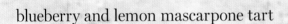

blueberry and lemon mascarpone tart

500g mascarpone*
2 tablespoons finely grated lemon rind
½ cup (80g) icing (confectioner's) sugar, sifted
375g blueberries
icing (confectioner's) sugar, for dusting
sweet shortcrust pastry
1½ cups (225g) plain (all-purpose) flour, sifted
125g cold unsalted butter, chopped
½ cup (80g) icing (confectioner's) sugar, sifted
3 egg yolks
2 teaspoons vanilla extract
1 tablespoon iced water

To make the sweet shortcrust pastry, place the flour, butter and icing sugar in a food processor and process in short bursts until the mixture resembles fine breadcrumbs. While the motor is running, add the egg yolks and vanilla. Add the iced water and process until the dough just comes together. Turn out onto a lightly floured surface, bring the dough together and flatten into a disc shape. Cover in plastic wrap and refrigerate for 1 hour.

Preheat oven to 180°C (350°F). Roll the pastry out between 2 sheets of non-stick baking paper to 3mm thick. Line a lightly greased 33cm x 9cm loose-bottomed rectangular tart tin with the pastry. Trim the edges and prick the base with a fork. Refrigerate for 30 minutes. Line the pastry case with non-stick baking paper, fill with baking weights or rice and bake for 10 minutes. Remove the paper and the weights and bake for a further 10 minutes or until golden. Set aside to cool.

While the tart is baking, make the filling. Place the mascarpone, lemon rind and icing sugar in a bowl and mix well to combine. Spread onto the base of the cooled tart shell, top with the blueberries and dust with icing sugar to serve. SERVES 8–10

peach tray tart

½ cup (60g) almond meal (ground almonds)
¼ cup (55g) caster (superfine) sugar
2 tablespoons white sugar, plus extra, for sprinkling
1 vanilla bean, split and seeds scraped
800g large yellow and white peaches, cut into wedges
1 eggwhite, lightly beaten
icing (confectioner's) sugar, for dusting
pastry
2½ cups (375g) plain (all-purpose) flour, sifted
¼ teaspoon baking powder, sifted
⅓ cup (75g) caster (superfine) sugar
270g cold unsalted butter, chopped
¼ cup (60ml) iced water
1 teaspoon vanilla extract

Preheat oven to 180°C (350°F). To make the pastry, place the flour, baking powder and sugar in a food processor and process to combine. Add the butter and process until the mixture resembles fine breadcrumbs. While the motor is running, gradually add the water and vanilla and process until the mixture comes together to form a smooth dough. Flatten into a disc shape, cover with plastic wrap and refrigerate for 30 minutes. Roll the pastry out between 2 sheets of non-stick baking paper to a 5mm thick rectangle roughly 30cm x 42cm. Refrigerate for 10–15 minutes or until firm. Place on a 30cm x 42cm baking tray and remove the top sheet of non-stick baking paper. Mix to combine the almond meal and caster sugar and sprinkle over the dough, leaving a 4cm border. Place the white sugar and vanilla seeds in a bowl and rub with your fingertips to combine. Add the peach wedges and toss to combine. Layer the almond meal mixture with the peach wedges, alternating colours, and fold the edges of the pastry around the peaches. Brush the edges with eggwhite and sprinkle with the extra white sugar. Bake for 40–45 minutes or until the pastry is cooked through and golden. Dust with icing sugar to serve. SERVES 6–8

peach tray tart

portuguese-style custard tarts

portuguese-style custard tarts

¾ cup (165g) caster (superfine) sugar
¾ cup (180ml) water
peel of 1 lemon
1 vanilla bean, split and seeds scraped
¼ cup (35g) cornflour (cornstarch)
1½ cups (375ml) milk
3 egg yolks
1 x 375g sheet all-butter puff pastry+, halved

Preheat oven to 200°C (400°F). Place the sugar, water, lemon peel and vanilla bean and seeds in a saucepan over low heat and stir until the sugar is dissolved. Increase heat to high and bring to the boil for 4 minutes or until thickened slightly. Remove the lemon peel and vanilla bean and discard.

Place the cornflour and ½ cup (125ml) milk in a large bowl and mix until smooth. Add the egg yolks and whisk to combine. Add the remaining milk and the sugar syrup and whisk until combined. Pour the egg mixture into a saucepan and place over medium heat. Bring to the boil and cook, whisking continuously, for 6 minutes or until the mixture is thickened. Set aside to cool completely.

Layer the halved pastry sheets on top of each other. Starting at the short end of the pastry, tightly roll into a log. Trim the edges and cut into 12 x 1cm rounds. Lay the pastry rounds flat on a lightly floured surface and roll out to 12 x 10cm rounds. Carefully press the pastry rounds into a 12-hole, ½ cup-capacity (125ml) lightly greased muffin tin. Divide the custard between the pastry cases and smooth the top. Bake for 25–27 minutes or until the custard is just blistered and golden. Allow to cool in tins for 5 minutes. Turn out onto a wire rack to cool completely. MAKES 12

+ *It's important to use an all-butter puff pastry to achieve the light, crispy pastry of an authentic Portuguese tart.*

strawberry, lime and coconut pie

2 cups (300g) plain (all-purpose) flour
¼ cup (55g) caster (superfine) sugar
145g cold unsalted butter, chopped
⅓ cup (80ml) iced water
2 cups (500ml) single (pouring) cream*, whipped
lime curd
1¾ cups (430ml) coconut milk
1 cup (220g) caster (superfine) sugar
⅓ cup (50g) cornflour (cornstarch)
80g unsalted butter, chopped
½ cup (125ml) lime juice
2 tablespoons finely grated lime rind
6 egg yolks
lime marinated strawberries
500g strawberries, hulled
2 tablespoons shredded lime zest
2 tablespoons lime juice
¼ cup (55g) caster (superfine) sugar

To make the lime marinated strawberries, place the strawberries, lime zest and juice, and sugar in a bowl and mix until well combined. Set aside.

Place the flour, sugar and butter in a food processor and process until the mixture resembles coarse breadcrumbs. While the motor is running, gradually add the water and process until the mixture just comes together. Turn the dough out onto a lightly floured surface and knead until smooth. Flatten into a disc shape, cover in plastic wrap and refrigerate for 30 minutes.

Preheat oven to 180°C (350°F). Roll the pastry out between two sheets of non-stick baking paper to 5mm thick. Line a lightly greased 23cm tart tin with the pastry, prick the base with a fork, line with non-stick baking paper and fill with baking weights or rice. Bake for 20 minutes, remove the paper and weights, and bake for a further 10–15 minutes or until the pastry is golden. Set aside to cool.

To make the lime curd, place 1 cup (250ml) coconut milk and the sugar in a saucepan over high heat and stir until the sugar is dissolved. Place the cornflour and remaining coconut milk in a small bowl and stir to combine. Pour the cornflour mixture into the saucepan and stir to combine. Reduce heat to medium, add the butter and whisk until melted and combined. Add the lime juice, rind and egg yolks and cook, whisking, for 8–10 minutes or until thickened. Pour the lime mixture into the tart shell and refrigerate for 2–3 hours or until set. Top the pie with the whipped cream and the lime marinated strawberries to serve. SERVES 6

strawberry, lime and coconut pie

HOW TO COOK lemon tart

basic lemon tart

sweet shortcrust pastry
1½ cups (225g) plain (all-purpose) flour
125g chilled unsalted butter, chopped
½ cup (80g) icing (confectioner's) sugar, plus extra, for dusting
3 egg yolks
1 tablespoon iced water
lemon filling
1 cup (250ml) single (pouring) cream*
2 eggs
3 egg yolks, extra
½ cup (110g) caster (superfine) sugar
½ cup (125ml) lemon juice

STEP 1 To make the sweet shortcrust pastry, place the flour, butter and icing sugar in a food processor and process until the mixture resembles fine breadcrumbs. With the motor running, add the egg yolks and process until combined. Add the iced water and process until the dough just comes together. Turn out onto a lightly floured surface and gently bring together to form a ball. Flatten into a disc shape, wrap in plastic wrap and refrigerate for 1 hour. Roll the pastry out between 2 sheets of non-stick baking paper to 3mm thick.
STEP 2 Preheat oven to 180°C (350°F). Line a lightly greased 22cm round loose-bottomed, fluted tart tin with the pastry. Trim the edges and prick the base with a fork. Refrigerate for 30 minutes. Line the pastry case with non-stick baking paper and fill with baking weights. Bake for 15 minutes, remove the paper and weights and bake for a further 10 minutes or until the pastry is light golden. Remove from the oven and set aside.
STEP 3 Reduce temperature to 140°C (250°F). To make the lemon filling, place the cream, eggs, extra yolks, sugar and lemon juice in a bowl and whisk to combine. Strain the mixture into a clean bowl.
STEP 4 Transfer the tart to a baking tray and carefully pour the filling into the tart shell. Bake for 30–35 minutes or until just set. Allow to cool at room temperature before refrigerating until completely set. Dust with icing sugar to serve. SERVES 4-6

RECIPE NOTES
You can make the pastry in advance. Simply roll out between sheets of non-stick baking paper to 3mm thick, cover with a double layer of plastic wrap and freeze flat for up to 1 month. Simply place in the fridge to thaw.

basic lemon tart

pink grapefruit tartlets

1 x quantity sweet shortcrust pastry (see recipe, page 394)
1 pink grapefruit, peeled and thinly sliced
1 cup (250ml) single (pouring) cream*, lightly whipped
grapefruit filling
½ cup (125ml) single (pouring) cream*
1 egg
2 egg yolks, extra
¼ cup (55g) caster (superfine) sugar
⅓ cup (80ml) pink grapefruit juice

Preheat oven to 180°C (350°F). Make the sweet shortcrust pasty, following step 1. Line 6 x 8.5cm round lightly greased, loose-bottomed fluted tart tins with the pastry and bake as per step 2. Set aside. Reduce temperature to 140°C (275°F).

To make the grapefruit filling, place the cream, egg, extra yolks, sugar and grapefruit juice in a bowl and whisk to combine. Strain the mixture into a clean bowl. Transfer the tarts to a baking tray and carefully pour the filling into the tart shells. Bake for 15–20 minutes or until just set. Allow to cool before refrigerating until set. Top with grapefruit and cream to serve. MAKES 6

lime and almond tarts

1 x quantity sweet shortcrust pastry (see recipe, page 394)
¼ cup (30g) almond meal (ground almonds)
fresh blueberries and icing (confectioner's sugar), to serve
lime filling
1 cup (250ml) single (pouring) cream*
1 egg
2 egg yolks, extra
¼ cup (55g) caster (superfine) sugar
⅓ cup (80ml) lime juice

Preheat oven to 180°C (350°F). Make the sweet shortcrust pastry, following step 1. Add the almond meal with the flour. Line 8 x 5.5cm x 10.5cm loose-bottomed fluted tart tins with the pastry and bake as per step 2. Remove from oven and set aside. Reduce temperature to 140°C (275°F).

To make the lime filling, place the cream, eggs, extra yolks, sugar and lime juice in a bowl and whisk to combine. Strain the mixture into a clean bowl. Transfer the tarts to a baking tray and carefully pour the filling into the tart shells. Bake for 15–20 minutes until just set. Allow to cool before refrigerating until completely set. Top with blueberries and dust with icing sugar to serve. MAKES 8

passionfruit tart

1 x quantity sweet shortcrust pastry (see recipe, page 394)
passionfruit filling
1 cup (250ml) single (pouring) cream*
2 eggs
3 egg yolks, extra
½ cup (110g) caster (superfine) sugar
2 tablespoons lemon juice
½ cup (125ml) passionfruit pulp (approximately 4 passionfruit)

Preheat oven to 180°C (350°F). Make the sweet shortcrust pastry, following step 1. Line a lightly greased 11.5cm x 34cm loose-bottomed, fluted tart tin with the pastry and bake as per step 2. Set aside. Reduce temperature to 140°C (275°F).

To make the passionfruit filling, place the cream, eggs, extra yolks, sugar and lemon juice in a bowl and whisk to combine. Strain the mixture into a clean bowl and stir through the passionfruit pulp. Transfer the tart to a baking tray and carefully pour the filling into the tart shell. Bake for 30–35 minutes or until just set. Allow to cool at room temperature before refrigerating until completely set. SERVES 4–6

lemon, coconut and raspberry tart

1 x quantity sweet shortcrust pastry (see recipe, page 394)
½ cup (40g) desiccated coconut
lemon filling
1 cup (250ml) single (pouring) cream*
2 eggs
3 egg yolks, extra
½ cup (110g) caster (superfine) sugar
½ cup (125ml) lemon juice
250g raspberries

Preheat oven to 180°C (350°F). Make the sweet shortcrust pastry, following step 1. Add the coconut with the flour. Line a lightly greased 22cm round loose-bottomed, fluted tart tin with the pastry and bake as per step 2. Remove from oven and set aside. Reduce temperature to 140°C (275°F).

To make the lemon filling, place the cream, eggs, extra yolks, sugar and lemon juice in a bowl and whisk to combine. Place half the raspberries in the tart shell. Strain the mixture into a clean bowl. Transfer the tart to a baking tray and carefully pour the filling into the tart shell. Bake for 30–35 minutes or until just set. Allow to cool at room temperature before refrigerating until completely set. Top with the remaining raspberries to serve. SERVES 4–6

DESSERTS

When it's a question of dessert, there's always room to be found for a sweet ending. From rich chocolate and decadent caramel to fruit or cream-based treats, there's no doubting you'll find your sweet tooth here.

caramel apples

soft caramels

caramel apples

8 wooden sticks
8 small red apples, washed and dried
1½ cups (375ml) light corn syrup
300g unsalted butter, chopped
2 cups (440g) caster (superfine) sugar
2 teaspoons vanilla extract

Insert a stick into the centre of each apple and set aside. Place 1 cup (250ml) corn syrup, the butter and sugar in a saucepan over medium heat and stir until well combined. Bring to the boil and cook for 8–10 minutes (do not stir) or until temperature reaches 140°C (275°F) on a sugar thermometer. Remove from the heat and stir in the remaining corn syrup and vanilla. Dip the apples into the caramel and place on a baking tray lined with non-stick baking paper. Set aside for 30 minutes or until set. MAKES 8

soft caramels

1 cup (250ml) double (thick) cream*
¾ cup (180ml) sweetened condensed milk
1 cup (250ml) light corn syrup
1 cup (220g) caster (superfine) sugar
¼ cup (60ml) water
60g unsalted butter, chopped

Place the cream and condensed milk in a small saucepan over low heat and stir until just warm. Set aside and keep warm. Place the corn syrup, sugar and water in a small, deep-sided saucepan over high heat and stir until the sugar is dissolved. Bring to the boil and cook (do not stir) until the temperature reaches 120°C (250°F) on a sugar thermometer. Reduce heat to medium, add the butter and warm cream mixture (the temperature will drop on the thermometer) and cook, stirring continuously, until the temperature reaches 110°C (230°F)+. Immediately remove the caramel from the heat. Carefully spoon into a lightly greased 20cm square tin lined with non-stick baking paper and allow to cool for 2–3 hours or until set. Do not refrigerate. Cut into squares to serve. MAKES 16
+ It's important to stir continuously when you have added the butter and milk to ensure the mixture doesn't stick to the sides of the pan, as this will give the caramel a burnt flavour.

chocolate caramel truffles

1 cup (250ml) single (pouring) cream*
½ cup (110g) caster (superfine) sugar
¼ cup (60ml) water
50g unsalted butter, softened
250g dark chocolate, roughly chopped
1 tablespoon butterscotch-flavoured schnapps
200g dark (70%) chocolate, melted, extra

Place the cream in a small saucepan over medium heat and bring to a boil. Remove from the heat and set aside.
    Place the sugar and water in a saucepan over low heat and stir until the sugar is dissolved. Increase heat to medium and bring to the boil. Cook for 6–6½ minutes or until a deep-golden+. Remove from the heat and, working quickly, add the cream and butter. Return saucepan to the heat and stir to combine. Place the chocolate in a bowl, pour over the caramel mixture and schnapps and stir gently until chocolate is melted and mixture is smooth. Place in a lightly greased 20cm square tin lined with non-stick baking paper and refrigerate for 2–3 hours or until set.
    Roll tablespoonfuls of the mixture into balls and place on a baking tray lined with non-stick baking paper++. Freeze for 1 hour or until firm. Dip the truffles in the melted chocolate and place on a tray lined with non-stick baking paper. Refrigerate for 1 hour or until set.
MAKES APPROXIMATELY 22
+ It's important the caramel is deep golden in colour, as adding the cream and butter will arrest the cooking process. If the caramel is too pale, it will have a weak flavour. And if it's too dark, it will taste bitter.
++ Dip a tablespoon in hot water and pat dry to help roll the mixture into balls. Use a skewer to help remove the truffles from the tablespoon.

chocolate caramel truffles

HOW TO COOK *truffles*

1
3

basic chocolate truffles

¾ cup (180ml) single (pouring) cream*
600g dark chocolate, finely chopped⁺
Dutch cocoa, for dusting

STEP 1 Place the cream in a small saucepan over high heat and bring to the boil. Place the chocolate in a bowl and pour the cream over. Place the bowl over a saucepan of simmering water, and using a metal spoon, stir until the mixture is smooth.
STEP 2 Pour into a lightly greased 20cm x 20cm metal tin lined with non-stick baking paper⁺⁺ and tap the tin (or smooth the surface with a palette knife) to even the mixture. Refrigerate for 2–3 hours or until firm.
STEP 3 Remove the truffle from the tin and bring to room temperature. Cut into 36 squares to serve. Dust with cocoa, if desired. MAKES 36
+ *It's important to finely chop the chocolate first so it melts evenly and quickly, without being on the heat for too long.*
++ *Be sure to line the sides of the tin with enough non-stick baking paper so that you can use the paper to lift the chocolate truffle from the tin.*

RECIPE NOTES
Chocolate is fragile and can burn easily, causing it to split and become grainy. Heating it in a bowl over a saucepan of simmering water is a gentle way of melting it, reducing the risk of this happening. Using a metal spoon or silicone spatula, rather than a wooden one that retains moisture, is also important, as moisture can also cause a grainy result.

basic chocolate truffles

almond and pistachio truffles

¾ cup (180ml) single (pouring) cream*
600g dark chocolate, finely chopped
¼ cup (60ml) almond-flavoured liqueur
1 cup (140g) shelled pistachios, toasted and finely chopped

Place the cream in a small saucepan over high heat and bring to the boil. Place the chocolate in a bowl and pour over the cream. Place the bowl over a saucepan of simmering water and using a metal spoon, stir until the mixture is smooth and well combined. Stir in the liqueur. Pour into a lightly greased 20cm x 20cm tin lined with non-stick baking paper and tap the tin to even the mixture. Refrigerate for 2–3 hours or until firm. Remove truffle from the tin and bring to room temperature. Cut into 18 even rectangles and sprinkle with the pistachios to serve. MAKES 18

milk chocolate and espresso truffles

¾ cup (180ml) single (pouring) cream*
2 tablespoons strong instant coffee granules
600g milk chocolate, finely chopped
Dutch cocoa, to coat

Place the cream and coffee in a small saucepan over high heat and stir to dissolve. Bring to the boil. Place the chocolate in a bowl and pour over the cream. Place the bowl over a saucepan of simmering water and using a metal spoon, stir until the mixture is smooth and well combined. Pour into a lightly greased 20cm x 20cm tin lined with non-stick baking paper and tap the tin to even the mixture. Refrigerate for 2–3 hours or until firm. Remove truffle from the tin and bring to room temperature. Cut into 25 even squares and using two forks, toss the truffles in cocoa to coat. MAKES 25

chocolate butterscotch truffles with almond praline

¾ cup (180ml) single (pouring) cream*
600g dark chocolate, finely chopped
¼ cup (60ml) butterscotch-flavoured liqueur
½ cup (110g) raw sugar
⅓ cup (25g) flaked almonds, toasted

Place the cream in a small saucepan over high heat and bring to the boil. Place the chocolate in a bowl and pour over the cream. Place the bowl over a saucepan of simmering water and using a metal spoon, stir until the mixture is smooth and well combined. Stir in the liqueur. Pour into a lightly greased 20cm x 20cm tin lined with non-stick baking paper and tap the tin to even the mixture. Refrigerate for 2–3 hours or until firm. Preheat oven to 200°C (400°F). Sprinkle the sugar evenly on a lightly greased baking tray lined with non-stick baking paper. Cook for 15 minutes or until the sugar is melted and golden. Sprinkle over the almonds and allow to cool completely. Transfer to a food processor and blend until finely chopped. Remove truffle from the tin and bring to room temperature. Cut into 36 even squares and sprinkle over the praline to serve. MAKES 36

salted dark chocolate truffles

¾ cup (180ml) single (pouring) cream*
600g dark chocolate, finely chopped
sea salt flakes, for sprinkling

Place the cream in a small saucepan over high heat and bring to the boil. Place the chocolate in a bowl and pour over the cream. Place the bowl over a saucepan of simmering water and using a metal spoon, stir until the mixture is smooth and well combined. Pour into a lightly greased 20cm x 20cm tin lined with non-stick baking paper and tap the tin to even the mixture. Refrigerate for 2–3 hours or until firm. Remove truffle from the tin and bring to room temperature. Cut into 18 even rectangles and sprinkle with salt to serve. MAKES 18

homemade dulce de leche

homemade dulce de leche

2 x 395g cans sweetened condensed milk

Preheat oven to 220°C (425°F). Place the condensed milk in an
ovenproof baking dish and cover tightly with aluminium foil. Place the
baking dish in a larger deep-sided baking tray and fill with boiling water
until it reaches ⅔ of the way up the sides of the dish. Bake for 1 hour
30 minutes–1 hour 45 minutes or until caramel in colour. Spoon the
caramel into a bowl and whisk until smooth. Spoon into sterilised
glass jars. Keep in the fridge for up to 1 month. MAKES 2 CUPS (500ML)

basic crêpes with lemon and sugar

1 cup (150g) plain (all-purpose) flour, sifted
2 tablespoons caster (superfine) sugar
4 eggs
1 cup (250ml) milk
1 cup (250ml) single (pouring) cream*
lemon wedges and extra caster (superfine) sugar, to serve

Place the flour and sugar in a large bowl and mix to combine.
Place the eggs, milk and cream in a separate bowl and whisk to
combine. Gradually whisk the flour mixture into the egg mixture
until smooth. Allow to stand for 20 minutes. Heat a lightly greased
22cm round, non-stick crêpe pan⁺ over low heat. Add ¼ cup of the
batter and swirl to cover the base of the pan. Cook for 2–3 minutes,
gently turn using an eggflip, and cook for a further 1 minute or until
just cooked. Place on non-stick baking paper and cover with a clean
tea towel. Repeat with the remaining batter. Serve with the lemon
wedges and sprinkle with the extra sugar. MAKES 16
+ You can use any size pan and make smaller or larger crêpes.

moscato and vanilla poached plums

1.5kg mixed plums
1.5 litres moscato (sweet sparkling wine)
2 cups (440g) caster (superfine) sugar
2 vanilla beans, split and seeds scraped

Using a small, sharp knife, cut a small cross in the base of each plum.
Place the moscato, sugar and vanilla bean and seeds in a large,
heavy-based saucepan over low heat and stir until the sugar is
dissolved. Increase heat to high and bring to the boil. Cook the
plums, in batches, for 1–2 minutes or until the skins start to peel
away. Remove plums with a slotted spoon and place in a bowl of iced
water, remove the skins and discard. Cook the syrup for a further
10 minutes or until thickened slightly. Remove from the heat and
allow to cool slightly. Return the plums to the syrup and allow to
cool completely before serving. SERVES 6–8

coeur à la crème

1 vanilla bean, split and seeds scraped
½ cup (125g) mascarpone*
80g cream cheese, softened
¾ cup (165g) caster (superfine) sugar
½ cup (125ml) double (thick) cream*
1 cup (280g) plain (natural) yoghurt

Place the vanilla seeds, mascarpone and cream cheese in the bowl
of a food processor and process until smooth. Add the sugar, cream
and yoghurt and process until combined. Line 6 x ½ cup-capacity
(125ml) porcelain heart-shaped moulds⁺ with 6 x 25cm squares of
damp muslin. Spoon cream mixture into moulds, smooth the tops and
fold over the excess muslin. Place moulds on a tray, cover with plastic
wrap and refrigerate for 6 hours or until firm. Carefully turn out
moulds and remove muslin to serve. SERVES 6
*Tip: Coeur à la crème means 'the heart of the cream' and is a traditional
French dessert. You can buy coeur moulds from specialty kitchenware
stores, or simply wrap the mixture in muslin and mould into hearts.
The muslin allows the moisture to drain but retains the shape of the heart.*

tray-baked berry meringue

500g strawberries, hulled
250g blueberries
250g raspberries
⅓ cup (75g) caster (superfine) sugar
150ml eggwhites (approximately 4 eggs)
1 cup (220g) caster (superfine) sugar, extra
2 tablespoons cornflour (cornstarch)
2 teaspoons white vinegar
1 cup (250ml) single (pouring) cream*, whipped

Preheat oven to 150°C (300°F). Place the berries and sugar in a
27cm x 36cm tin and toss to coat. Place the eggwhites in the bowl
of an electric mixer and whisk until stiff peaks form. Gradually add
the extra sugar, whisking well, until the mixture is stiff and glossy.
Add the cornflour and vinegar and whisk until just combined.
Top the berries with the meringue and bake for 45 minutes.
Serve with whipped cream. SERVES 6–8

basic crêpes with lemon and sugar

moscato and vanilla poached plums

coeur à la crème

tray-baked berry meringue

HOW TO COOK marshmallow

1 2
3 4

basic vanilla marshmallow

½ cup (125ml) warm water
2 tablespoons gelatine powder
1½ cups (330g) caster (superfine) sugar
⅔ cup (230g) liquid glucose*
½ cup (125ml) water, extra
1 vanilla bean, split and seeds scraped
icing sugar mixture
1½ cups (240g) icing (confectioner's) sugar, sifted
¼ cup (35g) cornflour (cornstarch), sifted

STEP 1 Place the warm water in an electric mixer, sprinkle over the gelatine and stir to combine. Set aside. Place the sugar, glucose and extra water in a saucepan over low heat and cook, stirring, until the sugar is dissolved. Increase heat to high and bring to the boil. Add a sugar (candy) thermometer and cook, without stirring, for approximately 5–7 minutes, until the temperature reaches 115°C (239°F) or soft ball stage.
STEP 2 With the mixer running on high, gradually add the hot syrup to the gelatine mixture in a thin, steady stream. Add the vanilla seeds and beat for 5–7 minutes or until thick and fluffy. Working quickly, spoon the mixture into a lightly greased 20cm x 30cm slice tin lined with lightly greased, non-stick baking paper⁺.
STEP 3 Using a spatula, smooth the top and cover with lightly greased non-stick baking paper⁺⁺. Refrigerate for 1–2 hours or until set.
STEP 4 To make the icing sugar mixture, place the icing sugar and cornflour in a bowl and mix to combine. Turn the marshmallow out onto a surface lightly dusted with some icing sugar mixture. Dust the knife in the icing sugar mixture and cut the marshmallow into squares. Dust the marshmallows with more icing sugar. **MAKES 40**
+ *Ensure you have enough baking paper hanging over the sides so you can lift the marshmallow from the tin once it has set.*
++ *For a perfect smooth finish to your marshmallow, place the base of a smaller rectangular tin over the top of the marshmallow (which is covered with lightly greased non-stick baking paper) and gently press down while smoothing to create a flat and even surface.*

RECIPE NOTES
Your marshmallows will keep in an airtight container dusted with icing sugar mixture, in the fridge, for up to one week. Be sure to take your marshmallows out of the fridge just before serving, to prevent them becoming sticky from the humidity.

basic vanilla marshmallow

classic pavlova

150ml eggwhites, at room temperature (approximately 4 eggs)
1 cup (220g) caster (superfine) sugar
1 teaspoon white vinegar
1 cup (250ml) single (pouring) cream*
⅓ cup (80ml) passionfruit pulp
250g strawberries, hulled and sliced
1 banana, sliced

Preheat oven to 150°C (300°F). Place the eggwhites in an electric mixer and whisk on high until stiff peaks form. Gradually add the sugar, 1 tablespoon at a time, waiting 30 seconds before adding another tablespoon. Once all the sugar is added, whisk for a further 6 minutes or until the mixture is stiff and glossy⁺. Scrape down the sides of the bowl, add the vinegar and whisk for a further 2 minutes or until glossy and combined. Place spoonfuls of the meringue onto a baking tray lined with non-stick baking paper to fill an 18cm circle⁺⁺. Reduce temperature to 120°C (250°F) and bake for 1 hour 30 minutes. Turn the oven off and allow the pavlova to cool completely in the oven. Place the cream in a bowl and whisk until soft peaks form. Top the pavlova with the cream, passionfruit pulp, strawberries and banana. SERVES 4–6
+ When the mixture is thick and glossy the sugar should be completely dissolved. To test, simply rub a little of the mixture between your fingertips. If it feels gritty continue to whisk.
++ To shape the pavlova, draw an 18cm circle on non-stick baking paper. Place the paper pencil-side down on the tray to ensure the pencil doesn't transfer to the pavlova.

sunset granita

mango granita
500g mango, peeled and chopped
2 tablespoons caster (superfine) sugar
1 cup (250ml) water
lychee granita
2 x 250g cans lychees in syrup, drained
¼ cup (60ml) lime juice
½ cup (110g) caster (superfine) sugar
2 cups (500ml) water
watermelon granita
1kg seeded and chopped watermelon
½ cup (110g) caster (superfine) sugar
1⅓ cups (330ml) water

To make the mango granita, place the mango in a food processor and process until smooth. Place the sugar and water in a saucepan over low heat and stir until the sugar is dissolved. Add the mango purée and stir to combine. Pour the mixture into a shallow 20cm x 30cm slice tin and place in the freezer for 1 hour. Using a fork, rake the top of the granita and freeze for a further 1 hour. Repeat every 3–4 hours until granita is set.

To make the lychee granita, place the lychees and lime juice in the bowl of a food processor and process until smooth. Place the sugar and water in a saucepan over low heat and stir until the sugar is dissolved. Add the lychee purée and stir to combine. Pour the mixture into a shallow 20cm x 30cm slice tin and place in the freezer for 1 hour. Repeat the method from the mango granita (above).

To make the watermelon granita, place the watermelon in the bowl of a food processor and process until smooth. Place the sugar and water in a saucepan over low heat and stir until the sugar is dissolved. Add the watermelon purée and stir to combine. Pour the mixture into a shallow 20cm x 30cm slice tin and place in the freezer for 1 hour. Repeat the method from the mango granita (above). Layer granita flavours into glasses to serve. SERVES 6

sunset granita

summer melon ices

strawberry and cranberry pops

creamy tropical pops

blueberry and yoghurt pops

basic sugar syrup

½ cup (110g) caster (superfine) sugar
¾ cup (180ml) water

Place the sugar and water in a small saucepan over low heat and stir until the sugar is dissolved. Increase the heat to high and bring to the boil for 1 minute. Set aside to cool completely. MAKES 1 CUP (250ML)

summer melon ices

½ cup (125ml) basic sugar syrup (see recipe, above)
2 tablespoons lemon juice
150g watermelon, seeded and chopped
150g rockmelon (cantaloupe), seeded and chopped

Pour the sugar syrup and lemon juice into a jug and stir to combine. Place the watermelon and half the lemon syrup into a blender and process until smooth. Pour the watermelon mixture into 8 x ⅓ cup-capacity (80ml) ice-block moulds, insert ice-block sticks and freeze for 4 hours.

Place the remaining lemon syrup and the rockmelon into a blender and process until smooth. Pour over the watermelon and freeze for a further 4 hours or until frozen. MAKES 8
Tip: When making layered ice blocks, always be sure that each layer is set before adding the next. Otherwise, all the colours will mix into each other,

strawberry and cranberry pops

1 quantity basic sugar syrup (see recipe, above)
1⅓ cups (330ml) cranberry juice
8 strawberries, sliced

Pour the sugar syrup and cranberry juice into a large jug and stir to combine. Pour half the cranberry mixture into 8 x ⅓ cup-capacity (80ml) ice-block moulds. Place 2 strawberry slices into each mould, insert ice-block sticks and freeze for 4 hours. Pour remaining cranberry syrup into moulds. Divide remaining strawberry slices between moulds and freeze for a further 4 hours or until frozen. MAKES 8
Tip: Some ice-block kits come with ice-block sticks that have holders or lids to keep the stick in place as the popsicle freezes. If you don't have these sticks, an easy way to keep them in place is to cover the moulds with foil and make an incision in the centre of each mould to place the stick.

creamy tropical pops

1 quantity basic sugar syrup (see recipe, left)
1 cup (250ml) coconut cream
100g chopped pineapple
½ cup (125ml) passionfruit pulp (approximately 4 passionfruit)

Place the sugar syrup, coconut cream and pineapple in a blender and process until smooth. Add the passionfruit pulp and stir to combine. Pour mixture into 8 x ⅓ cup-capacity (80ml) ice-block moulds, insert ice-block sticks and freeze for 4 hours or until frozen. MAKES 8

blueberry and yoghurt pops

375g blueberries
3 tablespoons caster (superfine) sugar
2 tablespoons lemon juice
1½ cups (420g) vanilla yoghurt
⅓ cup (80ml) passionfruit pulp (approximately 3 passionfruit)

Place the blueberries, sugar and lemon juice in a saucepan over high heat and bring to the boil. Cook for 10–12 minutes or until thickened. Remove from the heat and allow to cool completely.

Place the yoghurt in a bowl and fold through the passionfruit pulp and cooled blueberry mixture. Pour into 8 popsicle moulds, insert wooden ice-cream sticks and freeze for 4 hours or until set. MAKES 8
Tip: When removing ice-blocks from their moulds, allow the mould to stand at room temperature for a couple of minutes before placing a hot tea towel around the mould to help loosen the ice block. If the ice blocks are really stuck, you can run a palette knife gently around the edges.

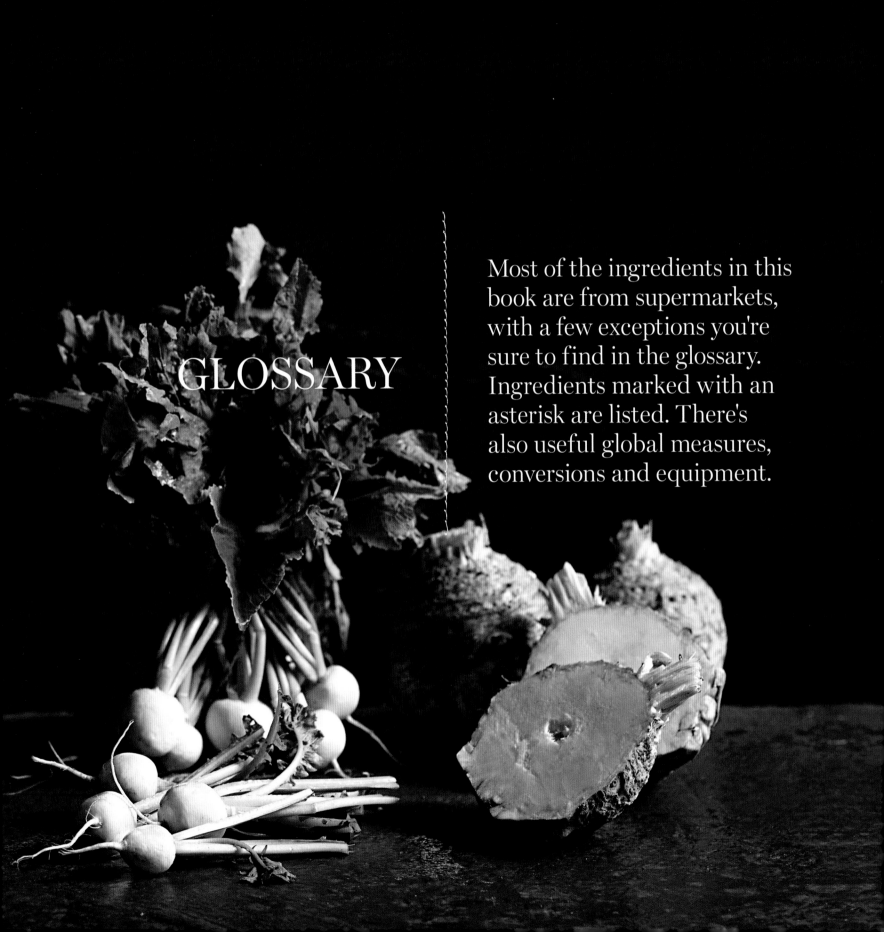

GLOSSARY

Most of the ingredients in this book are from supermarkets, with a few exceptions you're sure to find in the glossary. Ingredients marked with an asterisk are listed. There's also useful global measures, conversions and equipment.

apple eggplant

This variety of Thai eggplant is small and green (like a little Granny Smith apple) and also comes in a similar shape that is white and purple. They are commonly used in green and red curries where they absorb the flavours of the sauce. They have a thinner skin and a more subtle flavour than their purple European cousins.

arborio rice

Rice with a short, plump-looking grain that cooks to a soft texture while retaining a chalky interior. It has surface starch that creates a creamy texture in a risotto when cooked to al dente. Substitute with carnaroli, roma, baldo, padano, vialone or Calriso rice. Available from most supermarkets, specialty food stores and delicatessens.

asian greens

These leafy green vegetables from the brassica family are now becoming widely available. We love their versatility and speed of preparation – they can be poached, braised, steamed or added to soups and stir-fries.

bok choy: A mildly flavoured green vegetable, also known as Chinese chard or Chinese white cabbage. Baby bok choy can be cooked whole after washing. If using the larger type, separate the leaves and trim the white stalks. Limit the cooking time so it stays green and crisp.

broccolini: A cross between gai larn (Chinese broccoli) and broccoli, this green vegetable has long, thin stems and small florets. Sold in bunches, broccolini can be substituted for regular heads of broccoli.

choy sum: Also known as Chinese flowering cabbage, this green vegetable has small yellow flowers. The green leaves and slender stems are steamed or lightly cooked in soups and stir-fries.

gai larn: Also known as Chinese broccoli or Chinese kale, gai larn is a leafy vegetable with dark green leaves, small white flowers and stout stems. It should be steamed and served with oyster sauce as a simple side or added to soups, stir-fries and braises towards the end of the cooking time.

baking blind

Line the tart shell with non-stick baking paper and fill with baking weights, rice or beans. Bake for 15 minutes, remove the weights and cook for a further 10 minutes or until the pastry is golden and crisp.

black-eyed beans

Pale beans with an obvious black spot in the centre, these need to be soaked overnight before using. Black-eyed beans are common in southern US and Mexican cuisines.

blanching

A cooking method used to slightly soften the texture, heighten the colour and enhance the flavour of food such as vegetables. Plunge the ingredient briefly into boiling unsalted water, then remove and refresh under cold water. Drain well.

bonito flakes

Dried, fermented and smoked bonito fillets are very finely shaved and sold in bags as 'flakes'. They are one of the main ingredients in dashi, a broth that is the basis for soup such as miso. Dried bonito flakes can also be sprinkled on dishes such as agedashi tofu.

brioche

A sweet, buttery French yeast bread made in loaf or bun form. Traditionally dunked in coffee and eaten for breakfast. Available from specialty bread and cake stores and some supermarkets, brioche makes great bread and butter pudding.

char siu sauce

Commonly used in Cantonese cuisine to flavour pork, char siu contains sugar or honey, Chinese five-spice, soy sauce, red food colouring and sherry. Available from supermarkets and Asian grocery stores.

cheese

blue: The distinctive veins and flavour of blue cheeses are achieved by adding a cultured mould. Most have a crumbly texture and acidic taste, which becomes rounded and more mellow with age.

bocconcini: Small, bite-sized balls of the mild Italian cheese, mozzarella.

fontina: An Italian cow's milk cheese from the Piedmont region, it resembles soft gruyère with smaller holes and a richer, creamier and nuttier flavour.

goat's: Goat's milk has a tart flavour, so cheese made from it, sometimes labelled 'chèvre', has a sharp, slightly acidic taste. Immature goat's cheese is milder and creamier than mature cheese and is sometimes labelled curd.

gouda: This Dutch cow's milk cheese with a mild, sweet and fruity flavour has a red wax protective covering and is popular on breakfast tables in western Europe.

gruyère: An alpine hard cow's milk cheese resembling Swiss Emmenthaler, but with smaller eyes (holes from pockets of gas that develop during the fermentation process) and a more pronounced bite.

haloumi: Firm white Cypriot cheese made from sheep's milk. It has a stringy texture and is usually sold in brine. Available from delicatessens and some supermarkets.

manchego: Firm ivory-yellow cheese of Spanish origin made from sheep's milk. It has a subtle, buttery flavour.

mascarpone: A fresh Italian triple-cream, curd-style cheese, mascarpone has a smooth consistency similar to thick (double) cream. Available in tubs from specialty food stores, delicatessens and supermarkets, it's used in sauces and desserts such as tiramisu.

mozzarella: Italian in origin, mozzarella is the mild cheese of pizza, lasagne and tomato salads. It's made by cutting and spinning (or stringing) the curd to achieve a smooth, elastic consistency. The most prized variety is made from buffalo's milk.

parmesan: Italy's favourite hard grating cheese is made from cow's milk. The 'Rolls Royce' variety, Parmigiano Reggiano, is made under strict guidelines in the Emilia-Romagna region and aged for an average of at least two years. Its cousin, Grana Padano, mainly comes from Lombardy and is aged for at least 15 months.

ricotta: A creamy, finely grained white cheese. Ricotta means 'recooked' in Italian, a reference to the way the cheese is produced by heating the whey left over from making other cheese varieties. It's fresh and creamy and low in fat. Ricotta salata is a hard, salted ricotta that has been aged and dried. Find it at delicatessens and Italian grocery stores.

tallegio: This semi-soft cow's milk cheese has a pale, creamy interior and a washed rind. It has a strong yeasty flavour and pronounced aroma.

chervil

A herb relative of parsley with softer, delicate leaves and a slightly aniseed flavour and aroma.

chilli

There are over 200 different types of chilli in the world. By general rule of thumb, long red and green chillies are milder, fruitier and sweeter, while small chillies (sometimes called birdseye) are much hotter. Taking this into account, we specify either large or small chillies in our recipes. Remove the membrane and seeds for a milder result.

ancho: This is a dried Mexican poblano chilli with a sweet, fruity flavour and medium heat. You can find them at greengrocers, spice stores and online.

jalapeño: A medium-sized chilli that's picked when still green, jalapeños are often pickled and sold sliced or whole in brine and are common in Mexican and Tex-Mex dishes.

chilli bean paste

Made from salted black beans mixed with chilli, garlic and star anise, this is a pungent sauce of the Asian kitchen. It adds a great depth of flavour and is available from Asian supermarkets and grocery stores.

chilli jam

Thai condiment made from ginger, chilli, garlic and shrimp paste used in soups and stir-fries. It goes well with roasted meats, egg dishes and cheese. You can find many types of chilli jam in most supermarkets and Asian grocery stores.

chinese cooking wine

Similar to dry sherry, Shaoxing, Shao Hsing or Chinese cooking wine is a blend of glutinous rice, millet, a special yeast and the local spring waters of Shao Hsing, where it is made in northern China. It is sold in Asian supermarkets.

chinese five-spice powder

This fragrant blend of cinnamon, Sichuan pepper, star anise, clove and fennel seeds goes well with chicken, pork, lamb and beef and is an essential ingredient in red-cooked, or slow-braised, Chinese dishes. Five-spice is available at Asian grocery stores and in most supermarkets.

chorizo

Firm, spicy, coarse-textured Spanish pork sausage seasoned with pepper, paprika and chillies. Sold fresh or dried (like a salami) from butchers and most delicatessens.

coconut

A milky sweet white liquid made by soaking grated fresh coconut flesh or desiccated coconut in warm water and squeezing through muslin or cheesecloth to extract the liquid. Available in cans from supermarkets, coconut milk should not be confused with coconut juice, which is a clear liquid found inside young coconuts. It's popular in curries.

cornmeal

Ground from corn and similar to polenta, cornmeal is used to make bread, porridge, tortillas and more.

cream

The fat content determines the names of the different types of cream and the uses for which they are ideal.

double (thick) cream: Has a butter fat content of 40–50 per cent. It is sometimes called pure cream and is usually served as a dollop on the side of desserts.

clotted: Also known as Devonshire cream, this is the classic accompaniment for scones and strawberry jam. Clotted cream is made by heating unpasteurised milk very gently until it thickens. Store-bought versions are available.

créme fraîche: A fermented cream with a minimum fat content of 35 per cent and a tangy flavour.

single (pouring) cream: Has a butter fat content of 20–30 per cent. It is the type of cream most commonly used for making ice-cream, panna cotta and custard. It can be whipped to a light and airy consistency and served on the side.

thickened cream: Not to be mistaken for heavy or double cream, this is single or pouring cream that has had a vegetable gum added to stabilise it. The gum makes the cream a little thicker and easier to whip. It's ideal for creamy desserts or for topping cakes and pavlovas.

crystallised ginger

Essentially a candied version of fresh ginger, this can be sold in syrup or coated in sugar. It's mostly used in baking and can be found in most supermarkets or health food stores.

curry leaves

Sold fresh or dried, curry leaves function in much the same way as bay leaves or kaffir lime leaves, imparting a fragrance and aroma to a dish but removed before serving. With their slightly spicy, citrus aroma, fresh curry leaves are great in curries and chutneys.

dulce de leche

This is a thick milk caramel made from slowly heating and thickening sweetened milk. You can buy it in jars or make your own by gently boiling an unopened can of sweetened condensed milk (not a ring-pull can) for 2–3 hours. The longer it's cooked, the thicker, darker and more intense it becomes. It can be used as a filling for tarts, as a topping on cakes, or drizzled over ice-cream.

edamame

The Japanese name for baby soy beans, edamame are usually sold frozen in the pod. They can be quickly steamed or blanched and served simply as a snack with a little salt as they are in many Japanese restaurants, or they can be podded and tossed through salads and sides. Find them in the freezer section at Asian grocery stores.

eggs

The standard egg size used in this book is 60g. It is very important to use the right size eggs for a recipe, as this will affect the outcome of baked goods. The correct volume is especially important when using eggwhites to make meringues. You should use eggs at room temperature for baking, so always remember to remove them from the refrigerator about 30 minutes before you begin cooking.

eschalot (French shallot)

A member of the onion family, eschalots are smaller and have a milder flavour than brown, red or white onions. A popular ingredient in Europe, they look like small elongated brown onions with purple-grey tinged skins. Asian shallots are smaller again, with pinkish skins and grow in small clusters. They're used in curry pastes and also sold as fried chips to sprinkle over salads or noodle dishes.

fish sauce

An amber-coloured liquid drained from salted, fermented fish and used to add flavour to Thai and Vietnamese dishes. Fish sauce is used in curries to add pungency, as well as soups such as pho (beef noodle soup). Available from supermarkets and Asian food stores, it's often labelled 'nam pla'.

flour

Made from ground cereal grains, flour is the primary ingredient in breads, cakes and many other baked goods including biscuits, pastries, pizzas and pie cases.

cornflour (cornstarch): When made from ground corn or maize, cornflour is a gluten-free flour. It is often blended with water or stock to use as a thickening agent.

glutinous rice flour: This flour, also called sticky rice flour, is made from short-grain sticky rice and has a slightly chewy and elastic texture. You can find it at Asian supermarkets and grocery stores.

'00' flour: A superfine flour that makes for soft and stretchy dough. It contains less gluten than normal flour, resulting in a softer product. It's commonly used to make fresh pasta or cakes.

plain (all-purpose): Ground from the endosperm of wheat, plain white flour contains no raising agent.

potato (starch): As its name suggests, potato starch is extracted from potatoes and can be used to make dumplings and noodles. It's available from Asian supermarkets and grocery stores.

rice: A fine flour made from ground white rice. It is used in baking and Asian cooking to give a crispy coating to fried foods.

self-raising (self-rising): Ground from the endosperm of wheat, self-raising flour contains raising agents including sodium carbonates and calcium phosphates. To make it using plain flour add 2 teaspoons of baking powder for every 250g of flour.

tapioca: Made from the sweet cassava root, tapioca flour is used widely as a thickening agent in pies and soups, and can also be made into dumpling dough. Find it in some supermarkets and Asian grocery stores.

galangal

A rhizome with pink skin and a knobbly exterior, galangal is related to ginger but has a milder flavour. It's used widely in Thai cuisine, especially in soups and pastes. You can find it at greengrocers.

ghee

An Indian version of clarified butter made by heating butter and separating the clear liquid from the milk solids to increase the temperature at which you can cook with it. It has a high smoking point.

gow gee wrappers

Chinese in origin, these round, thin sheets of dough are available fresh or frozen. They can be steamed or fried. Fill them with meat and vegetables to make dumplings, or use as a crunchy base for nibbles.

green mango

Unripe or green mangoes have a sour flavour and are used in Southeast Asian cuisine in chutneys and salads. They are popular in Thai-style salads.

green onion (scallion)

Both the white and green part of this small bulbed, mild onion are used in salads, as a garnish and in Asian cooking. Sold in bunches, they give a fresh bite to dishes.

green papaya

Like green mango, unripe papaya has a starring role in Thai salads, where it is shredded and served with a dressing of lime, fish sauce, palm sugar and chilli. This popular dish is called som tam.

harissa

A North African condiment, harissa is a hot red paste made from chilli, garlic and spices including coriander, caraway and cumin. It may also contain tomato. Available in jars and tubes from supermarkets and specialty food stores, harissa enlivens tagines and couscous dishes and can be added to dressings and sauces for an instant flavour kick.

hoisin sauce

A thick, sweet Chinese sauce made from fermented soybeans, sugar, salt and red rice. Used as a dipping sauce or marinade and as the sauce for Peking duck, hoisin is available from Asian grocery stores and most supermarkets.

horseradish

A pungent root vegetable that releases mustard oil when cut or grated. It oxidises quickly, so use immediately after cutting or cover with water or vinegar. Fresh horseradish is lovely grated over beef or roast pork; find it at greengrocers. You can also find the grated product in jars or sold as horseradish cream in supermarkets.

hummus

Popular dip of the Middle East made by blending cooked chickpeas (garbanzos) with tahini, garlic and lemon juice. It's served with all manner of grilled meats, flatbread and salad. Available in tubs from supermarkets.

kaffir lime leaves

Fragrant leaves with a distinctive double-leaf structure, used crushed or shredded in Thai salads and curries. Available fresh or dried from greengrocers and Asian food stores.

laksa

This spicy curry-like soup made with coconut milk, vermicelli noodles, bean curd and prawns is of Malaysian origin with Chinese and Indonesian influences. The laksa base is made with chillies, spices, ground shrimp, lemongrass and ginger and is commonly sold in jars or tubs as a paste. Find it in most supermarkets and Asian grocery stores.

lemongrass

A tall, lemon-scented grass used in Asian cooking, and particularly in Thai dishes. Peel away the outer leaves and chop the tender root-end finely, or add in large pieces during cooking and remove before serving. Available from Asian food stores and some greengrocers.

miso paste

A traditional Japanese ingredient produced by fermenting rice, barley or soybeans with salt and fungus to a thick paste. Used for sauces and spreads, pickling vegetables or meats, and mixing with dashi soup stock to serve as the ever-popular miso soup. Miso comes in white, red (brownish in colour) and black varieties. White miso has the sweetest flavour. Available from some supermarkets and Asian food stores.

mushrooms

button: This tender little mushroom tightly closed around its stalk is the young form of the commercial field mushroom. White and mildly flavoured, it can be used raw in salads, but is tastier when cooked in stews, stir-fries and pasta sauces.

enoki: This Japanese mushroom has a long white stalk with a small bulb at the end. It goes well in soups, salads and stir-fries and should only be added at the very end of the cooking time.

oyster: This shell-shaped mushroom, sometimes called abalone, has a delicate flavour and tender bite. Colours range from pearly white to apricot-pink. Tear rather than cut and cook gently, whether simmering in soups, pan-frying or grilling. When eaten raw, they can trigger an allergic reaction.

pine: Also known as saffron milk caps, these large-capped mushrooms are a pretty orange hue and are found growing around pine trees, hence their name. They have a nutty favour and firm texture that keeps its shape when cooked. You can find them at some greengrocers and farmer's markets.

porcini: Available fresh in Europe and the UK and sold dried elsewhere, including Australia and the US. They have an almost meaty texture and earthy taste. Soak dried porcini mushrooms before using, and use the soaking liquid if desired. Frozen porcinis are becoming more readily available. Like the dried variety, they're available from specialty food stores.

portobello: This large flat mushroom is closely related to the white field mushroom but has a nutty, rich flavour and brown flaky skin. A mature version of the Swiss brown, its meaty texture makes it suitable for robust cooking styles.

shiitake: A tan to dark brown mushroom with a meaty texture and rich earthy taste akin to wild mushrooms. Its dried form, found in Asian food stores, gives the most intense flavour.

swiss brown: A button version of the portobello and a more flavoursome substitute for the common white mushroom. Use Swiss browns in pasta sauces, risottos or braises.

noodles

bean thread: Also called mung bean vermicelli, cellophane or glass noodles, these noodles are very thin and almost transparent. Soak them in boiling water and drain well to prepare for use.

chinese wheat: Available dried and fresh in a variety of thicknesses. Fresh noodles need to be soaked in hot water or cooked in boiling water. Dried noodles should be boiled before use. Good for stir-fries.

dried rice stick: Fine, dry noodles that are common in Southeast Asian cooking, particularly salads. Depending on their thickness, rice noodles need only be boiled briefly, or soaked in hot water until pliable.

fresh rice: Available in a variety of thicknesses, including thin, thick and rolled. Use noodles that are a few days old at most, soak in hot water for 1 minute, and drain well to prepare for use.

soba: Japanese-style noodles made from buckwheat flour. Used in soups and salads and also eaten cold.

nori

Thin sheets of dried, vitamin-packed seaweed used in Japanese-style dishes and to wrap sushi. Available in packets from supermarkets and Asian food stores.

olives

Black olives are more mature and less salty than the green variety, which are picked when they are unripe. Neither variety is edible as it comes off the tree as olives are bitter and must be cured first, usually by soaking them in lye then pickling in brine or salt. Choose firm olives with good colour.

kalamata olives: Of Greek origin, the large, fleshy Kalamata olives have an intense flavour, which makes them the ideal choice for Greek salads and for use in tapenades. They are sometimes sold split.

ligurian/wild olives: Usually labelled or sold as Ligurian olives, wild olives are uncultivated and grow close to the ground in clusters. This small variety of olive can range in colour from pale mustard to dark purple and black. The thin flesh has a nutty flavour that makes them a great substitute for peanuts. Niçoise olives are similar in size as well as flavour.

pancetta

A cured and rolled Italian-style meat that is like prosciutto but less salty and with a softer texture. It's sold in flat pieces or chunks, or thinly sliced. It can be eaten uncooked or used in pasta sauces and risottos.

paprika

Spice made from ground, dried capsicum. Originally from Hungary, it comes in mild (sweet), smoky and a hot Spanish version called 'pimenton'. Adds flavour and vibrant colour to meat and rice dishes.

pastry

Make your own or use one of the many store-bought varieties which are sold frozen in blocks or ready-rolled into pastry sheets. Defrost in the fridge before use.

puff: This pastry is time-consuming and quite difficult to make, so many cooks opt to use store-bought puff pastry. It can be bought in blocks from patisseries or bought in both block and sheet forms from supermarkets. Butter puff is very light and flaky, perfect for a sweet pie.

pickled ginger

A popular Japanese condiment, pickled ginger or 'gari' is commonly served with sushi and sashimi to cleanse the palate. It is usually made with young ginger that's been pickled in sugar and vinegar. It's sold in pouches or jars from Asian grocery stores.

puy lentils

This small slate-green lentil gets its name from the region it is grown in – Le Puy in France. It is highly regarded in cooking because it holds its shape and has a lovely peppery taste.

quince paste

Also known as membrillo for its Spanish origins, this intensely aromatic paste is made by boiling quinces, lemon juice and sugar to a thick condiment. It's commonly served on a cheese platter where it cuts through strong blue cheeses and cheddar, but it also pairs well with roasted meats, such as pork. You can find it in supermarkets and delicatessens.

red curry paste

Buy good-quality pastes in jars from Asian food stores or the supermarket. When trying a new brand, it is a good idea to add a little at a time to test the heat as the chilli intensity can vary significantly from brand to brand. Red paste is usually mild.

rosewater

An essence distilled from rose petals, rosewater is one of the cornerstone flavours of Indian, Middle Eastern and Turkish tables. It's usually used in sweets and is the distinctive flavour in Turkish delight (lokum).

saffron

The world's most expensive spice is made from the dried stigmas of a purple crocus flower. A quarter of a million flowers have to be hand-picked to produce 1kg of saffron. Fortunately a little bit of saffron goes a long way and a small pinch is usually enough to colour and flavour a dish for six. The threadlike filaments should be soaked (steeped) in hot water, milk or stock to release maximum yellow colour and honeyed flavour before adding to the other ingredients.

salted black beans

Also known as Chinese black beans, these are black soy beans which are fermented and preserved in salt. They generally need to be soaked in water or at least rinsed before adding to a recipe. You can also buy them as a ready-made sauce, popular in stir-fries. They are not the same as South American, Spanish or Portuguese black beans.

sashimi-grade fish

Sashimi-grade means the freshest fish available. They are line-caught and therefore have no bruises. It's best to buy a centre piece from the fillet as it won't have veins, skin or blood lines. To ensure freshness you should buy your fish from the market the day you're going to eat it. You can pop it in the freezer for 20 minutes before thinly slicing.

semolina

A flour made from ground durum wheat, semolina is the base ingredient for pasta, breakfast cereal, sweet puddings and Middle Eastern cakes.

shiso leaves

Sometimes called perilla, this herb comes in both green and purple leafed varieties. It has a slight peppery flavour and is often used to to wrap ingredients. The micro variety makes a pretty garnish. Find it at some greengrocers and Asian markets.

shrimp paste

Made from small fermented shrimp and often called blachan, this pungent paste is used in stir-fries and curries to give a lovely depth of flavour. It's available from Asian supermarkets and grocery stores.

sichuan peppercorns

Not a pepper but dried berries with a spicy, tongue-tingling effect that are sold whole. Toast in a hot, dry frying pan until fragrant before crushing or grinding.

silver beet (swiss chard)

A vegetable with large green leaves and prominent white, red or yellow stalks. It can be used in salads, soups, pies and steamed as a green vegetable. Not to be confused with spinach which has a smaller leaf.

speck

This smoked German-style ham is from the top side of the leg and is sold as a flat piece or slab in delicatessens. If unavailable, use flat pancetta or smoky bacon.

spring onion

With a more pronounced bulb than the green onion (scallion), the spring or salad onion is great in salads, soups and stir-fries or slow-cooked until caramelised and puréed or served whole.

star anise

Small, brown seed cluster that is shaped like a star. It has a strong aniseed flavour and can be used whole in savoury dishes or used ground in sweet dishes.

stock

Quality stocks are available in supermarkets or make your own.

beef stock

1.5kg beef bones, cut into pieces
2 onions, chopped
2 carrots, chopped
2 stalks celery, chopped
assorted fresh herbs
2 bay leaves
10 peppercorns
2.5 litres water, or to cover

Preheat oven to 220°C (425°F). Place the bones on a baking tray and roast for 30 minutes. Add the onion and carrot and cook for 20 minutes. Transfer the bones, onion and carrot to a stockpot or large saucepan. Add the remaining ingredients.

Bring to the boil and simmer for 4–5 hours, skimming regularly. Strain the stock and use. Refrigerate for up to 3 days or freeze for up to 3 months. Makes 1.5–2 litres

chicken stock

1.5kg chicken
1 onion, chopped
2 cloves garlic, chopped
2 stalks celery, chopped
1 carrot, chopped
4 bay leaves
1 teaspoon black peppercorns
2.5 litres water, or to cover

Place the chicken, onion, garlic, celery carrot, bay leaves, peppercorns and water in a stockpot or large saucepan over high heat. Bring to the boil, cover and reduce the heat to low. Cook for 1 hour or until the chicken is cooked through. Use a large metal spoon to occasionally skim the foam from the surface. This removes impurities so the finished stock will have a cleaner, sweeter flavour and clearer appearance. Remove the chicken from the stock, strain the stock discarding vegetables. Refrigerate the stock for up to 3 days or freeze for up to 3 months. Makes 1.5–2 litres. You can skin and shred the chicken by scraping it with a fork for use in salads or sandwiches.

vegetable stock

2.5 litres water
1 parsnip
2 onions, chopped
1 clove garlic, chopped
2 carrots, chopped
300g cabbage, roughly chopped
3 stalks celery, chopped
assorted fresh herbs
2 bay leaves
1 tablespoon peppercorns

Place all the ingredients in a stockpot or large saucepan and simmer for 2 hours, skimming regularly. Strain and use, or refrigerate for up to 4 days or freeze for up to 8 months. Makes 1.5–2 litres
Tip: For a more intense flavour, roast the vegetables prior to simmering them.

sugar

Extracted as crystals from the juice of the sugar cane plant, sugar is a sweetener, flavour enhancer and food preservative.

brown sugar: Processed with molasses. It comes in differing shades of brown, according to the quantity of molasses added. This also affects the taste of the sugar, and therefore the end product. You can find it in light and dark varieties.

caster (superfine): The fine granule of this sugar gives baked products a light texture and crumb, which is important for many cakes and light desserts. Caster sugar is essential when you want the sugar crystals to dissolve in eggwhites for meringue.

Demerara: With its large crystals, rich golden colour and mild caramel flavour, this is the sugar to use if you want a pronounced crust on baked goods or a distinctive flavour in coffee. If unavailable, substitute with a mixture of 3 parts white sugar to 1 part brown sugar.

icing (confectioner's): Regular granulated sugar ground to a very fine powder. It often clumps together and needs to be sieved before using. Use pure icing sugar not icing sugar mixture, which contains cornflour (cornstarch) and needs more liquid.

palm: Made from the sap of various palms, this hard sugar is sold in blocks or pieces ranging in colour from light to dark (which has a more intense flavour). It's used widely in Southeast Asian cooking in sweet-sour dishes and in desserts.

raw: Light brown in colour and honey-like in flavour, raw sugar is less processed than regular white sugar. It can be used in baking where it lends a more pronounced flavour and colour to the finished product.

sumac

These dried berries of a flowering plant are ground to produce an acidic, purple powder popular in the Middle East. Sumac has a lemony flavour and is great sprinkled on salads, dips or chicken. Find it at greengrocers and some supermarkets.

tahini

A thick paste made from ground sesame seeds, tahini is used in Middle Eastern cooking in sauces and dressings and is a key ingredient in the popular dip, hummus. It is available in jars from Middle Eastern grocery stores, health food shops and supermarkets.

tofu

Translated as 'bean curd', tofu is a high-protein food popular across Asia. Made by coagulating the milk of soy beans and pressing the curd into blocks, tofu comes in several grades. according to the amount of moisture that has been removed. Silken tofu is the softest, with a custard or junket-like texture. Soft tofu is slightly firmer with the texture of raw meat, while dried or firm tofu has the texture of, and cuts like, a semi-hard cheese. It's great in soups, stir-fries and salads.

tomato paste

This rich concentrate of tomatoes is sold in cans, jars, tubes and tubs. It's used whenever an injection of strong tomato flavour is needed in sauces and stews.

tomato purée (passata)

This is made by removing the skins and seeds from ripe tomatoes and blending the flesh to make a rich, tomato sauce. Passata is an Italian term for skinned and seeded tomatoes which have been passed through a sieve to make thick, pulpy sauce. Sugo is made from crushed tomatoes so it has a little more texture than passata.

tomato sauce (ketchup)

A sweet, acidic bottled sauce made with strained tomato juice, salt, sometimes garlic and onion, lemon juice or vinegar and sweetener, which may be sugar or fruit such as apple, pear or grapes. It's a common condiment for sausages and steak.

treacle

The syrup produced from the refining process applied to sugar, treacle can come as a pale syrup known as golden syrup or a darker, more molasses-like version with a bitter flavour. It's mostly used in puddings and baking, like the famous English dessert, treacle tart.

turmeric

This vibrantly orange root is commonly used in Indian cuisine and is usually ground, dried and sold as a powder to flavour curries. You can find fresh turmeric in Asian grocery stores and some greengrocers.

vanilla beans

These cured pods from the vanilla orchid are used whole, and often split and the tiny seeds scraped into the mixture, to infuse flavour into custard and cream-based recipes. If unavailable, substitute 1 vanilla bean with 1 teaspoon pure vanilla extract (a dark, thick liquid – not essence).

vanilla extract

For a pure vanilla taste, use a good-quality vanilla extract, which is a dark, thick liquid, often containing seeds, not an essence or imitation flavour, or use a real vanilla bean, split and with the seeds scraped.

vinegar

The name of this weak solution of acetic acid comes from the French term *vin aigre*, meaning sour wine. However vinegar can be distilled from sources other than wine that include cider, rice and grain alcohol.

balsamic: A rich, dark colour and a sweet, mellow, almost caramel flavour distinguish balsamic vinegars from other wine vinegars. Made from trebbiano grapes in Modena, Italy, it is aged for five to 30 years, or more. The older the balsamic, the better (and more expensive) and the less you'll need to use. Cheaper ones may need to be balanced with some sugar. It can't be used as a substitute for regular vinegar. It also comes in a white variety, which is perfect to use when you don't want to discolour salads or vegetables.

cider: Made from fermented apple juice, cider vinegar's golden brown colour and mellow acidity is a good match for pork or chicken and can be used to cut the sweetness of caramelised apple.

malt: Produced from ale made from malted barley, this vinegar is typically light brown in colour. Used in pickles, some argue it's the natural partner for fish and chips.

rice: Made from fermenting rice or rice wine, rice vinegar is milder and sweeter than vinegars made by oxidising distilled alcohol or wine made from grapes. Rice wine vinegar is available in white (colourless to pale yellow), black and red varieties from Asian food stores.

sherry: To be labelled sherry vinegar, this product must be made from sherry from the Cádiz province of Spain and aged in oak for a minimum of six months. Its nomenclature is protected by European Union law.

white balsamic: Made from the same grape variety (trebbiano) as regular balsamic, white balsamic is paler, thinner and less sweet than the dark variety. It is often used to avoid the discolouration the dark variety causes.

wine: Both red and white wine can be distilled into vinegar for use in dressings, glazes, sauces and preserved condiments such as pickles. This is the vinegar to use in the classic French dressing, vinaigrette.

wasabi

Often called Japanese horseradish although it is a different plant, wasabi belongs to the brassica family. It's usually made into a paste used in making sushi and as a condiment for Japanese dishes. It has a very strong, hot flavour. Available from Asian food stores and supermarkets.

white anchovies

These Spanish anchovies called 'boquerones' are filleted and marinated in white vinegar and olive oil, giving them a sweet, mild taste. They are popular as a tapas dish on their own and are great in robust salads.

wonton wrappers

Chinese in origin, these square or round thin sheets of dough are available fresh or frozen. Filled with meat and vegetables to make dumplings, they can be steamed or fried. They are also versatile enough to use as a crunchy base for nibbles or a cheat's ravioli.

za'atar

Middle Eastern spice mix containing dried herbs, sesame seeds and sumac. It's often used as a crust for grilled meats.

EQUIPMENT

bakeware

baking dishes: Use ceramic for cooking dishes that need a more gentle heat, such as lasagne and vegetable bakes. Use metal, a much better conductor of heat, for cooking meat.

pie dishes: Choose from metal or ceramic – metal gives a crisp, dry crust, while ceramic gives a softer one – and opt for deep dishes that will hold a generous filling. A lip on the dish makes securing a pastry top much easier.

ramekins: These ceramic cups are not only useful for cooking soufflés in, they can also be used for individual pies and bakes. Place ramekins on a baking tray before transferring to the oven shelf so they are easier to handle when hot.

baking dishes, trays and racks

cooling racks: Not only for cooling cakes, tarts and pies, racks are used to elevate a roast in a baking dish – having the meat on a rack allows the heat to flow around the entire surface, and prevents the meat from sitting in the fatty pan juices during roasting.

metal baking dishes: These vary in type and quality from thin aluminium to thick, heavy duty stainless steel. Choose a deep stainless steel dish if possible; it will last a lifetime and has a good, even cooking surface.

metal baking trays: Flat metal baking trays are great all-rounders – bake cookies, biscuits and galettes on them, use them under the grill (broiler), or use them in the preparation and assembly stages of cooking.

frying pans and wok

deep frying pans: Fantastic for stir-frying vegetables and making pasta sauces – just toss the pasta through in the pan.

shallow frying pans: Good for cooking eggs and pancakes, simmering a sauce or searing a steak. Choose a frying pan with a thick base for even cooking and an insulated handle that won't heat up during cooking. A non-stick surface will minimise the amount of oil you will need when cooking.

wok: Not essential, depending on your cooking style. A wok works best on a gas flame, which heats the base and sides – essential for good stir-frying. If you only have electric hotplates, it may be easier to stir-fry in a deep frying pan. A wok is also good for deep-frying. Choose stainless steel with a wooden handle if possible and season the wok before using it. By seasoning an uncoated metal wok at high heat with salt and oil, you'll help prevent food from sticking to it and the wok from becoming rusty.

knives and peelers

knives: The three most important knives a cook can have are a small paring knife, a cook's or utility knife and a serrated edge or bread knife. All do a variety of kitchen tasks. Choose a knife that feels well weighted in your hand.

peeler: A sharp vegetable peeler cuts the work of peeling a mountain of vegetables in half. Choose a good-quality peeler with a sharp blade. A wide one is good for peeling large vegetables such as pumpkin and for making vegetable ribbons. Also handy is a julienne peeler that shreds vegetables into very fine ribbons – very useful for Asian salads and slaws.

zester: My favourite tool. When removing the zest from lemons, limes and oranges, use just a little pressure so that you are only removing the outer flavour-filled zest from the fruit, not the bitter white pith.

measuring equipment

measuring cups: Get a set that has 1 cup, ½ cup, ⅓ cup and ¼ cup measures. To measure dry ingredients with accuracy, fill generously and level off with the back of a knife. Cup measures differ between countries, so check the origin of the recipe you are using. For recipes in this book, consult the conversion chart on page 434.

measuring spoons: Get a simple set that has 1 tablespoon, 1 teaspoon, ½ teaspoon and ¼ teaspoon measures. Level off the spoon after filling with dry ingredients for accuracy. Spoon measures differ between countries as for cup measures, see above.

measuring jugs: Essential for measuring liquids. Get one that has ml (fl oz) as well as cup measures. Measure the liquid at eye level on a flat surface for accuracy.

scales: Indispensable for fast and accurate weighing of ingredients. Whether digital or conventional, a simple set will do.

power tools

blender: A handy tool for puréeing soups, making a quick pesto or salsa verde. Heavy duty glass jugs are a must. A stick blender is perfect if you make lots of soups (and is also less messy than pouring soup into a blender!).

food processor: Use it to make pastry, blend foods, mix cakes, make breadcrumbs, cream butter and sugar, chop anything. The best all-round power tool if you only have room or budget for one.

prep-ware

grater: I prefer a sturdy multifunctional box grater with various surfaces providing different grating options, rather than a different grater for each purpose. Choose stainless steel if possible and keep the fine surfaces clean with a small brush.

mixing bowls: Glass, metal or ceramic, a set of mixing bowls is essential. Glass and ceramic bowls may be preferable, as there is no limit to the time acidic ingredients such as lemon juice, vinegar and tomatoes can be kept in them (acidic contents may react with a metal bowl and acquire a metallic taste).

saucepans

Choose stainless steel saucepans with a thick base for even heat distribution and tight-fitting lids for a good seal. Invest in a few saucepans of better quality rather than a set of lesser-quality ones. Have a small size for sauces, a medium size for curries and vegetables and a larger one for boiling pasta.

tins

Aluminium (aluminum) tins are fine to use for baking, but stainless steel will last longer and won't warp or buckle. Always measure tin widths at the base, particularly when it comes to baking.

Bundt: A decorative tin with fluted sides and a hole in the middle. A Bundt tin is used for dense cakes with a heavy batter. The hole in the middle allows the heat to penetrate the cake from all sides, making it cook faster.

muffin: The standard sizes are a 12-hole tin, each hole with ½-cup (125ml) capacity, or a 6-hole tin, each hole with 1-cup (250ml) capacity. Mini-muffin tins have a capacity of 1½ tablespoons. Non-stick tins make for easy removal, or line with paper cases.

round: The standard sizes for round tins are 18cm, 20cm, 22cm and 24cm. The 20cm and 24cm tins are the must-haves of this collection.

springform: The standard sizes for round tins are 18cm, 20cm, 22cm and 24cm. The 20cm and 24cm round tins are the must-have members of the range.

square: The standard sizes for square tins are 18cm, 20cm, 22cm and 24cm. If you have a recipe for a cake cooked in a round tin and you want to use a square tin, the general rule is to subtract 2cm from the size of the tin. For example, you would need a 20cm square tin for a recipe calling for a 22cm round cake tin.

utensils

spoons: From wooden to metal to slotted, you need a variety of spoons for a variety of kitchen jobs. Keep your sweet and savoury wooden spoons separate so that the flavour of heavy spices doesn't taint a delicate custard or cake. Keep a large metal spoon for folding and serving.

tongs: Essential. Use them to toss pasta, turn steaks or chicken, mix or serve a salad.

whisk: When you're making a light soufflé, a smooth sauce or combining eggs, a medium-size whisk with sturdy wires is a must.

spatula: For turning, flipping and delicately removing or serving large wedges of food, I find a long, wide spatula the best.

spoonula: This spatula and spoon in one is great for baking cookies and cakes.

THANK YOU

This compilation book is testimony to the incredibly engaging body of work the *donna hay magazine* team has produced over the years – pages and pages of visually stunning, inspiring and hunger-inducing work it is, too! It's also a celebration of what we do best and that's taking tried and true classics and family favourites and giving them a new twist with modern flavours, textures and ingredients.

I can't thank our food team past and present enough – Steve, Justine, Siobhan, Jess, Kirsten and Jane – for producing the flavour-packed recipes you see in these pages. To Steve and Justine in particular, whose exquisite styling brings each dish to life, I want to thank you for helping produce content that looks as good as it tastes!

To the current team Mia, Drina, Evelin, Anthony, Abby and Dolores, who make the wheels go around and produce amazing content in their respective roles day in, day out – thank you. To my managing editor Mel, thank you for helping curate this book, ensuring the recipes are accurate and the words are beautifully crafted.

And lastly, a very special thanks has to go to the talented Chi Lam, art director extraordinaire, whose keen eye and inspiring design work have helped weave this book into the beautiful and collectable tome you have before you. Chi, you are amazing!

At the age of eight, Donna Hay skipped into a kitchen, picked up
a mixing bowl and never looked back. She later moved to the world
of magazine test kitchens and publishing, where she established
her trademark style of simple, smart and seasonal recipes all
beautifully put together and photographed. It is food for
every cook, every food lover; every day and every occasion.

Her unique style turned her into an international food-publishing
phenomenon as a best-selling author of 22 cookbooks, publisher of
the bi-monthly *donna hay magazine* and the number one iPad app
in Australia, newspaper columnist, creator of the donna hay for
Royal Doulton homewares collection plus a food range, and owner
of her online store. Donna is a working mum to two beautiful boys.

Donna's first television series, *Donna Hay – fast, fresh, simple.*,
a 13-part half-hour cooking series for The LifeStyle Channel in
Australia and various international networks, brought her approach
to food to life for viewers in over 32 countries.

Books by Donna Hay include: *Fresh and Light*; *simple dinners*;
a cook's guide; *fast, fresh, simple.*; *Seasons*; *no time to cook*;
off the shelf; *instant entertaining*; and the *simple essentials* collection.

donnahay.com

donnahay.com

For more of Donna's cookbooks and recipes,
as well as her homewares and kitchen collections,
and a bake-at-home range, visit donnahay.com